THE
ENGLISH
GAME

A JOURNEY OF DISCOVERY
IN THE HOME OF FOOTBALL

IVAN AMBROSIO

pitch

First published by Pitch Publishing, 2025

1

pitch

Pitch Publishing
9 Donnington Park,
85 Birdham Road,
Chichester, West Sussex,
PO20 7AJ
www.pitchpublishing.co.uk
info@pitchpublishing.co.uk

A CIP catalogue record is available for this book
from the British Library.

ISBN 978 1 83680 141 2

Typesetting and origination by Pitch Publishing

MIX
Paper | Supporting
responsible forestry
FSC
www.fsc.org   FSC® C013604

Printed and bound in the UK on FSC® certified paper in line
with our continuing commitment to ethical business practices,
sustainability and the environment.

Printed and bound by CPI Group (UK) Ltd, Croydon, CR0 4YY

CONTENTS

Before We Start. 9
Preface by Claudio Ranieri 11
Preface by Andrea Pettinello 13
Introduction 15
Premise 19
The plane tickets that changed my life: 20 February
    2013 and 25 March 2013. 21
This is the letter I wrote (in very poor English) asking
    for a trial as a footballer 22

Chapter 1: Learn to Dream 23
Yorkshire and the Humber 27
The Home of Football 28
Welcome to Sandygate: The World's Oldest
    Football Ground. 35
The Blades 39
In Memory of the 97 42
Remember the 56. 46
Don Revie in Command 51

Chapter 2: Face Your Fears 55
North East 61
There's Only One Bradley Lowery. 62
The Men from the North. 66
Ahm Coming Home, Newcastle 71

Chapter 3: Believe in Yourself. 75
North West. 79
Welcome to Ewood Park 80
We Are Burnley from the North 84
The Theatre of Dreams 88
The Red Rebels. 92
The Class of 92 96
93:20 101
The People's Club 105
This Is Anfield .110

Chapter 4: Stay Patient and Trust Your Journey . . . 115
West Midlands 119
Welcome to Stoke-on-Trent: City of Rain and Wind . 120
Out of Darkness Cometh Light 126
This Is Villa Park 130
My Border Collie 135

Chapter 5: Be the Farmer of Your Life 139
East Midlands 143
The Story of a Dream 144
Welcome to Derby 148
In Memory of Brian 151

Chapter 6: The Importance of the Little Things . . . 155
East of England 159
The Finest Stand in England 160
The Family Club 164
Mythical Bill 169
The Old and Glorious Oak Tree 176

Chapter 7: Watchword: Sacrifice 181
London 185
Liberté, Égalité, Fraternité 187
Wembley Stadium, 17 November 2015 187
We Are Tottenham from The Lane 190
The Invincibles 195
Long Live the Boleyn 199
A Friendship in the Name of Crystal Palace 204
The Legend of Corinthian Football Club 209
The Real Dons Are Here 216
Farewell Griffin Park 222
Craven Cottage: England's Most Beautiful Stadium . 226
Blue Is the Colour 231

Chapter 8: Be Kind to Yourself 237
South East 241
Brighton, Home of the Seagulls 242
Welcome to York Road: Home of Maidenhead
    United FC 246
My story on Maidenhead United's Match Programme 250

Stand Up if You Love Wycombe 251
Ohhh Vito Mannone, ...255
ohhh Vito Mannone 255
Ours 260

Chapter 9: Find Your Own Way. 265
South West 271
Together, Anything Is Possible. 272
The Romans 276
Welcome to Ashton Gate: The Home of the Robins. .279
Colin: The Gentle Giant 284
A Lesson in Generosity. 290
Welcome to Garrison Field: The Home of the
    Smallest Football League in the World 294

Chapter 10: To You, Your
Dreams and Your Happiness 299
Between a Dream and Reality 301
It All Started Here!. 302
One Step from the Dream 308
Best Day of My Life 316
What's Left … .321

Afterword by Filippo Galli: English Grounds,
    Those Temples of Football 325
To Bradley and Giuseppe, My Life Coaches. 327
There's Only One Bradley Lowery. 329
The Strongest Person I Know 331

Acknowledgements. 333
My journey, encapsulated in over 300 stadiums 337
216 matches lived on my skin, from 2014 to 2025,
    chasing my dreams. 341
Recommended books 350
Photographic copyright. 351

Dedications

To Mum and Dad, for always giving me the freedom to choose, for passing on healthy life values and for teaching me to keep going despite difficulties.

To my brother, hoping that you can realise all your dreams. I hope the future will enable us to spend a lot more time together. So far, it's never been enough.

To Eleonora, my life partner. You've always been there for me in the difficult moments. I'll try to give you the very best part of me. I hope it can always be like this, every day of our life.

To Giuseppe B., who unknowingly taught me the importance of facing life with courage and a positive mindset. You're a wonderful example. #AvantiSempre (Always Forward)

To little Bradley Lowery, for teaching me to smile in the hardest times. Your memory and your example will live within me forever.

To my nan, Anna, who went to heaven while I was in the stands at the Boleyn Ground.

To my nan, Maria, who went to heaven while I was on the plane, flying towards my new life in Manchester.

To those who have always been there, come rain or shine.

To those who held out their hand and let me into their lives. This book is dedicated to you. Without your help, I'd never have done it.

I love you all.
Ivan

'Origins should never be a barrier to success. A modest start in life can be a help more than a hindrance.

Sir Alex Ferguson

BEFORE WE START ...

IT'S BEEN over four years since I first published this book in Italian, and more than five years have passed since I finished writing it. Time flies, as Eleonora would say, but a friend once told me that even though time passes, it's up to us to make it meaningful and unique. And that's exactly what I've tried to do over these past five years—through ups and downs, smiles and tears, joys and sorrows, new beginnings and farewells, successes and failures. This is life, and that's precisely why it's beautiful—always, despite everything.

Over the past five years, I've often found myself flipping through the pages of this book—always in the silence of the night. While Eleonora slept, I would quietly reread the stories of my travels and the stories of the people I met along the way, and I often found myself reflecting on the journey and the decisions I made—mostly brave, and often risky.

Well, as you'll see when reading the book, when I published it in Italy on March 6, 2021, at the age of 27, I had a dream of becoming a professional football coach, and without even a high school diploma, I could count the people who believed in me on the fingers of one hand. And yet, nearly four years after that March 6, 2021, so much has changed in my life.

I completed my high school diploma and, incredibly, went on to graduate with a First-Class Honours from St Mary's University in Twickenham in partnership with Chelsea FC.

I also earned my UEFA B coaching licence and had the privilege of working with both Fulham FC and Chelsea FC, living my dream day after day. Over these past four years, I also had the incredible opportunity to launch my own football academy in the heart of London, called Strive FC, and fulfilled the lifelong dream of playing at both Craven Cottage and Stamford Bridge. In fact, at Craven Cottage, I even scored a fantastic goal. Yet, even after all these years, I still struggle to believe whether all of this is real or just a dream. I also coached there, and every time I look at the photos and videos, I can hardly believe it.

Reflecting on the things I've done over these past four years, I could never forget the moment when Marco contacted me to create a documentary about my journey in England, or when, in June 2022, I managed to bring Upton Park FC to Naples and recreate the Anglo-Italian Cup.

I could continue, but I'll stop here. As of today, I'm completing an MSc in Advanced Performance Football Coaching with the University of South Wales, working at the Crystal Palace FC Academy, and studying to complete the UEFA A coaching licence—a course I've dreamed of attending for many years. On June 7, 2025, I'll have the honour of marrying Eleonora, and I couldn't ask for anything more from life. Now, I bid you farewell and wish you a wonderful journey through my journey. And when in the following pages you will read about dreams, determination, hopes, and goals, you'll understand that believing in my biggest dreams was the right choice... I hope you will do the same.

Thank you for your support. With love,
Ivan
London, 10 April 2025

PREFACE BY CLAUDIO RANIERI

The Stadium –
Football's Never-Never Land

THE FIRST time in a football ground is like a child's first Christmas. Its impact is so great that it either stays with you for the rest of your days or you reject it forever. In most cases the first time for a football fan is a memory so vivid that it takes on a mystical air. We have all read legendary accounts – of existential import much greater than the practical essence of the game – transformed into masterpieces of sporting literature: novels, poems, songs, philosophical tracts, films.

The pull of the stadium is membership of a great common home. There's physical separation, obviously, but it's not necessarily the exploits of the footballer-actor that trigger the applause or the boos. The mechanism can be inversely proportional. I can assure you that in my career I have experienced a plethora of these moments, good and bad alike, in Italy, in England, in every corner of planet football.

Every ground has its own shape and structure, features that can make all the difference in the context of a match. This is one of the reasons why no two matches are the same. And don't think that a manager or a midfielder is unaware of all this; it's there in the eyes of those watching you, in their manifestations of joy and despair, in the personal rituals of those who are there, always waiting to discover their Christmas surprise.

A journey to the stadiums, as this book recounts, is above all a journey into the soul of the supporters, those who constitute the unwritten DNA of every club – its history, its qualities and its faults.

In England more than anywhere – probably because each club has its own ground, shared with no one else – this in-built factor is the common home passed down from father to son, from grandmother to granddaughter, from friend to friend. It's a never-never land, the one always reached at the rising of the sun: the match.

Enjoy the journey.
Claudio Ranieri

PREFACE BY
ANDREA PETTINELLO

WHEN I first met Ivan, I was a bit sceptical. Plenty of other lads had managed the feat of visiting football ground after football ground, watching hundreds of matches and spending sleepless nights to catch the early train and pursue the dream floating in front of them. So I wondered what was so special about Ivan. And I continued to do so because, despite my initial scepticism, his infectious enthusiasm had begun to rub off on me.

As time went on, I was lucky enough to go with him on some of these journeys, getting lost in England's remotest outposts in search of crumbling stadiums – in many cases half abandoned and often so small and nondescript that they could easily be mistaken for local parks. And it was on one of those long treks with Ivan that I actually understood the meaning of all the words he had said to me and that I'd naively underestimated.

It wasn't so much a matter of visiting every ground in England (or, in any case, most of them) as undertaking a long journey of self-discovery, putting yourself to the test every day and seeking what's good in people. That's because Ivan, aside from the usual and comprehensible initial communication problems, always (and I mean always) managed to get everyone to believe in his dream.

It was about courage, about having the brass neck to introduce yourself to a stranger with: 'Hi, my name's Ivan and I'm going to write a book.' Put yourself in his shoes for a second. Wouldn't you be at least a bit embarrassed? Wouldn't you feel uneasy at having to explain in a foreign language, to people you have just met, how important they have just become in the fulfilment of a stranger's dream? It might seem obvious and easy enough, but I can assure you that, faced with much less, most of us would have given up at the first sign of difficulty.

Ivan's not like that. He succeeded in enchanting everyone with his story, and in so doing has taken us with him on a long pilgrimage made up of closed doors, unexpected refusals, unanswered calls and wind-ups.

However, it's also made up of smiles, long embraces, coffees that turned into lunches or dinners, shared values, television appearances and the unconditional support of those who always believed in him.

I sincerely hope that in reading this book you too can join Ivan on his journey. Don't read it just for the sake of ticking yet another book off your list and then stick it on a shelf or stow it in a cupboard with a stack of others. Let Ivan take you on a route that many may already have followed but that he will bring to life from the word go.

This is the story of a dream. A dream nurtured by a boy who loves life and who decided to make it unforgettable.

Andrea Pettinello
Friend of Ivan and founder of the Il Calcio Inglese
community

INTRODUCTION

WRITING THIS book was far from easy. In fact, it was damned hard. There were times when I thought I couldn't finish it, felt like giving up. Then I said to myself, giving up is for losers. So, it was nose to the grindstone, 12 hours a day, for over a year. I challenged myself, page after page, story after story, all laced with tears and smiles.

Despite the difficulties, going back and reliving the last few years of my life has been uplifting. It seems like yesterday when I found myself alone and bewildered in the middle of Victoria station, carrying two bags and a heart full of hopes. It was 20 February 2013 when I left home to pursue my dream of playing football in England. I'd just turned 19. It was just over a month later when I returned home with my heart broken and pockets empty – London had crushed all my dreams.

Despite that, before boarding the plane to go home, eyes full of tears and heart full of sadness, I looked up at the London sky and made a promise: 'Dear London, everything you've taken from me in the last few weeks, I'm going to get it back. I'll come back here and fulfil my dreams. You see if I don't …' That was 25 March 2013.

Two years later, I did go back. Not to London, but to Bowness-on-Windermere, a splendid town in the Lake District. My long journey of discovery in English football began there, jumping from one train to another and trudging mile after mile on foot to see the football grounds that had always fascinated me. For years I'd admired them in photographs and on television, and all of a sudden I was standing right in front of them, often rendered speechless by the thrill of their history. From Stamford Bridge to Craven Cottage, from the Boleyn Ground to Goodison Park, from Kenilworth Road to the City Ground, from Fratton Park to little Sandygate. Spending more than four years on a journey to discover the roots of English football was a sensational experience.

Although my ambition had been to experience those grounds as a player, walking to them and in them has been the most enjoyable journey of my life. The thought of having set foot in the places where trod legends such as Brian Clough, Don Revie and Sir Alex Ferguson is in itself an enormous satisfaction. Experiencing those places had always been a dream of mine, and no matter if my ambition to be a footballer came to nothing. What does matter is fighting for your dreams, every day of your life.

The aim of this book is not just to tell the story of English football as it has never been told; it's to leave something positive, something healthy in the mind of the reader. It may not give you answers, but it will make you ask yourself the right questions.

I'm not a writer by trade, but I've put this work together with all the love in my heart, word after word, in the hope of stimulating curiosity and the desire to organise a journey to England. To the place where football is much more than a sport. It's feeling part of a family, it's supporting your club even when they lose, it's drinking a beer while watching your local team, irrespective of the league they play in.

In England, football is going to the match by car, bus, train or on the Underground, it's walking – before and after the match – among the away supporters, respecting each other and perhaps sinking a pint in the same pub. It's walking outside the ground and breathing in the air smelling of onions and the beloved hot dogs. It's buying a match programme from an old fellow who's been a supporter of that club since childhood, it's finding yourself peering into the windows of the houses that have surrounded the ground for more than a hundred years.

Football is this and much more. In the pages of the book you have in your hands, you'll be able to read of the best adventures I've ever lived through. We'll start in the north of England and end our journey in the Scilly Isles, home to the smallest football league in the world. The book is divided into nine chapters, one for each of the nation's regions. Then there's a tenth chapter, but I'll let you discover that one for yourselves ...

At the beginning of each chapter I'll tell you about some of the experiences I've had, from the obstacles I found along the way to what I eventually achieved. Not to put myself at the centre of attention, but to show that if you want something enough, anything in life is possible. If I managed to achieve it, I'm sure you can too, whatever your dreams and objectives.

In the pages of this book there's nothing copied and pasted from the internet, only what life brought me – encounters with legendary figures and the memories of a wealth of precious stories that I heard as I made my way around the country.

Before leaving you to read those stories, besides thanking you for the trust you place in me, I'd like to repeat one last thing, especially for younger readers. Believe in your dreams and have the courage to face what life throws at you.

Reach out to others and try to act with love in your heart. If you can do that, life itself will be the best journey you can ever make.

Ivan

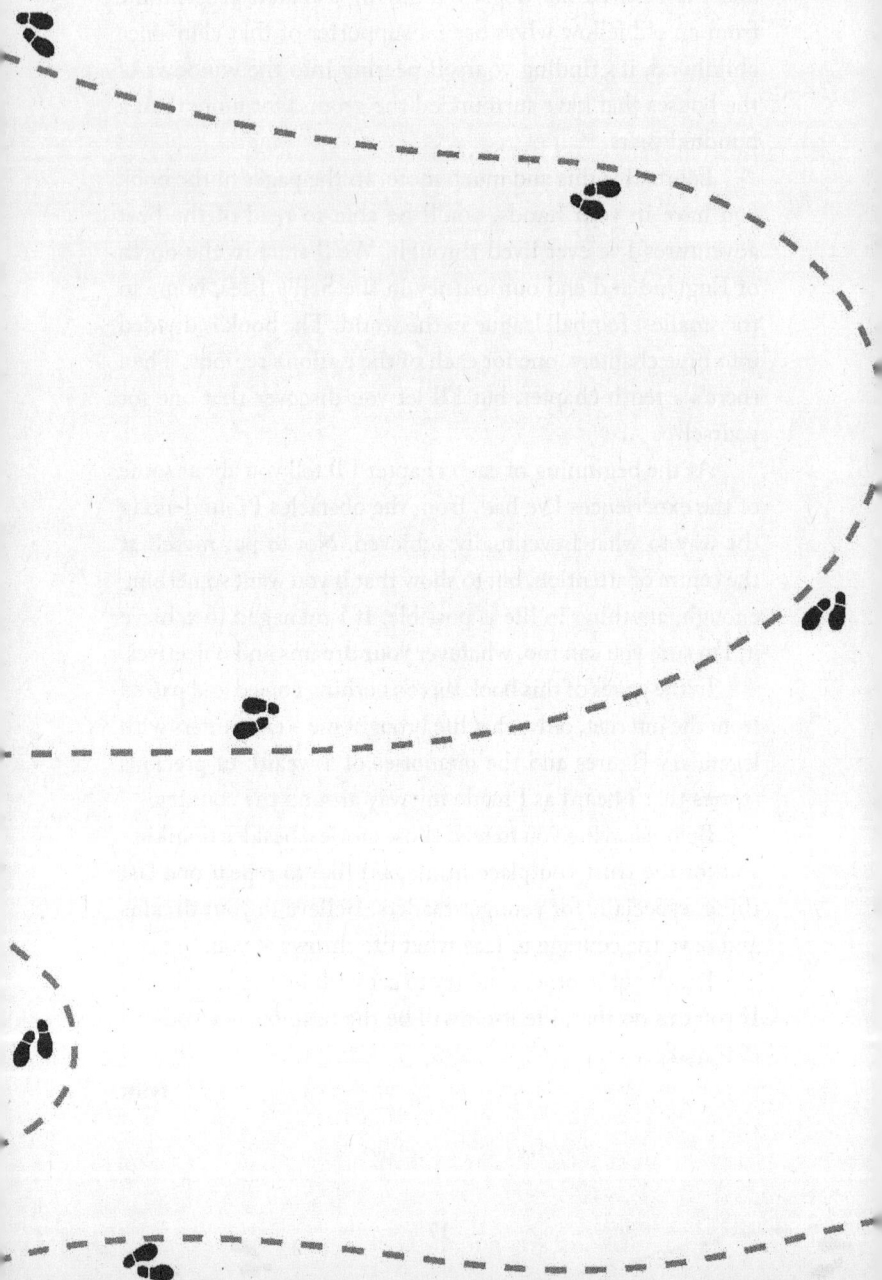

PREMISE

IN THE pages of this book you'll be able to read about the best things that have ever happened to me. I'll be taking you on a tour of England during which, hand on heart, I'll try to communicate something special, something beneficial.

But before starting on the unforgettable episodes of the journey that completely changed my life, I'd like to make one thing clear. Everything I've recounted in these pages is just a small part of the marvellous world I explored, full of fine people and fascinating stories to discover.

The further into the book you go, the more you'll realise that some big clubs aren't featured. This is because they didn't elicit in me the same sort of response as the ones I've included – but not because they have no history or stories to tell. It's because, not wanting to bore anyone, after months of careful thought I opted for quality rather than quantity.

Not only that, this book also isn't a guided tour of all the football grounds in England, but an account of the long journey I undertook to discover football and myself. Although some of the trips and some of the stories may appear similar, I can assure you that the excitement they aroused in me along the way was always strong but never the same.

Making no attempt to hide my romantic side, during the writing I gave free rein to the emotions and sensations I felt on the journey – smiles, tears, unforgettable encounters, awe-inspiring grounds and much more.

I've given it my best, investing five years of my life in this personal project and realising the dream I'd always had. My hope is that you too will be able to experience what's in here and – who knows? – achieve much more than I have.

THE PLANE TICKETS THAT CHANGED MY LIFE: 20 FEBRUARY 2013 AND 25 MARCH 2013

easyJet

AMBROSIO/IVAN
Naples (Term1)
London Gatwick
EZY8530 20FEB 12:15 16

Please go straight to departure
If you're late we won't wait!

Boarding Pass B 2 1.35

easyJet

AMBROSIO/IVAN
Naples (Term1)
London Gatwick
EZY8530 20FEB 18

Booking Ref ELYP5HX

Boarding Group 2 6C

easyJet **Boarding Pass**

TRAVEL DATE
25 MAR 2013
MON

FLIGHT NUMBER
EZY3249

GATE CLOSES
05:40

SEAT NUMBER
25B

FROM
(STN) London Stansted

TO
(NAP) Naples

FLIGHT DEPARTS
06:10

PASSENGER
AMBROSIO, IVAN Mr

EL5MNN5 S600

Please don't be late, the rest can't wait

21

THIS IS THE LETTER I WROTE (IN VERY POOR ENGLISH) ASKING FOR A TRIAL AS A FOOTBALLER

Hello.

I' m Ivan Ambrosio and I'm was born on 13 December 1993 in Naples.. I'm playing to football for when I was 10 years old, but where I lived, the football culture never had serious consideration.. I'm here in England since 20 February, I'm alone and with a lot of hope, because I want to give a great change to my life, learning the english language and playing to football. I say you that the desire to play is very much, that I'm in the land that I love and in a place totally different from where I was, than I think that the possibilities will be more and than I put the best of me in every thing that I do. In few words, with this letter, I ask you to give me the possibility to do a proof for see if can play at these levels. Certainly it was better that I say you in words, but still I don't know speak in english, I hope that you understand me and that you give me this possibility,because for me my life has no sense without football.. I hope that you will do me this new challenge..

Thank you!

Striker - Foot right - 1.82 cm - 78 kg -

Ivan Ambrosio

Ambrosio Ivan

Cognome AMBROSIO
Nome IVAN
nato il 13/12/1993
(atto n.)
( )
Cittadinanza ITALIANA
Residenza
Via
Stato civile STATO LIBERO
Professione STUDENTE

CONNOTATI E CONTRASSEGNI SALIENTI

Statura m. 1,80
Capelli CASTANI
Occhi CASTANI
Segni particolari

Firma del titolare

lì

impronta del dito indice sinistro

IL SINDACO

CHAPTER 1
LEARN TO DREAM

Good timber does not grow with ease; the stronger the wind, the stronger the trees.

J. Willard Marriott

LET'S GET one thing straight from the start – it takes courage to dream. Dreaming is far from simple; at times it's complicated and to be honest it can be pretty tiring. Having a strong belief in something can lead to stress, attacks of nerves and even a breakdown, but I can assure you there's nothing better than fighting for your dreams. Waking up in the morning with something to believe in is one of those feelings that make you come alive, properly alive. Sometimes you can feel tired and worn out by all the attendant worries, but that's par for the course.

I'll be honest with you, brutally honest. Dreaming requires sacrifice, dedication, infinite abnegation, enormous responsibilities, organisation, attention to detail, patience and optimism, and above all it takes the one resource that we all have in equal measure but of which there's never enough – time. Once it's passed, time doesn't come back. That said, the good thing is that its management is entirely in our hands.

I could talk for hours about organising your time, but the one thing I want to say in simple terms is that you should employ your time as you really want to. You'll say that's not easy, especially under certain circumstances, but I believe that, in due course, if you give all of yourself, anything is possible. If, that is, you really want it. I've always thought that life is a matter of choices, black or white. Those stuck in between are idlers, pessimists, people who do nothing but complain all day, never getting a grip on their lives.

I have a vivid memory of the day when, as a dreamer with a capital D, I decided to leave my comfort zone and put myself on the line in the journey of a lifetime. I was 19 when I left everything to pursue my greatest dreams. By everything, I mean school, the football team I played for, my family, my friends, a well-paid job, the girlfriend I had at the time and all the certainties offered to me by that normal life. The desire to experience those far-off dreamed-of places led me to abandon all the security I had, and before long I began to discover a new part of myself.

Since that day, I've faced and lived through extraordinary experiences. I've travelled roads I could never have imagined. Travelling for four years of my life opened my mind and made me a better man.

My mission in this world is not just to realise my greatest dreams; above all else, it's to give love and to be ready always to help others, whatever the circumstances.

Obviously, with each step taken, between one success and the next, there have been plenty of problems along the way, but my determination to make it has always prevailed over everything and everybody.

Failures, fears, mistakes made, sudden tumbles, tears, pain, sleepless nights, enormous sacrifices, things you have to give up and do without, your alarm going off in the middle of the night, endless hours of work, doors being slammed in your face – I could go on – are all part of life. But without those things you wouldn't develop, and without development there can be no change ...

I think I've said enough, but there's one more thing I want to add. Have the courage to get out of that damned comfort zone and go to meet your dreams, be they great or small. Leave that job you can't stand, go and live in that city you've always dreamed of, organise that journey you've been putting off all your life, throw yourself into the project that only you believe in. In other words, do what you've always dreamed of.

Don't be afraid of making mistakes and failing – the problem isn't when you fall, it's when you stand still for fear of getting hurt. Be hungry for your dreams and for life, because this is the only one we've got. Be young and foolish, be kind to the world and open your hearts to life. Only this way will you learn to dream, and rest assured that once you start you'll never stop ...

London, 9 December 2019

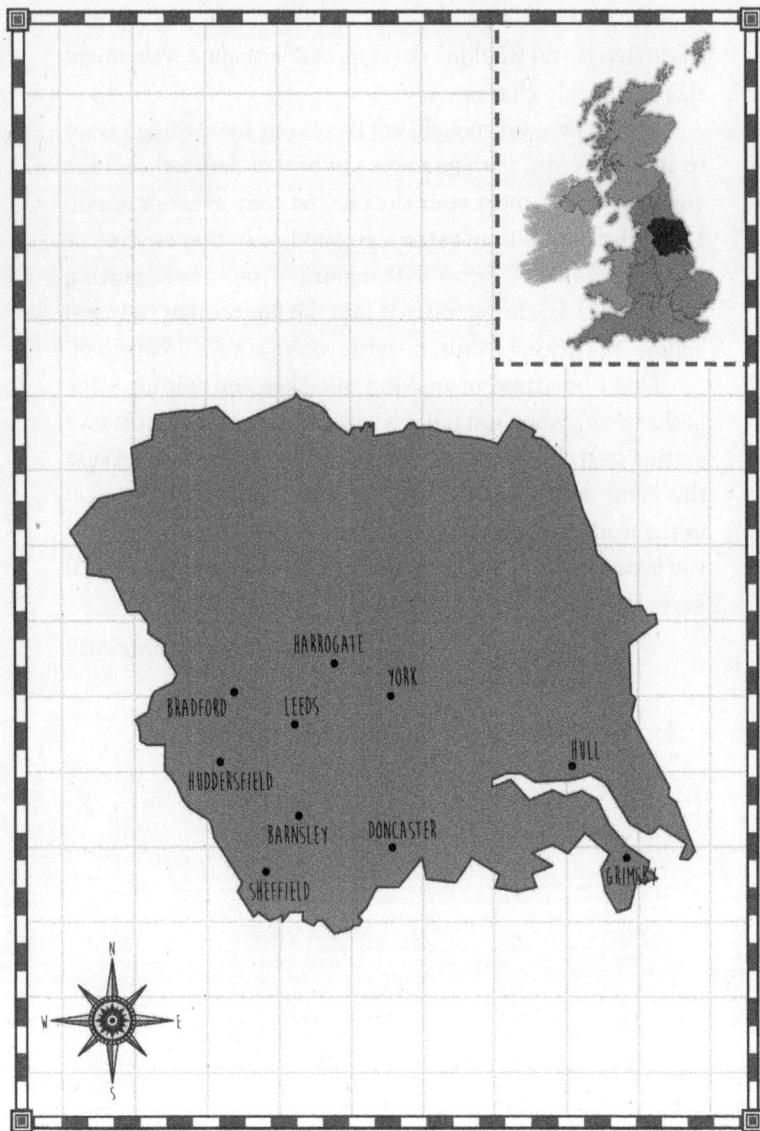

HARROGATE

YORK

BRADFORD

LEEDS

HULL

HUDDERSFIELD

BARNSLEY

DONCASTER

GRIMSBY

SHEFFIELD

YORKSHIRE AND
THE HUMBER

I love England, infinitely. I've always felt at home in that wonderful land, right from day one. And experiencing it and discovering it with my own eyes has only augmented this infinite love.

London apart, I think that York is England's finest city by far. It has a rich and fascinating history, visible still in its narrow streets, where time seems to have stopped. The Minster dominates the city, just as the endless green moors stamp their authority over the whole county.

Not far from York is the pretty spa town of Harrogate, also well worth a visit. To the south, in Sheffield, where football is a religion and the steel industry lifted the city to world renown, a walk through the streets evokes a different emotion. The beautiful game was born right there, and that in itself is reason enough.

I have much more to tell, and many stories await you in the pages that follow. Sit back and enjoy the ride – my journey to discover English football starts here.

THE HOME OF FOOTBALL

If I asked you to choose between watching a match played by Sheffield FC and spending hours and hours kicking a ball in their home ground, let's say with a good friend of yours, which would you go for? I've been lucky enough to do both.

If I had to choose, I assure you that I'd have much preferred the second option. Not just because there's nothing better than playing football with a good friend, but doing it on the home pitch of the oldest club in the world is not something that happens every day. On that particular day, life gave us a helping hand. When we got to the ground we found an open door and a punctured-looking ball lying in a goal net, giving Giuseppe and me one of the most exciting moments of our long journey. And this was just the beginning of the adventure.

That summer, in 2016, kicking a ball around on the pitch of the Coach and Horses Ground, I felt happier than I'd ever been.

I went back to Sheffield three years later. Not with Giuseppe this time, but with Lucio, my accomplice in many adventures. I was there, again in the summer, not to kick a ball but to watch a match between Sheffield FC and Hallam FC. Not just any match, but football's oldest derby.

Take your seats, the train bound for Sheffield is about to leave. The next stop is the unassuming Coach and Horses Ground – home to the world's first football club.

⚽⚽⚽

'Hi, Ivan, pleased to meet you. Come in, today you're our guest. In here is the little room with all the photos and trophies in our history. I've got a few things to take care of now, but don't worry. Make yourself at home. Enjoy your day!'

That's how Richard, chairman of Sheffield FC, introduced himself. Up to then I'd been given a good many warm welcomes around the country, but being received with such open kindness by the world's oldest football club was something special. It gave me such a stupendous feeling, because in this life I've never received anything for free, because I've worked hard day and night to achieve what I've always wanted and dreamed of.

Difficulties have always arisen, but it's up to us to keep bad thoughts at bay and make room for positive ones. I've always believed that an optimistic outlook is the first step towards a happy life – for me that's not a cliché, it's how it is.

For years I'd wake up every morning with my head full of bad stuff, thinking about all the things I didn't have. Then one day somebody shouted right in my face that the life I was leading was sickening, and it was true. It was true because I appreciated nothing of what was around me. I had no time for my mother, my father, even my brother. Having a meal with my family meant nothing to me. I didn't appreciate the beauty of a ray of sunshine or a blue sky. I appreciated nothing of what life was giving me, and what's worse was that I failed to appreciate the days I had. I threw them all away, thinking that sooner or later someone would give them back to me. Fat chance. Nobody gives back the time we've wasted, nobody puts right the mistakes we've made, but this is the very reason we can develop and get better.

I've done it and will continue to do so, step after step, problem after problem. I've worked hard to make myself better, I've shed tears when I felt the need and I've never shied away from my mistakes, just tried to find solutions for them. Solutions that led me, day by day, to nurture my dreams more and more, without knowing whether they'd ever produce anything.

Nurturing is far from simple, as was confirmed when Richard began to tell me his story and his club's history. At that moment, as his words touched my heart, my mind's eye was full of images of myself in February 2013, when I was washing dishes in a London restaurant, and of a few weeks later, when I was faced with the first and biggest failure of my life.

Even then, though, instead of throwing in the towel I redoubled my efforts, by concentrating not on my failure but on the second chance that life was offering me. To start afresh, start better and pursue my dreams along another path, with better organisation and more determination.

Think about this for a moment: what would have happened if I hadn't tried? Where would I be today if I'd given up on my dreams? These are difficult questions to answer. Looking back on those years, only one thing is certain: England changed my life.

If I'd given up, I wouldn't have written the book you're reading. There would have been no adventures to relate and no other dreams to pursue. So I say, open up that box where you've locked away your greatest wishes and go after them, just as Richard did in 2001 when he became chairman of Sheffield FC.

Since then, with passion and dedication, he has been true to the values espoused by William Prest and Sir Nathaniel Creswick in 1857 when they founded the first club in the history of football: Integrity, Respect and Community. Sound and healthy values, these.

But I wanted to know more about the past of that great little club. I wanted to discover its history, go back in time and imagine myself in the streets of Sheffield with William Prest and Sir Nathaniel Creswick. I wanted to feel part of a bygone age, and as I listened to Richard's words I got flashes of actually being there with them ...

One day in the summer of 1857 William Prest and his close friend Nathaniel Creswick went out for a walk in the English countryside. Their conversation centred on cricket and fencing, which in those days were the sports most popular with the well-off sons of Sheffield.

At one point they started to talk about the new game that was developing in some of England's state and private schools – the game of football. Aware of the fact that various forms of the game had been tried out around the world, but unaware that they would be the men who founded what is today's best-loved sport, as cricketers they thought that one of the best ways to keep fit during the winter would be to play this new game. The problem was that in those days football was played only in some schools, and each school applied different rules – in some cases the rules were even decided on the day of the match by the two team captains.

As time went by, the two men developed some ideas to give the game a more structured form, and with the help of the Sheffield committee they wrote to all the state and private schools to inform them that a new set of rules were going to be introduced in the interests of the better development of the game of football.

The first of these was: 'The game shall be commenced by a place kick from the centre of the ground.'

The first brick, which would change the game of football forever, had been laid. A few days later, on 24 October 1857 to be exact, Nathaniel and his friend William announced the birth of the first football club in the world: Sheffield Football Club.

I could hardly contain my excitement. Listening to Richard was like going back in time, and when the players of Sheffield

FC and Hallam FC went on to the pitch to warm up, I realised how fortunate I was to be there with them.

It's not just that this was the oldest club in the world: I was there talking to one of the successors of its two founders. The men who had played a crucial part in forging a new era, but who also provided some of the rules and innovations known today the world over, which are applied every day, from the street to the best-known stadiums in the world.

After establishing that the kick-off would take place in the centre of the pitch, the other innovations were: the corner kick, the foul, the free kick, the throw-in, the crossbar and – of crucial importance – a red or blue cap to be worn by every player so as to avoid confusion by distinguishing the two teams during the match.

Red and blue, the same colours worn on that cool July afternoon, under the excited gaze of over 300 spectators, by the players running after that magic ball. To celebrate not just the first two football clubs in history but, above all, the 159th match of the world's oldest football derby, of which the first was played at Sandygate, Hallam FC's ground, on Boxing Day 1860 and won by Sheffield FC by the score of two goals to nil.[1]

The Sheffield FC members had to wait three years to play that match, since Hallam FC wasn't founded until 1860. Up to then the only games played had been within the club. The married men would play the bachelors and the professional people would play a team of farmers, all playing and training with those rules and innovations of their own creation.

As the years passed, football and its rules began to evolve. In 1863, in London, the English Football Association was founded. Three years later, for the first time ever, Sheffield

---

1   Since 1860 it has been customary to play football matches on Boxing Day.

FC ventured outside their home city to play two matches, the first in Nottingham and the second in London, where the practice of heading the ball came into the game. In 1867, under the famous Sheffield Rules, the world's first knockout competition was held: the Youdan Cup. The legendary FA Cup first saw the light of day a few years later, in 1871.[2]

In those years, novelty and innovation came thick and fast. New clubs were springing up like mushrooms all over the country. And with them came a generation of supporters, swept up in a growing wave of popular enthusiasm. Football was able to bring together people from all walks of life, giving rise to hopes and dreams in supporters of all ages, exciting young and old alike, regaling them with joy and suffering, tears of sadness and smiles of happiness.

Smiles in which I was incessantly wreathed that July afternoon in the neat and charming setting of the Coach and Horses Ground, with which I was by then quite familiar but whose simplicity struck me as almost surreal – the pitch in the grounds of the Coach and Horses pub, the old gentleman selling tickets at the turnstile, and the club shop, as tiny as it was splendid. Non-league grounds have always held more fascination for me than the classic Premier League arenas, not only because they've retained the flavour of football as it was but also because it was there that the most remarkable and exciting stories originated.

As happened to me when, with the score at 4-0 to Sheffield FC, the referee blew the final whistle and Richard told me to go on to the pitch with him. From then on, to be honest, it's all a bit of a blur. One thing I do remember amid all the emotion is the awarding of the home side with the Alan Cooper Memorial Trophy – Richard took off his precious

---

2   The Sheffield Rules were the first rules of the game, in force from 1858 to 1877.

club scarf, put it round my neck and said, 'Ivan, you give the boys the cup!'

Those years of travelling round England were full of many other experiences just as memorable. Dreams come easily to me, but I could never have imagined finding myself awarding a cup to the oldest club in the world after watching them play (and win) the 159th edition of such an important and little-known derby. Not just any derby, the derby that every lover of the game should experience at least once in their life: quite simply, the 'World's Oldest Derby'.

WELCOME TO SANDYGATE: THE WORLD'S OLDEST FOOTBALL GROUND

It was just over half an hour before kick-off. The two teams were on the pitch, and I could see they were enjoying themselves. As I watched them I felt a touch of sadness at not being able to take the field myself and show everyone that I could have worn the No.9 shirt without a problem. I wished I could have been one of them, boots on my feet and that historic blue shirt on my back, fighting for a club more than a hundred years old. A club far from the limelight, playing in the most obscure of the English leagues and embodying one of the most inspiring stories ever told. One of the stories whose discovery requires a train journey to Sheffield and from there to Sandygate Road, home to Hallam Football Club since 1804. A place like no other – simply the world's oldest football ground.

❀❀❀

I first found myself at Sandygate Road one day in December 2016. It was cold, and a wild wind blew at me all day long. It was two days before the umpteenth Christmas I'd be spending away from my family, but the happiness of that day made me forget everything …

The half-hour bus ride separating the centre of Sheffield from that tiny historic ground was a tonic for the eyes and the spirit, soothed by the sight of the green hills picked out in sharp detail. It felt like being in a film, a short but intense journey made unforgettable by the roofs of the characteristic terraced houses. A journey to discover days gone by, difficult to relive but one I tried to imagine when I found myself outside the old Plough Inn, standing opposite the tiny entrance to the ground.

Unfortunately, everything was shut. There wasn't a soul in sight, but rather than going away empty-handed, as I usually did, I decided to look for another way in. The Catholic church of St Francis of Assisi, standing next to the ground, is separated from it by a stone wall about six feet high. When I was a boy I used to kick footballs all over the place, and I'd climbed hundreds of walls like that one. So, having made sure the coast was clear, I quickly scaled it and in the blink of an eye I was right inside the ground.

Silence reigned supreme. The only sound was the keening of the wind as it swept impetuously through the surrounding trees. The sky, greyer than ever, promised nothing but rain and more rain. Oblivious to all that, as happy and curious as a little boy, I explored every nook and cranny of that inner sanctum. Walking across the centre circle I suddenly noticed something I'd never encountered in a football ground before.

Seemingly perfect, the pitch was on a slope, the like of which I'd never seen. I'd heard about sloped pitches before, but seeing that one and standing on it was an experience I'll not forget. Struck by that strange new sensation, I wondered what it would be like to play there, running around a pitch that was anything but normal.

As fate would have it, a few moments later I found out, thanks to a ball I retrieved from the branches of a tree behind one of the goals. Blithely ignoring anyone who might have seen me, I played with that ball for an hour, imagining myself in an age long past. In an age when, in that very place where I was playing, on 26 December 1860, football's first derby match was held between Hallam FC and Sheffield FC – the clubs who wrote an indelible page of history remembered to this day.

And in my own way I saw that history. First by playing unhindered on the grass of Sandygate, then, three years later, by putting my hands on the world's oldest football trophy: the glorious, the unknown Youdan Cup, which came into being on 16 February 1867.

As well as a football enthusiast, Thomas Youdan was the owner of a theatre in the centre of Sheffield. After coming to the conclusion that playing nothing but friendly matches left something to be desired, he had the idea of financing the manufacture of a modest trophy that would be played for by 12 teams.

Just over a fortnight after the cup's appearance, on 5 March 1867, Hallam FC went down in history as the first team to win it, a feat proudly remembered to this day. Their success was achieved in front of 2,000 spectators in the now-famous setting of Bramall Lane. With a 2-0 victory over Norfolk Club, the boys in the blue shirts watched John Charles Shaw – founder, player and club captain – proudly lift the trophy.

Shortly thereafter, however, the cup somehow got lost – it vanished into thin air and wasn't seen or heard of for over a century. In 1997 it was spotted by a Scottish antique dealer, who contacted the club and sold them their precious trophy.

Despite its history, Hallam FC is a club far removed from the attention of the big television channels. Which is a pity, considering the simplicity and warmth to be enjoyed by spending a day in the splendid setting of Sandygate. A special place with extraordinary people who spend their free time working for the club without getting a penny, who do it out of undying passion for the game of football. A passion that on one October afternoon, at a league match against Nostell Miners Welfare FC, my friends Fabio and Giuseppe and I witnessed with our own eyes, after being welcomed to the club.

Club volunteer Sharon, together with Hallam FC chairman Steve, made us feel at home, offered us something to drink and took us on a tour of the club's history, showing us photographs and various memorabilia.

Hallam FC owes its existence to John Charles Shaw and the 300-plus members who in 1860 belonged to Hallam Cricket Club, founded as long ago as 1804. Since its inception, the cricket team had played its matches there at Sandygate and had its headquarters at the Plough Inn.

The Plough is a historic pub for the city of Sheffield. It was there that Hallam FC was founded and there that the footballers would gather before and after the matches, using it first as a changing room and then as a place to relax with a pint or two. A pint that on that October afternoon I didn't have to drink away from the terraces, as is the case in every Premier League ground these days, but took with me right beside the pitch, leaning on a small steel crash barrier as I watched those lads give battle on the sloping field. A slope like that, and a ground that's been there for more than two centuries – it's a unique experience.

And it's a ground on which I've had the honour of chasing a football, grinning uncontrollably and with my mind going back in time, picturing myself alongside John Charles Shaw in the discovery of a football long gone. A moment that I've tried, in my own small way, to relive. Not wearing those historic club colours, but at least kicking a ball in the place where it all started.

So now I can say I've played, at least once, in the world's oldest football ground.

THE BLADES

In the Cricketers Arms, traditional watering hole for Sheffield United fans, the atmosphere was electric. All fired up for the new season, Blades shirts on and pints in hand, the supporters sang and sang at the top of their voices.

Their eyes shone with belief, displaying an unbreakable bond I'd rarely seen before – not just with the colours, which were part of their identity, but above all with the city itself, to which they were so proud to belong. A city with a wealth of stories to tell, many of which were set right there, at Bramall Lane, a stone's throw from the pub. Sacred to every supporter, the ground is home to relics and photographs of unrepeatable times – some in black and white, many others in red and white.

On that blazing early August afternoon those two colours made me feel as if I belonged to those people, supporters who couldn't wait for the season to start. People who nine months later would be celebrating promotion to the Premier League, so nothing would have been better than spending the entire season at their side. Not just to feel part of them, but to experience the spectacular setting of Bramall Lane, the oldest professional football ground in the world.

⚽⚽⚽

My eyes were pricking with tears and shivers ran up and down me. Three months was too long to have been away from the packed ranks inside the ground. So when the 24,000 fans in Bramall Lane burst into the 'Greasy Chip Butty' song, my emotions got the better of me and the passion of those people transported me into their world. An unbelievable experience, to be sure, but it was actually the best thing that could have happened to me. Seeing men, women and children feel so alive and so ecstatic in belting out the song that stood for their identity, their city and their club – it was like entering another dimension. A dimension that can't be explained in writing, nor by word of mouth, because to capture the true essence of the support at Bramall Lane you have to be there, to feel it on your skin. Over 160 years of history around you, which you can sense before you go through the turnstiles, with small round plaques marking the buildings along Cherry Street, overlooked by the magnificent Tony Currie Stand. Red plaques to commemorate important events in the club's history, to remind any passer-by that they're not in the presence of just another football ground, but a place that turned football into an institution: this was the venue of the first floodlit football match in history.

A visit to the ground makes it clear. Bramall Lane was the first real home of football for the city of Sheffield. The home that in those early years became the headquarters of Sheffield FC and Sheffield Wednesday. It then became the permanent home of Sheffield United, founded in March 1889. In the first 30 years of its existence the club won the FA Cup four times and the First Division title once, but since 1925 it has been unable to put any major silverware in the trophy cabinet at Bramall Lane. The cupboard may be bare, but all the lean years have done nothing to dull the fans' commitment.

I saw living proof of this during the Blades' Championship match against Swansea City when, in the 62nd minute, George Baldock smashed the ball into the net to put his team into the lead. The supporters went wild, jumping for joy as if they'd just won the title. Then, in little more than 20 minutes, Swansea turned the game around and claimed all three points, but none of the home supporters lost heart. They left Bramall Lane solidly behind their lads, letting loose with another refrain of the 'Greasy Chip Butty' song and showing the whole world that no defeat, no missed trophy would ever change their love for their team and their colours.

This is a historic club, passion for which has been passed down through the generations for 130 years, from father to son, grandfather to grandchild – with the oldest pointing the way to Bramall Lane and reminding the youngsters that there will never be anything better in the world than Sheffield United.

One curious and well-known fact about Bramall Lane is that it started life as a cricket ground and was used for cricket as well as football matches until 1973. Until that time the adjoining football stadium had only three stands, the fourth side being open to the cricket outfield. The ground acquired its current form in 1975 with the opening of the new (Tony Currie) stand.

IN MEMORY OF THE 97

It's a sad thing to say, but every time I think of Sheffield Wednesday the first thing that comes to mind is that ill-fated day, 15 April 1989. It was a Saturday afternoon. On the neutral ground of Hillsborough, the FA Cup semi-final between Liverpool and Nottingham Forest was due to kick off at 3pm. The referee blew the whistle to start the game right on time, but what happened in the minutes that followed has gone down as one of the darkest and most painful episodes in the history of English football. Below is a brief summary of what has come to be known as the Hillsborough disaster.

⚽ ⚽ ⚽

I'll never forget the first time I set foot in Sheffield. On that summer's day in 2015 high winds and driving rain welcomed me to a city of workers, famous for its steel industry and as the birthplace of football. Football not just as a sport, but a way of life. Something that bestows hope on an entire population, split in two and always ready to follow their respective colours around the country. Colours that in the north of the city shine blue and white for Sheffield Wednesday, who owe their existence to members of the Wednesday Cricket Club.

This new team was founded on 4 September 1867. The main aim of the Cricket Club members was to keep the players busy during the winter months, when the willow and the leather are in mothballs. In the first 30 years of its life, the club known as Sheffield Wednesday played at four different venues, spending some time at the historic Olive Grove ground before settling at Hillsborough in 1899.

Hillsborough is not the same as other grounds. It stands in the suburb of Owlerton, which I've visited a couple of times, always with a heavy heart. With sadness at the thought of the worst tragedy ever to have struck English football, a tragedy that took the lives of 97 people and broke the hearts of an entire nation that only four years earlier, in May 1985, had to face the Bradford City fire (in which 56 people died) and the Heysel disaster in Brussels, in which Liverpool supporters were involved and 39 Juventus fans died. There's a small plaque in memory of those fans at Anfield. A few yards from that is a bigger memorial bearing the names of the Liverpool supporters who lost their lives at Hillsborough's Leppings Lane end, designated for them on that day and subsequently written into history for the saddest of reasons.

The Leppings Lane end is skirted by the River Don and shrouded in complete silence. Not only on that rainy morning in 2015 but, above all, a few years later when I returned to Hillsborough for a Championship match against Brentford. To me that night the match was of secondary importance – as I looked around I tried to go back in time, picturing myself there on the terrible afternoon of 15 April 1989. In those days English football grounds were not the ultra-modern stadiums we see today, and although Hillsborough was considered one of the best grounds in the country, nothing and nobody was able to prevent that awful tragedy.

It was caused by a serious error on the part of the police. To ease the pressure of the mass of Liverpool fans trying to get through the seven turnstiles at the Leppings Lane end, match commander Chief Superintendent David Duckenfield gave the order to open Gate C and let over 2,000 fans on to the terraces in time for kick-off.[3] A kick-off that the police decided not to postpone, and by the time the thousands of supporters started to flood through Gate C, disaster was inevitable.

---

3   Before the Hillsborough tragedy, most English football grounds had large sections of terracing. Nowadays terraces are mainly confined to non-league grounds.

Given the perfect modern design of the English stadiums we know today, that disaster is hard to imagine, but it can be seen on a multitude of video clips and the few – brutal – photographs taken at the scene. Ninety-six people were killed, crushed and suffocated by the mass of supporters allowed to charge through Gate C and bear down on those already standing on the terraces waiting for the match to start.

The pictures of the ground as it was on that terrible day show precious little of what could be called safe or reliable. The fencing divided the spectators on the terraces into pens, and the few emergency exits provided were far too narrow. Hundreds of fans managed to escape the carnage that day by climbing the fencing that separated them from the pitch, others by being hauled up from the terraces by the people in the stand above. A stand packed with supporters who looked on in horror at the disaster that would change the face of English football forever.

On the basis of the findings of the Taylor Report, since then all professional clubs have had to modernise their grounds and replace the old terracing with seats to avoid further episodes of that kind.

In the aftermath of the disaster, the police, particularly in the person of David Duckenfield, did all they could to lay the blame at the feet of the Liverpool supporters, lying systematically for over 20 years and falsifying dozens and dozens of documents.

It wasn't until September 2012, thanks to an independent commission of enquiry, that the Report of the Hillsborough Independent Panel produced considerable new documentary evidence and brought to light a great many details that had been deliberately hidden for more than 20 years. Horrifying details that told the true story of what had happened on that fateful day. A day that the victims' families will never be able to forget. Not only because David Duckenfield and the police force deployed that day have never been held criminally liable for their actions but because nothing and no one will bring back the 97 people lost that day to their families.

Those lost loved ones are remembered and commemorated every year at Anfield on 15 April, first in the reverent silence of a whole community and then to the unmistakable notes of 'You'll Never Walk Alone'. An anthem to life and to love. In memory of those who have gone but who live in everybody's hearts.

Final note: Over 30 years later, the only individual to have received a criminal conviction is Graham Mackrell, former club secretary of Sheffield Wednesday, for failing to take reasonable care to ensure that the turnstile allocation and ticketing arrangements for the Leppings Lane end of Hillsborough did not result in large crowds building up. In May 2019 he was sentenced to a fine of £6,500 and ordered to pay costs of £5,000.

The 2012 panel found that the Liverpool supporters were in no way responsible for the disaster – a conclusion given further weight by the 2016 inquest, which stated that those same supporters had been unlawfully killed. In the consequent trial, held after it had been established that a criminal action had led to the death of a person, the jury was unable to reach a verdict in the case against David Duckenfield. The Crown Prosecution Service was granted leave to retry the case in October 2019, before a different jury. On 28 November 2019, after 13 hours of deliberations, the jury in Preston Crown Court found David Duckenfield not guilty of gross negligence manslaughter. Amid a series of collapsed cases, acquittals and trials yet to be held, thus far only Graham Mackrell has received a conviction. (Final note courtesy of Indro Pajaro, author of the book *15 Aprile 1989. La verità sul disastro di Hillsborough.*)

REMEMBER THE 56

You could feel the people's passion straight away. Men, women, children and sprightly oldsters, no matter what the age difference, were all united by those colours, sewn on to them like a second skin. I was astonished to see the number of people wearing something – anything – with Bradford City colours: shirts, shoes, caps, full club strip and boots for toddlers, wigs in club colours, kids' faces painted claret and amber, and a well of devotion in all their eyes. Passion that swept over me as the two teams took the pitch, devotion that made me well up.

It was an August afternoon when I finally found myself in a place I'd wanted to visit for so long. A place renowned not for the trophies won or the football played there, but for one of the most awful tragedies the history of football has ever had to recount.

⚽⚽⚽

I'd woken up at five o'clock that morning, I remember it well. The journey to Bradford would be a long one, and as the brightening London sky announced a new day, I picked up my backpack and set out for the station, still sleepy and pretty tired out by long hours of work. But the happiness and euphoria of moments like that seemed to sweep everything away – fatigue, problems, things missing, things needed; a rush of adrenaline went through me every time. For years I'd been soldiering on without the things that a lad in his early 20s should be enjoying. A carefree life, good times with friends, all-night parties, seeing more of your family, a few days' holiday by the sea and, if possible, something more to eat than a plain bread roll or, on a good day, one filled with odourless taste-free salami.

That was my lunch on most of the journeys I made, and no matter how long and winding the road, I can assure you that I'd do it all again. I'd go back to every town and every football ground without regretting any of it for a second.

Perhaps I'd avoid repeating some of the mistakes I made, but now that I think of it, they were useful too. To err is human, and if you don't make errors, you can't learn from them. I've always thought that the mistakes we make can give rise to fresh opportunities to achieve what we want the most.

To my way of thinking, the difference between someone who's happy and someone angry with life is the attitude you have towards existence. To fall is normal, it's par for the course, but the difference lies in how you get up and how you react to difficulties. In those days, when I couldn't afford more than a plain bread roll and a tiny room in one of the most run-down parts of Manchester, what kept me going and stopped me from giving up was the motivation to change my life and fulfil my biggest dreams.

Facing problems head-on and laughing in the face of my troubles was the best thing I could have done. If I hadn't done that, now I'd have no stories to tell and no other dreams to pursue, just pathetic and endless unhappiness. Unhappiness that comes over you when you abandon your dreams, letting in the fear and feelings of insecurity that all of us are prey to. These feelings can be ironed out and overcome bit by bit, climbing one step at a time and not looking up at the heights you have to scale.

Which is what I did, starting from a job washing dishes and facing a whole range of difficulties, and after a few years being able to set foot in all the grounds I'd dreamed of visiting, and even writing a book with the best stories from those visits. Stories that inspired me and touched my heart. Among these, though, sad to say, is one of the most dreadful tragedies ever to have struck football. It was 11 May 1985 when that disaster changed the history of English football. It happened there, in the proud stadium standing silently before me on that August morning – Valley Parade, home of Bradford City.

There was no one about. Just a cool early August breeze and the years of history speeding past in my mind's eye. I looked around, set my phone on silent mode so as not to be disturbed and walked towards the reception.

Gayana was there making the final preparations to receive all the people who would soon be arriving. As soon as I'd told her my story and the journey I was making, without a second thought she opened the doors of that historic ground and gave me a guided tour of her world. Walking along the corridors under the Main Stand, looking at picture after picture, I had the impression of reviewing the entire history of the club, with each season's shirt carefully hung on the wall alongside photos of City's FA Cup Final victory as long ago as 1911.

Fascinating as it was, though, my attention was directed elsewhere, and Gayana wasn't slow on the uptake. I wasn't there for the standard conducted tour, but to find out more about that terrible day, a day seared into the memory – as she told me on the terraces shortly afterwards – of every Bradford City supporter.

'Just here was the stand that caught fire on that terrible 11 May 1985. I shudder every time I think about it. I'm sorry.'

Gayana had been happy to show me around the ground, but as soon as I asked her whether she knew anything more, sadness showed in her eyes. It was sadness that came from the heart, but slowly she began to tell me what happened that afternoon ...

It was supposed to be a celebration – we'd won the Third Division title. Everything was going to start at the end of the match, but at about 4.220 huge flames began to shoot up from Block G. Dozens and dozens of people, people of all ages, literally threw themselves on to the pitch, some of them covered in flames. The fire was probably caused by a cigarette, because in those days smoking was allowed at matches. In less than ten minutes the whole stand went up in flames, killing 56 people. Including a girl, my cousin.

I didn't know what to say. To be honest, there isn't much you can say at a moment like that. As she spoke, Gayana gazed at the pitch, holding back the tears. For a few seconds we were silent, and when I apologised for bringing back such distant memories, she attempted a smile and went on with her painful story:

Her name was Moira Helen Hodgson. She was only 15. She worked for the club too, selling match programmes right there in that bloody stand. She would have been all right if she hadn't dropped her pouch with the money in it. It seems unbelievable now that she went back just to get that bit of change. She should be here with us, but she's gone ...

I was shocked. At that moment no words would have made any sense, so I put a hand on her shoulder in the hope of giving her some strength and sympathy.

On that August afternoon, a few hours after hearing that terrible story, I was bowled over by the feeling of warmth inside Valley Parade. The feeling of a whole community, a passion beyond all logic, expressed by over 18,000 spectators in the ground. That's right, 18,000 people for a match in League One. A match whose final whistle saw the home side go down by two goals to nil. Aside from the result, what struck me was the mass of fans around the pitch, people of all ages singing out their support for the club from the first second to the last. Support I was surrounded by in the heart of the Kop Stand, with drums, flags flying in the wind and chant after chant to the rhythm of tireless hand-clapping, as my gaze was constantly drawn from the field of play to the Main Stand.

That's where the disaster happened, and as the referee brought the match to a close and the fans began to make their way home, I sat where I was, waiting for the ground to empty. I stayed there in silence for more than ten minutes, trying to picture myself there on that fateful day in May 1985, trying to fathom the pain and fear in the eyes of those who were there. Pain that nearly 40 years has not faded from the minds and the eyes of those people – it will live forever in the gaze and memory of anyone who has set foot in Valley Parade.

DON REVIE IN COMMAND

The Championship match between Leeds United and Stoke City had finished several hours earlier, and although the train carrying me back to London was about to reach the station, my head was still ringing with the sound of 'Marching On Together', the anthem belted out at full volume by all the home fans at Elland Road – a spine-tingling experience.

On that hot August afternoon, at the first league match under renowned manager Marcelo Bielsa, Elland Road and its 34,126 spectators had me spellbound. Just mingling with those fans, who would have laid down their lives for Leeds United, was a rare privilege. Even today, when I hear mention of Leeds United, it's hard not to go back in time and relive one of the most engrossing adventures English football has ever given me …

⚽⚽⚽

The sun rising over the city of Leeds beat rudely on uncurtained window panes as a blue sky bade me good morning and reminded me that a new experience was in store. A gentle breeze caressed my face as soon as I walked out of the room where I'd spent the night. The warm rays of the Yorkshire sun filled me with a deep feeling of peace. My dear old backpack, veteran of countless trips, was particularly heavy that day, but my only concern was to squeeze the most from every second of that new experience.

I quickly got past Leeds Bridge and, quite suddenly, as I was trying to find a bus to the ground, I found myself walking along Hunslet Road. I reached the end of the road in the serene conviction that I was heading in the right direction. I was wrong. Looking around for some sign or other, my eye was caught by the blue of a small round plaque, fixed to the wall of Salem Chapel, built in 1791. At the bottom of the plaque were the words 'Leeds United FC was founded here in 1919'. I stood staring at it.

As I did so, open-mouthed, shivers went down my back at the thought of standing on the very spot where a club as legendary as Leeds United had been founded (or rather re-founded) almost a century before. I say that because from 1904 to 1919 the Yorkshire town was represented by Leeds City FC, which was dissolved as a result of financial irregularities and succeeded by the club everyone knows today – Leeds United Football Club.

The bus ride from the city centre to the ground was a silent one, since I was the only passenger. I encountered the same silence a short time later at the top of a small hill at the end of Marley Terrace, close to Elland Road. The only sounds to be heard were the rustle of the wind in the trees and the boisterous shouts of some children in the nearby streets, wearing the shirts of their beloved club as they kicked a ball around. They shouted out the names of their heroes after every goal they scored. Just as I'd done as a boy.

Our heroes are the players who have inspired our dreams and will always do so, no matter how much time passes and how old we grow. What matters is to hold on to the desire to believe in something, as did the legendary Billy Bremner and Donald George Revie – from simple lads whose bread and butter was football. As the years went by, it was here at Leeds that they grew into heroes.

The greatness achieved by these two mythical figures becomes clear as you leave the hill and walk towards Elland Road – the ground bulks larger and more imposing as you approach, and then you see their statues, standing in constant guard over their legendary home.

It was about two and a half hours before kick-off when I sat down at the foot of Don Revie's statue, imagining the years when he and his men made Leeds United great. As the supporters gathered in their hundreds, the club shirts they were wearing began to paint the stadium walls white.

Before going for a pre-match drink, several fans, especially older ones, came to pay homage to the statue, as if to implore Don Revie to come back and make history again. The history he made still lives in the hearts of the people here, and I could see it reflected in the eyes of the massed ranks of supporters as Elland Road rang with their rousing chorus of 'Marching On Together'.

That excitement was still with me when, after the match, thanks to Lorenzo and my friend Andrea, I was given the chance to go on to the pitch and lay my hands on the grass in that glorious ground, to walk on the very spot where Don Revie and his loyal band of men laid the foundations, in 1961, of one of the finest stories English football has ever told.

As I sat down on the bench, my mind began to travel back in time to the days when Don Revie and his team achieved greatness. Before their names were written into football's Hall of Fame, though, the early days had been far from easy. In April 1962, in their final match of the season, it was only by beating Newcastle United by three goals to nil at St James' Park that Leeds avoided a disastrous relegation to the Third Division.

The following season brought some important changes – the traditional yellow and blue club colours were abandoned to make way for an all-white strip (like Real Madrid's) and, more importantly, Don Revie drilled it into the heads of everyone under his command, from the players to the kit men, that Leeds United had to be one big family. As per Billy Bremner's ethos, everybody would have to have the same values, and above all Leeds United would come before everything and everyone, including themselves. Exactly as is written on the outer façade of Elland Road's main stand: side before self, every time.

As the years went by, Don Revie's iron will and the development of quality players brought up through the youth system bore fruit in the form of a tight-knit squad that set up a remarkable winning cycle, running from 1968 to 1974. That was the year when Revie left Leeds United to manage the England team. But his name will remain forever in the hearts of the people of the city on the strength of the trophies he brought to Leeds: two First Division titles, two Inter-Cities Fairs Cups, a Charity Shield, a League Cup and an FA Cup.

In that FA Cup Final, played at Wembley on 6 May 1972 in front of 100,000 spectators, Leeds United beat Arsenal 1-0 thanks to a goal by Allan Clarke, whose path I happened by pure chance to cross on that August afternoon outside Elland Road. Staring at him for a few moments, I lost myself in his eyes, the eyes of a man who had played a leading part in the golden years of Don Revie's Dirty Leeds, years in which the people of Elland Road celebrated unforgettable triumphs.[4]

Although figures like Don Revie and Billy Bremner are no longer to be seen in that part of the world, the people of Leeds will continue to support their club in the hope of a return to glory. Putting Leeds United before everything else and roaring out 'Marching On Together'. Every time I hear it, the shivers will come back ...

---

4 Dirty Leeds was a nickname given in the 1970s to Don Revie's team. He's said to have ordered his players to play as hard and dirty as necessary in order to win matches.

CHAPTER 2

FACE YOUR FEARS

*The cave you fear to enter holds
the treasure you seek.*

Joseph Campbell

IT SEEMS only yesterday that I found myself faced with the first big failure of my life. I remember every single thing about it. It was the night of 23 March 2013. It was cold and there wasn't a soul to be seen on the streets of London. My eyes were full of sadness and pain, only too aware that my dream of playing football in England was about to end.

Sat on the pavement outside Victoria station, waiting for the bus that would take me to the airport, two heavy bags beside me and my eyes brimming with tears, I scanned the London sky in search of answers. In a few hours I'd be back home, leaving my hopes and dreams in the city I loved so much.

I was 19 at the time, still beardless, and the only thing I wanted was to play football in the stadiums that had always fascinated me. I really believed I could, and I'd left everything and everybody to pursue that dream, but nothing went according to plan.

It took just 32 days to go from the dream of playing football in England to returning to the village where I grew up, feeling the world crashing down around me as I realised I'd failed. But I've travelled many roads since that day.

Broken-hearted, I decided to give up on my dream of being a footballer. I began to work as hard as I could to get enough money to go back to the country where I felt I belonged. Step by step, I found myself facing up to my greatest fears, and two years after that first and great failure I found the courage to pack my bags again and leave all my insecurity behind me. My one hope? To fulfil my dreams. That was 11 March 2015.

More than anything else, almost every day, I struggled with myself, repeating to myself that the problem isn't failing, but abandoning your ambitions out of fear of failure. Fear should never stop you fighting for what you want, because where there's fear, there will be unhappiness, and where there's unhappiness, there's no life. In my case, though, the fear of another failure was always alive; at every turn I found the courage to fight, facing life head-on and putting myself on the line every day.

Now that I think back, almost seven years after that great failure, I can say that it was worth finding the courage to face my fears. Leaving everything to pursue my dreams was the right choice to make. It was the right thing to do because it gave me the chance to develop by going out to see the world. I lived in England for more than four years, I learned English, I visited hundreds of football grounds all over the country and I watched over 130 matches in the places that had always sparked my dreams.

I discovered the nation that I love in its every corner, I attended courses for coaching badges conducted in a language that I'd never had the chance to study. I started working as a coach, I found myself telling my story on television and achieved my ambition of playing football for an English team.

I worked as a waiter for a whole season at Stamford Bridge, in the private box assigned to the family of Callum Hudson-Odoi, and with them I watched almost all of Chelsea's matches. Above all, I had the honour of working at the club's training ground at Cobham, living day by day with all those lads who made the sacrifices necessary to realise what was my greatest dream.

I met some wonderful people. One of them is Eleonora, and I hope with all my heart to have made my family proud.

Little by little, I've gained increasing confidence in my own abilities. I've got to know my inner self and found a way to develop as a man and as a person. I've had the chance to strike up relationships with people from all over the world. I've lived in the Lake District, in Manchester and then in London. I've done all manner of jobs. From dishwasher to barista, from farmer to electrician, from shop assistant to barman. From mechanic to bookie's cashier, from tour guide to pizza man, from waiter to burger flipper in a McDonald's in Manchester.

I've met some of the greatest legends in English football. I've experienced this, and much else besides. I've found the courage to face my biggest fears and, more than anything else, I've known what happiness is – and for me it's freedom.

What if I'd never tried? What would have happened? If I'd been afraid of failing, where would I be today? As I've said before, these are difficult questions to answer, but I want to say one last thing.

Being afraid is normal. Failing, making mistakes, falling down and getting hurt are part and parcel of life. The development of every individual starts precisely there: with hard falls and failures. And from there come the greatest lessons.

There's one thing I've always believed. At the end of the day, as Denis Waitley said:

Failure should be our teacher, not our undertaker.
Failure is delay, not defeat. It's a temporary detour, not
a dead end. Failure is something we can avoid only by
saying nothing, doing nothing and being nothing.

So how are you living your life? Are you facing your fears?

London, 5 February 2020

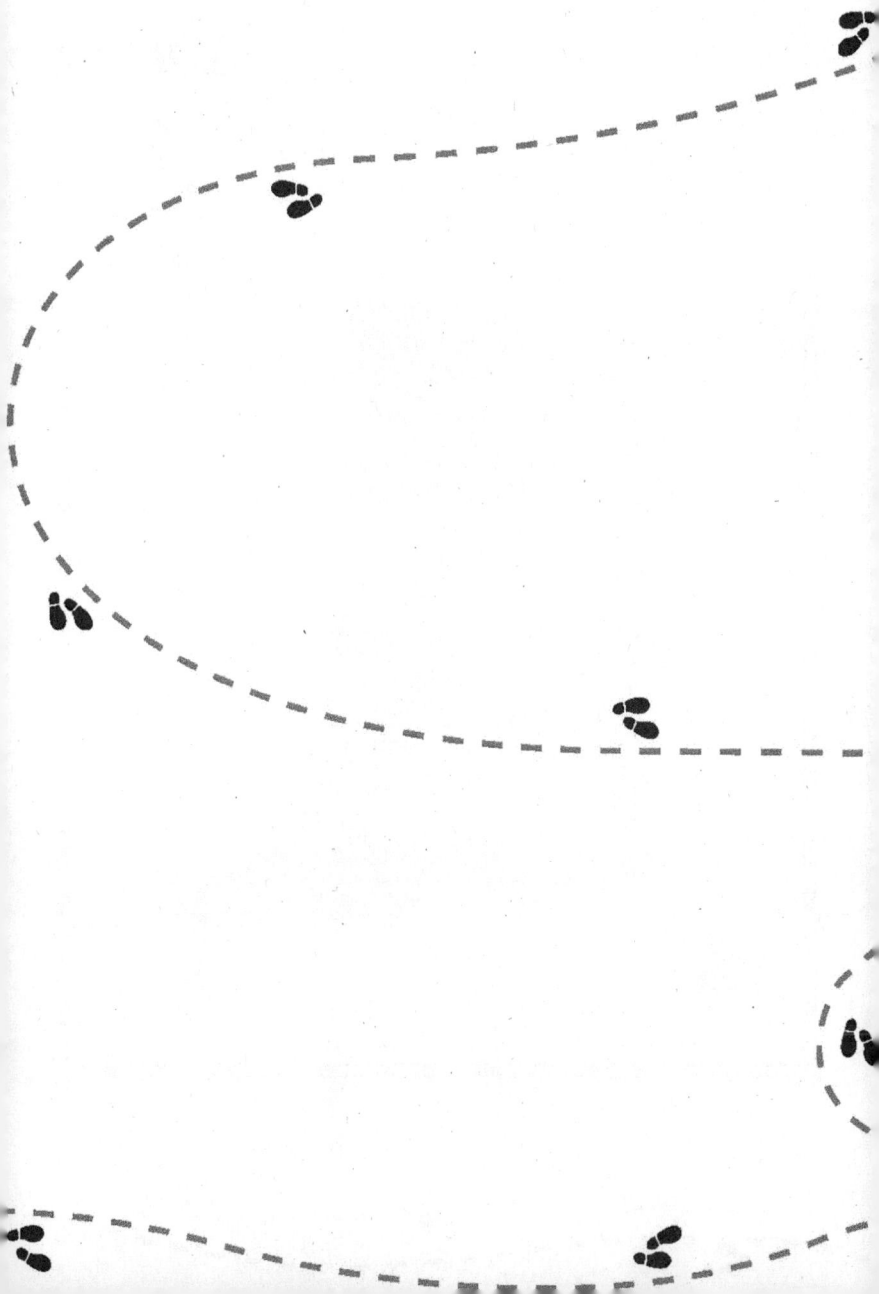

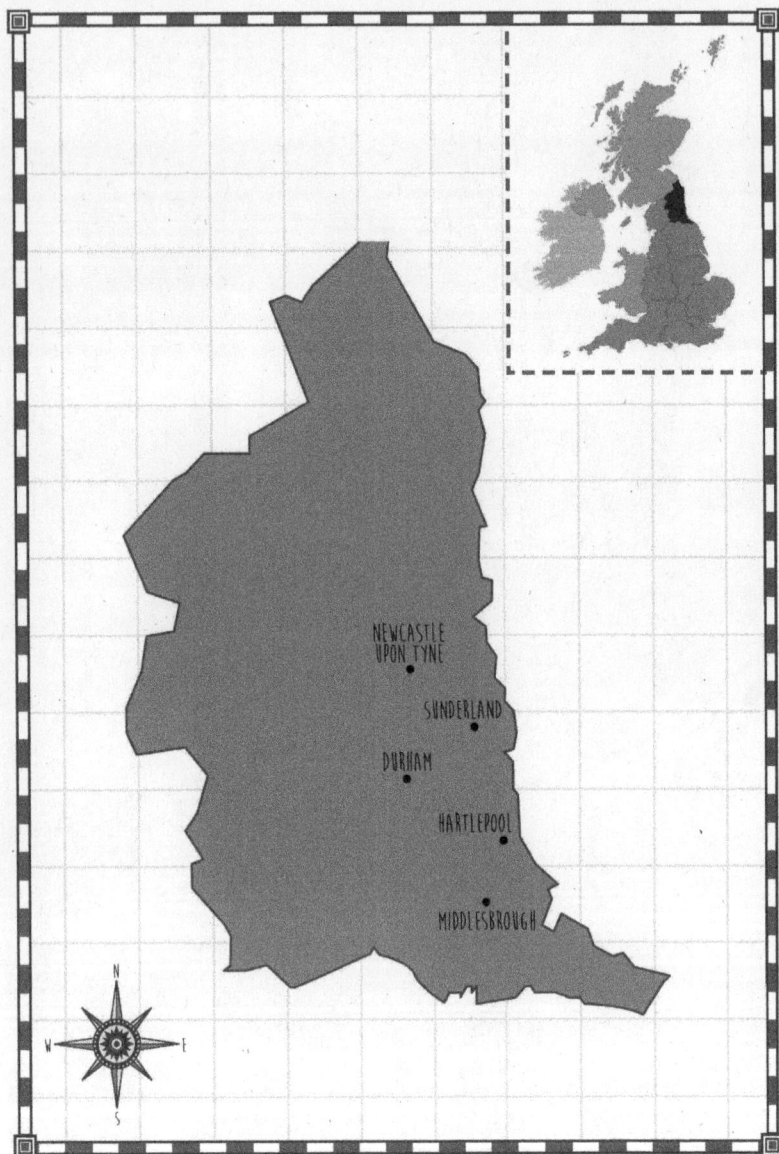

NEWCASTLE
UPON TYNE

SUNDERLAND

DURHAM

HARTLEPOOL

MIDDLESBROUGH

NORTH EAST

Passion, beer and football. The North East of England is without doubt one of the best places in which to get first-hand experience of real English football. The rivalry between Newcastle and Sunderland can only be understood by going to that corner of the country. For the people there, nothing can equal their club and their city, irrespective of the division they play in. And, I would add, the incessant rain.

But the North East is not only home to Sunderland and Newcastle. Not only can it boast many other clubs but it's also the birthplace of men who have written football history. Among the greatest of them are Sir Bobby Charlton, Sir Bobby Robson, Brian Clough, Alan Shearer, Bob Paisley and Don Revie, all of whom rose from nothing to become legends of world football.

It's also a place to which I have very strong ties, not only because of what football means there but especially because of a remarkable and moving encounter I had with Bradley Lowery. A boy who left an indelible mark on my life, difficult to explain and impossible to forget.

The memory of my journey to the North East is encapsulated in these things: little Bradley, Alan Shearer's Newcastle United, my dear friend Alan Simpson's Sunderland, and a great little club with an extraordinary history, standing at a stone's throw from the cold North Sea …

THERE'S ONLY ONE BRADLEY LOWERY

'Where are you going to sleep tonight?' asked Alan, after sinking his umpteenth pint of the day.

'We'll be in Newcastle. First thing tomorrow morning we're leaving for Glasgow,' I blandly replied as I emptied my glass.

'What? Newcastle?' he grinned. 'I don't even go shopping there! We're from Sunderland and around here there's no better place!'

'Oh my God. Sorry, Alan …' I was afraid I'd put my foot in it.

'Not to worry. Howay, I'll show you what my world's like – the land of the Black Cats!'

⚽ ⚽ ⚽

The Colliery Tavern, hard by the Stadium of Light, was crammed with fans. The beer was flowing like water and the chanting and singing lent the place an air of romance. Wearing her beloved club's shirt, a little girl held on tight to her dad's hand, and as thousands of supporters converged on the entrance to the ground, Alan stopped in front of the statue of local legend Bob Stokoe. It was there, eyes shining, that he began to tell me one of the best stories of his glorious club …

> You know, Ivan, for those of us who were born and raised here, Sunderland is more than just a football team. Sunderland is our life and our hope. It's our only light on the long grey days of rain. Sunderland's always been a working-class city, and 5 May 1973 is considered by far the best day of our lives. I was seven at the time, just a boy, but I remember every single minute of that fantastic day.

After we beat Manchester City in the quarter-finals and then Arsenal in the semis, we found ourselves in the FA Cup Final up against the mighty Leeds United. We were in the Second Division then, and getting to Wembley and playing in front of 100,000 spectators was an incredible prospect. Nothing less than a dream come true.

The day before the match, my dad went down to London along with thousands of other supporters. Me, my mum and my sister went to see it at my grandma's, because she had a better telly than us. Right from the kick-off, I was just a bag of nerves – until, out of nowhere, what I'd been hoping for actually happened. They'd been playing for just over half an hour when our Billy Hughes took the ball up towards the corner flag, and some of our biggest lads were running into the area. You could cut the tension with a knife.

In grandma's house everything went quiet. Wor Billy Hughes had a quick look up and belted the ball into the middle of the area ... Vic Halom couldn't control it and the ball ran to our number ten, Ian Porterfield, who stopped it with his left knee and smacked it in under the bar! Roars of joy and celebration coloured the grey skies of Sunderland, and the way all the family hugged each other made everything seem more overwhelming. We were 1-0 up against Leeds United. Leeds!

We couldn't believe it. As the minutes ticked by and Leeds laid siege to our goalmouth, an unbelievable double save by our keeper Jimmy Montgomery had us shouting as loud as we had for our goal. That save was probably the best I've seen in all the years I've been watching football.

The last minutes were torture. It seemed the time would never pass, every Leeds attack was like a stab in the heart.

Then, at long last, the full-time whistle came. I was over the moon, tears in my eyes. Mum told us to put our coats on and get our scarves so we could go into town and celebrate with everyone else. The streets were a sea of red and white. Tears of joy filled the eyes of hundreds and hundreds of people who, for a day, had realised their biggest dream. Our Sunderland had beaten the mighty Leeds United. What an atmosphere. What a day. What a team – my team!

Marvellous though the story was, I didn't know what to say. I was stunned, as I was every time I heard about such thrilling experiences. Then the cold east wind, sweeping down on us from the North Sea, reminded us that it was time for the match.

Kick-off was approaching. As the South Stand filled with red and white, the chants that had been accompanying the players on to the pitch suddenly stopped and the Stadium of Light fell silent …

Little Bradley Lowery was gone. He'd died a few weeks before. His passing was marked by a minute's silence, which ended with a prolonged burst of applause. The whole ground joined in a chant just for him – 'One Bradley Lowery, there's only one Bradley Lowery, one Bradley Lowery, there's only one Bradley Lowery' – to let him know we were with him.

Thinking back, I remember that when I looked up I saw that the grey clouds had gone and the blue sky seemed full of life, just as Bradley had been whenever he was running after a football …

Bradley had been taken from us, but he'd left an indelible mark, not only in the hearts of the people of Sunderland but in those of millions of people for whom a song or even a thought will let him know he'll always be one of us.

That day the match took second place. The general feeling was so strong that it got the better of me, and not even the couple of pints bought for me by Alan and his mates after the game did much to get my feet back on the ground.

'Ivan, no matter what division we're playing in, here we're a family. Come back whenever you like. This is your home. You're one of the family now. Please never forget that.'

That was his goodbye to us. With Giuseppe, my friend and fellow traveller, I headed for the station, and amid the sadness and smiles we shared along the way we knew that we'd experienced something memorable.

Sunderland was a special journey – a never-ending journey, because it will stay with me for the rest of my life. Sunderland stands a few miles south of the renowned Newcastle, a city where, according to Alan and his fellow supporters, you don't even go to shop.

As the Newcastle train pulled out of the station, I couldn't help feeling moved again, first of all for Bradley and then for the people we'd just left, so simple and so full of passion. A passion I'd made my own for an evening, and as I set foot in Newcastle, deep down it felt a bit like a betrayal …

In memory of Bradley Lowery, who left us on 7 July 2017 at the age of six.

Your smile will always be with me.

THE MEN FROM THE NORTH

Alan, chairman of North Shields, gave me a hug as if we'd been lifelong friends, astonished to see me back there three years after we first met. It was great to see him again. And the feeling was exactly that of embracing an old mate.

Sat in the comfortable chairs of the ground's clubhouse with a hot cup of tea, in little more than an hour he told me the history of North Shields, the story of the desperate times his beloved Sunderland were going through and, above all, of the awful tumour he'd recently fought off, facing the battle with all his strength and determination. A determination that had carried him through the darkest moments of his illness, his gaze constantly fixed on the club of which he's chairman and that he has run with love and boundless passion since the early 1990s. A passion given tangible form by the clubhouse walls, lovingly decorated down to the smallest detail.

It was right there, three years before, that I'd heard a remarkable story, one that began in England in 1969 and passed through Italy, an adventure marked by memorable victories. The story was brought to life by Alan's recollections and the pages of a dusty album that chronicled the events of the most important year in the history of that great little club.

Hold tight, this new journey will take us back in time in the discovery of North Shields Football Club. Not just any club, but one of the smallest and most fascinating in the North East.

❇ ❇ ❇

I remember everything about that morning. Newcastle United were going to play Aston Villa in the evening, but so as not to waste a minute of that day my friend Andrea and I decided to explore some of the obscure little football grounds scattered along the coastline near the cold North Sea. It was 20 February 2017, a date I had reason to remember. Four years earlier, that was the day I left home to pursue my dreams in the land that gave us football. Only a few weeks later, though, as I've already related, all my hopes lay in ruins and I was staring in the face of the first and worst failure of my life.

But since that day, and thanks to that failure, my life has changed. As I've grown, I've become stronger, more positive and more determined to face the difficulties that life has consistently thrown at me as the years pass. Some of these have seemed insurmountable, but each time I've faced them with the conviction that I'd prevail, following my own rules – more often than not achieving results I never could have imagined.

Which is a bit like what happened when Andrea and I were walking towards the seemingly deserted Daren Persson Stadium, accompanied by the seagulls' cries and the sighing of the wind. The ground is located in the middle of a park, just a stone's throw from the sea.

In my eagerness to experience the place, I was perfectly prepared to climb over one of the small wooden gates surrounding the pitch so I could run on a piece of the grass that has been the scene of all my greatest daydreams. Then, to my amazement, shortly after our arrival, I actually trod that grass – after I'd told my story to the kind-looking man who rolled down his car window and asked us, somewhat mystified, what had brought us to North Shields on a freezing Monday morning.

That man was Alan. He unhurriedly got out of his car and opened the doors of his home, welcoming us into the cosy clubhouse and, above all, letting us run as free as children on the pitch of that charming ground.

It had a charm of times past, marked by simplicity. The benches and tiny stands were built entirely with red brick and solid wooden supports, displaying to anybody who happened to pass the infinite beauty of non-league football. Far removed from the cameras of the big broadcasters, it's a unique world where football is still the people's game. Where tickets cost a few quid, and, above all, where the players don't race to get away from the fans after a match but stop to spend time with them, to sink a pint and have a natter in the clubhouse. A clubhouse that in non-league football stands for unity, belonging, generosity, history and an awful lot more.

I found that out as soon as Alan asked us to stay a bit longer, because he was about to tell us a remarkable story. It unfolded in 1969, the year of North Shields Football Club's astounding ride to triumph in the FA Amateur Cup. Launched as long ago as 1893 and played until 1974, the Amateur Cup gave non-professional clubs the chance to challenge each other and make a name for themselves in the history of the game.

On 12 April 1969 the Amateur Cup Final was played between North Shields and Sutton United in front of 47,000 spectators, at Wembley no less. The final whistle of a hard-fought encounter saw North Shields emerge as 2-1 winners. Players and supporters alike had the honour of celebrating their win in the very place where, three years before, Bobby Moore's England team had stood on top of the world.

For the club and the fans of North Shields, that victory was worth every bit as much as England's World Cup triumph. They'd written their name in the history of English football, making the whole of Tyneside burst with pride.

Immediately after their exploits at Wembley, North Shields received an invitation to play Almas Roma for the Coppa Ottorino Barassi, a trophy organised from 1968 to 1976. It was conceived with the aim of pitting the winners of the FA Amateur Cup against their counterparts from the Coppa Italia Dilettanti, the tie to be played over two legs – home and away.

That chance to experience European football gave small amateur clubs a taste of greatness. In the first leg, played in England on 25 September 1969, North Shields scored two goals without reply, a result that put them in a strong position for the second leg, but on 11 October (in Rome's Stadio Flaminio) a 2-0 win for the Italians left the teams tied.

To this day, though, that result is remembered and recounted as an act of daylight robbery. The Italian referee allowed the match to go on until Almas Roma managed to level the scores. Not only was the equaliser scored no less than ten minutes after the end of normal time but the referee was seen jumping for joy because of it. As often happened in those days, the cup and the medals were awarded on the toss of a coin: one team would get the trophy for a year, the other medals they could keep for good.

North Shields captain Ronnie Tatum won the toss. Without a second thought, he left the cup to Almas Roma and chose the medals for the players to keep.

Which is a bit like all the match programmes and photographs carefully conserved in the album I had the privilege of picking up and leafing through with my own hands. Not only does it recount the successes of that unforgettable year, it bears witness to the bond that grew between the club's legendary manager Frank Brennan, the players, the fans and the whole town of North Shields. A workers' town and a workers' team, made up of men first and players second, ready to fight for the colours and the club of which Alan is chairman. A special chairman who came to the club when I was yet unborn, above all when the club was verging on financial collapse. Luckily the collapse was averted, but unfortunately, to pay off some of its debts, the club had to sell Appleby Park, its traditional home.

Despite all their adversities, despite relegation to the 11th tier and the lack of a ground they owned, in 1997

North Shields managed to lay the groundwork for a home they could call their own. A tiny stadium that set a record of 1,500 spectators on 28 March 2015 for the FA Vase semi-final against Highworth Town FC. North Shields won the match and flew to Wembley to play the final against Glossop North End.

The final act of the competition ended with a 2-1 win for North Shields, which brought not only joy and celebration for the fans but also £25,000 into the club's coffers, a sum immediately invested in ground improvements and the construction of the clubhouse that Alan wished to donate to the entire community. A clubhouse I had the honour of discovering, an insight into one of the most inspiring football stories 'Made in England'. These are stories I'll take with me wherever I go, repeating to whoever cares to listen that every great dream in life can be made to come true.

As was proved by that great little club from the North East – as complete unknowns they went all the way to Wembley, lifted cups to the sky and shouted to the whole world what they were, are and always will be – the Men from the North!

AHM COMING HOME, NEWCASTLE

The banners, the chants, the continual hand-claps, the children wearing the shirts and scarves of their beloved club, the grit of the older fans and the passion you could read on the faces of the many youngsters who had grown up in the city's streets. The warmth and passion of everyone there, the deafening boos heaped on the opponents, the despair over a chance missed and the anger over a ball lost. The fervour of the Gallowgate End, beating heart of the Geordie fans. The jubilation at going one goal up, the incessant songs of devotion to their warrior chief Rafa Benítez.

The chants and songs swept me off my feet, overwhelming me so much that I found myself singing for the colours that had always had me spellbound. The colours that one Monday night in February made me feel part of a special people – one that could live without anything, but never, never ever without football. Not so much a game, more a religion.

Quite simply, their daily bread. Take your seats, one of the best places in the whole of England awaits us. Our next stop is St James' Park, home of Newcastle United Football Club.

⚽⚽⚽

There were still over two hours to go before kick-off, and although it was a Monday evening the whole of the Geordie support was already out in the Toon. Streets flooded with fans, from the heart of the city in Grey Street all the way to the metro exit of St James, by far the finest metro station I've ever seen. I say this on the strength of the giant pictures of Newcastle supporters and players adorning the walls, welcoming anybody getting off a train with the club's badge and colours. Colours bearing witness to decades of glorious history.

It's a history rich not so much in trophies as in unadulterated passion, a feeling that everyone should experience first-hand at least once in their life. Not only to be able to talk about it but to feel part of a community proudly representing the city on the banks of the Tyne. A city that lives for football and beer, which in this part of the world mean happiness.

It struck me as soon as I went through the door of the Strawberry Pub, which stands right beside the majestic St James' Park. It was so packed that I had to fight my way to the bar. After ten minutes I finally got my hands on a pint of Newcastle Brown. Songs and chants swirling around me, I edged away from the bar cradling the pint against my shoulder – like you do when you're trying to burp the baby – to prevent any spillage in the event of an inadvertent shove.

The pub walls oozed history, dominated by shirts and photos of local legend Alan Shearer, born and raised kicking a ball in the shadow of St James' Park. For a whole decade (1996–2006) the fans witnessed their fellow Geordie rack up goal after goal as he lived his greatest dream – playing for the club he'd always loved. In doing so he became the Premier League's all-time top scorer with 260 goals, 206 of which were in a Newcastle shirt – also a club record. A record marked in 2016 by the unveiling – at the behest of former chairman Freddy Shepherd – of a statue of the local football-mad boy made good. And in Shearer's testimonial match, on 11 May 2006, his fans saw his last goal in club colours, scored at the Gallowgate End.

And just there, outside the Gallowgate End of the ground, stands the statue of another club legend, Sir Bobby Robson. When Bobby Robson fetched up at St James' Park, in September 1999, Newcastle were languishing at the bottom of the Premier League. In that and the following seasons he pulled them out of trouble, took them into the upper echelons of the league and led them into Europe. He won no silverware, but he won the supporters' hearts.

On that Monday night in February, St James' Park was filled with 50,000 people, not for a European match but for a Championship fixture against Aston Villa. It was a crucial match for them, but then again they all were. The atmosphere was crackling, making it one of the most electrifying evenings I've ever spent. Not just because of the non-stop singing and chanting and the mega-banner unfurled over our heads a few seconds before kick-off but for the force of the devotion you could see in the eyes of everyone there, enamoured of the colours they'd give their lives for. Lives that wouldn't be worth as much without Newcastle United. A club that lives on unbridled passion, the very feeling evoked by the memorable words of Bobby Robson in a statement that's one of the finest I've ever read:

> What is a club in any case? Not the buildings or the directors or the people who are paid to represent it. It's not the television contracts, get-out clauses, marketing departments or executive boxes. It's the noise, the passion, the feeling of belonging, the pride in your city. It's a small boy clambering up stadium steps for the very first time, gripping his father's hand, gawping at that hallowed stretch of turf beneath him and, without being able to do a thing about it, falling in love.

He hit the nail on the head. The magic of football, at least in this city, is summed up in those heartfelt words.

My experience of St James' Park and all the Geordie support was more than just a joy – I count it as a privilege, a memory that will stay with me for good. I'll not forget those streets and the stands packed with fans who on that Monday night stole my heart and made me feel part of their great family. A special family. The Toon Army of St James' Park.

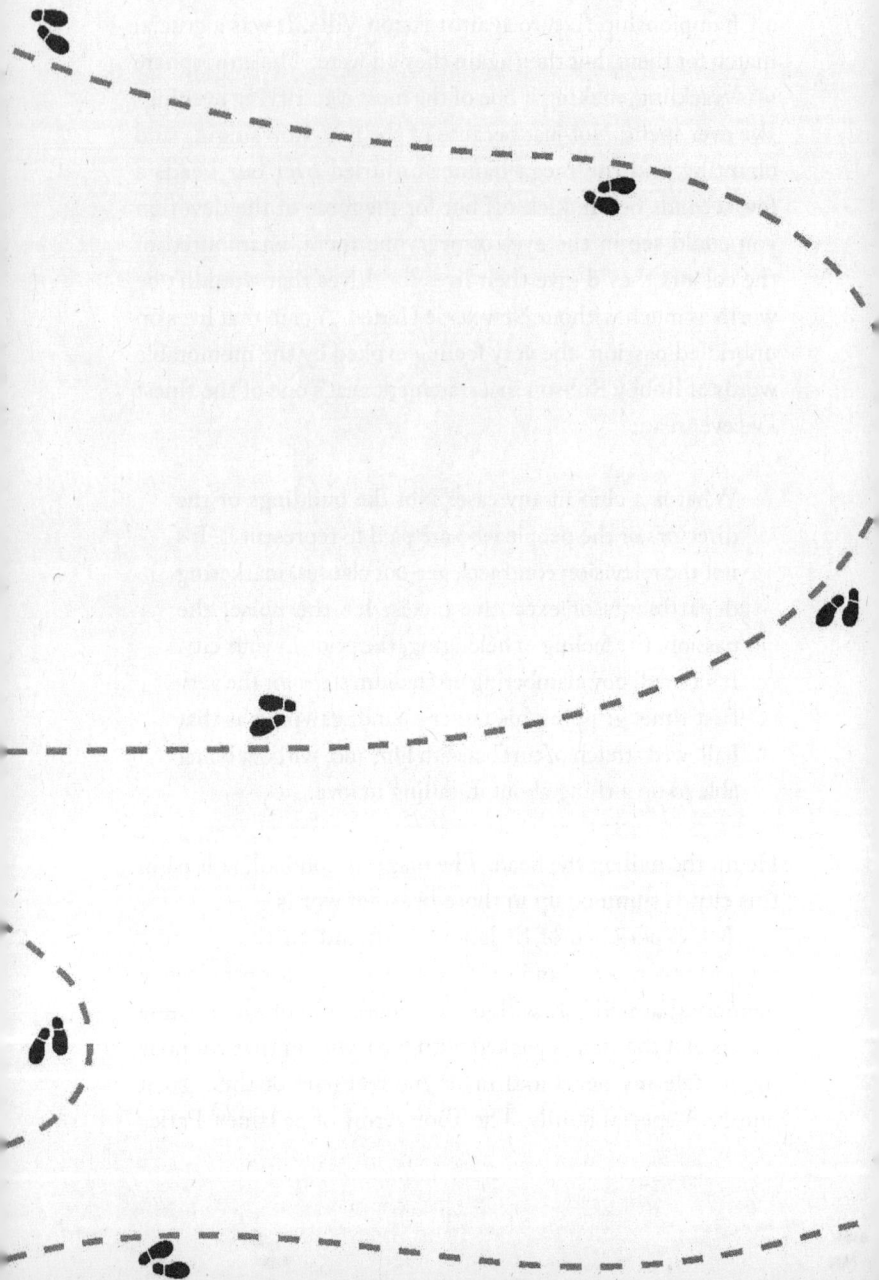

CHAPTER 3
BELIEVE IN YOURSELF

They are able because they
think they are able.

Virgil

I'VE SPENT the first part of my life nurturing my biggest dreams, going against everything and everybody. I've been told many times to get my feet back on the ground, find a 'normal' job and forget England and all its football grounds, give up the ambition to be a football coach. I've been told, eye to eye, that in England I'd only ever be a kitchen hand because washing up was all I'd be able to do. They laughed in my face when in March 2013, at just 19 years old, I was confronted with the biggest failure of my life. They told me that dreams are for fools, like leaving home to seek my fortune in England with no job, not even knowing the language. They told me I was good for nothing apart from dreaming …

Everything's been said about me, to my face and behind my back. They tried to shoot me down in the hope of shattering my dreams. Not because they were particularly nasty, simply because they were (and probably still are) unhappy people. Unhappiness breeds spite, and where there's spite there's no love. Have the courage to face all the people who try to do you down, smile in their faces and wish them all the best.

Have the courage to believe in yourselves, because no one else is going to do it for you. Surround yourselves with the right people, as they'll be your safe haven.

I'm talking to you. Love yourself, respect yourself and nurture your dreams. That's the only way to find happiness.

London, 28 November 2019

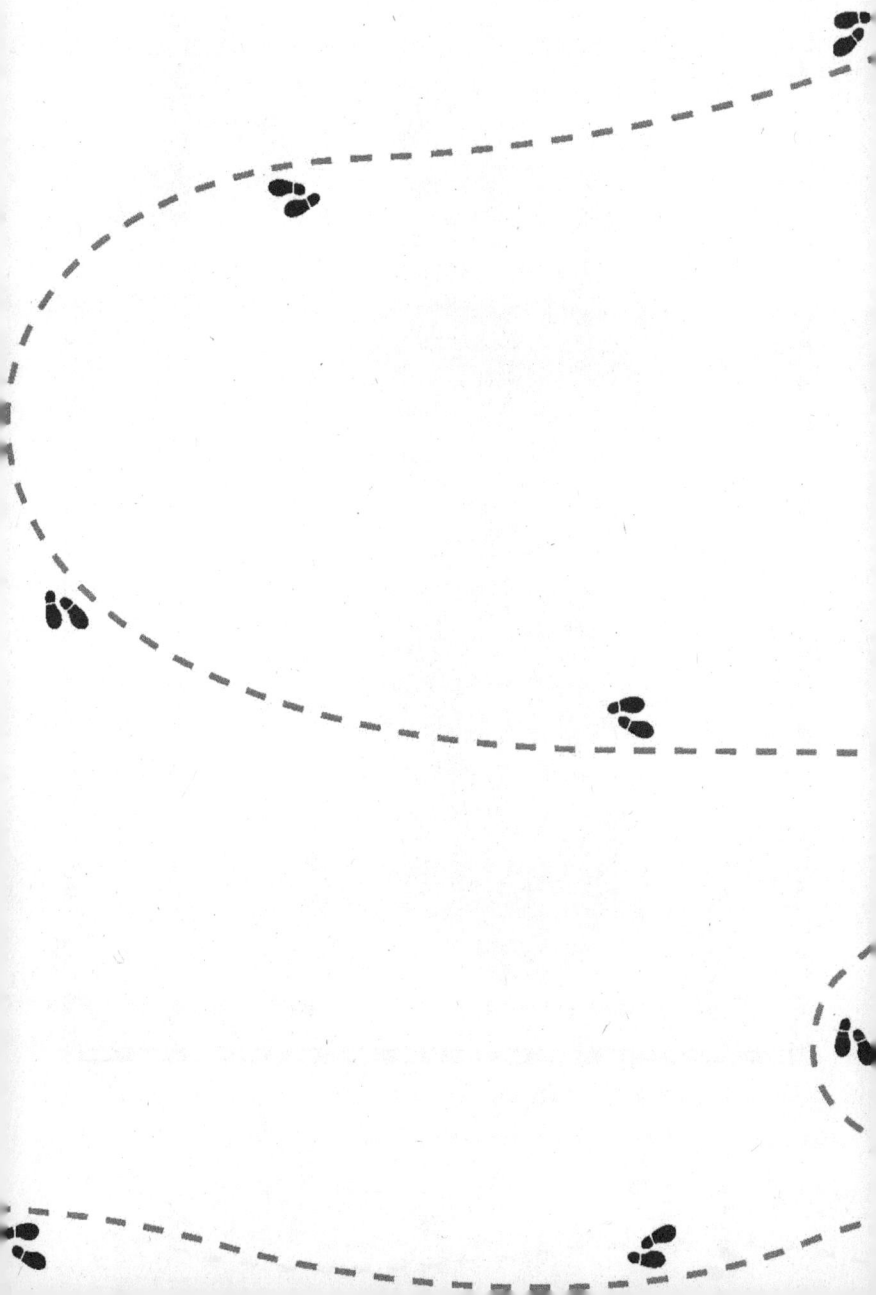

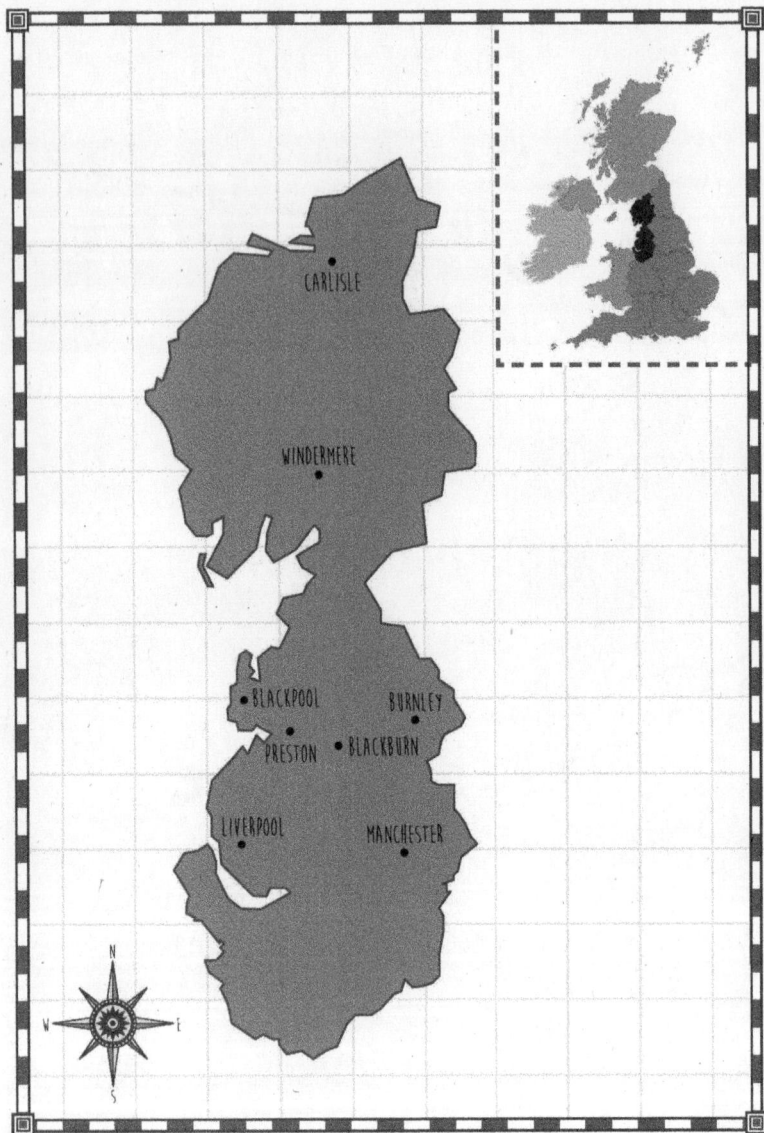

NORTH WEST

Whenever I think of the North West, I can't help thinking of Bowness-on-Windermere, a delightful town in the Lake District, and Manchester, the city where football reigns supreme. Living in those places, for about a year and a half, was the best thing I could have done – little by little they helped me to develop, making me into the man I am today.

As well as being the area that formed my character, though, the North West is home to dozens and dozens of clubs steeped in history, with the fascination of their own stadiums. To name only a few: the two Liverpool clubs, the two main clubs in Manchester, the Blackburn Rovers of the young Alan Shearer, and Preston North End when they were known as the Invincibles.

In the heart of Manchester stands the National Football Museum, a must-see for any football fan. Its historical exhibits are of incalculable value. For music lovers, the North West is also famous for being the home of The Beatles and Oasis, who need no introduction. Their songs have often accompanied me on my travels.

The North West is all this and a lot more. I'll be telling you some of its stories. Others you'll have to discover for yourselves, first-hand, in the cold and the rain. It was there that my journey began …

Here I'd like to remember the 22 precious lives lost on 22 May 2017 in the bombing of the Manchester Arena. Having lived in the city for six months, I felt my blood run cold when I saw what it was going through. Since that tragic day, every time I go to Manchester I make the time to visit Victoria station and its memorial to the people whose lives were cut terribly short. We will remember you.

WELCOME TO EWOOD PARK

The poverty was all too visible. That evening in early October the gardens behind the houses on Bolton Road looked sad and neglected, just one consequence of the everyday difficulties and lack of opportunities the town of Blackburn offers its people.

Opportunities and hope that a little boy wearing a Blackburn Rovers shirt would seek in football, for him and his family. I watched him for at least ten minutes as he enjoyed playing with his friends. He lived right there, in one of those red-brick houses with a scruffy backyard, within sight of Ewood Park's Jack Walker Stand. And it's there, in the heart of the stand, that pride of place is given to the Premier League trophy won by Blackburn Rovers in 1995, a piece of silverware, which, that evening, as Fabio and I made our way to the station, we saw glittering in the darkness. We thought of that boy admiring it every day from the window of his house with the run-down yard – every morning when he woke up and every night as he went to bed. Probably with the dream of playing for it and perhaps even winning it – there, at Ewood Park, wearing the blue and white of Blackburn Rovers, with his name to go down in history …

⚽⚽⚽

It didn't take long to understand that Blackburn isn't the same as other places. Its people's passion and love was there to see in their eyes, which were mostly tired out by long hours of work. For anybody not born and raised in those streets, it's not easy to grasp what it means to support Blackburn Rovers. Supporting that Lancashire club means belonging to a strong identity and a solid community. A community of people used to hard work, to soldiering on through life's hardships and waiting for their team's next match, killing time until it comes.

How? Drinking the day's umpteenth beer and thinking about the glories of times past. Of distant times that on the walls of the Fox & Hounds, a few yards from Ewood Park, I had the impression of reliving. Those walls seemed to be talking to me. Picture after picture showed the club's much-missed chairman Jack Walker and the one and only Alan Shearer.

Walking down Alan Shearer Way, within sight of the entrance to Blackburn's ground, I was taken back in time. I pictured the thousands of people who had walked that road before me. I conjured up the few but memorable moments of glory recorded there. The most recent was the work of Jack Walker, who took over as club chairman in January 1991. Multi-millionaire industrialist and diehard Rovers fan, he bought the club with the aim of taking it into England's elite. He refurbished the ground, built a new sports centre and engaged the services of Liverpool hero Kenny Dalglish as coach.

Brought to Ewood Park in October 1991, Dalglish took over the team when they were in the Second Division. After less than a season, in the following May, he got them promoted to the newly formed Premier League. In the next two seasons Blackburn finished in fourth and then second place, behind Alex Ferguson's Manchester United. At that time United ruled the roost every season, but on 14 May 1995 they had to take second place to Blackburn Rovers, who finished the final day one point ahead of them. That day gave the supporters and dear old Jack Walker one of the greatest joys of their lives: after 80 long years, Blackburn Rovers were back at the pinnacle of English football.

On that October afternoon, thanks to the friendly help of Rob Gill, the club's communications officer, I had a chance to relive that story. Guided by his devotion to Blackburn Rovers, not only did I discover a wealth of stories from their past, I was even able to climb to the pinnacle – literally – of Ewood Park. There, standing on the roof of the stadium, I felt like I was touching the sky. The significance of that inebriating moment was as plain to see in my eyes as in those of my fellow adventurer Fabio. When our journey began we could never have imagined such an experience. Not even in our wildest dreams could we have seen ourselves at the topmost point of that stadium, over a century old. From there, taking care not to fall from the narrow swaying stairway, we went down to the press room and then the changing rooms, where everything was shipshape for the Championship match to be played that evening against Sheffield United.

Such was the excitement of that afternoon, I have to say that the match paled into insignificance. In fact, when we were taken from the changing rooms on to the field of play, we forgot about it altogether as the club photographer took the pictures that I'll treasure forever in my box of souvenirs. More like a trunk than a box, to tell the truth, and every time I open it I'll be taken back to Ewood Park. One of the most memorable moments of that day was when Rob opened the doors of the boardroom, the very heart of the club, where he began to tell us its story.

It's a story that started in 1906, as the beguilingly small room we were standing in was built piece by piece – and today its condition is as impeccable as it was upon its completion. As I carefully observed everything around me I was struck by the obsessive attention paid to the smallest detail, with rows of ancient badges from the clubs of those days fixed to the boardroom walls. As if all that wasn't enough, Rob then started on another story: club legend Ronnie Clayton, who clocked up more than 500 appearances in a Rovers shirt, and during his apprenticeship was given the job of keeping the boardroom neat and tidy. One day, as he was polishing the badges hanging on the walls, he had an idea. He took the colours of local rivals Burnley, hung them up near the door, and thus made sure they'd be hidden from view whenever the door was opened.

With our heads spinning from the day we'd had the honour of experiencing, and all Rob's stories, before leaving we went back to the heart of the Jack Walker Stand, ascended a flight of steps and stood right in front of the coveted Premier League trophy. The prestigious piece of silverware lifted in triumph by Alan Shearer, Kenny Dalglish and the other champions that day in May 1995 was there shining before my incredulous eyes.

Our memorable day came to a conclusion soon afterwards as we said goodbye to Rob in front of the statue of the great Jack Walker, a man who gave a dream to a whole community. A chairman, but above all a supporter. A man who believed in his dreams and, at least for a while, took Blackburn Rovers to the top of England.

WE ARE BURNLEY FROM THE NORTH

I can still remember the first time I ever heard of Burnley. I must have been 16 or 17. At that time England seemed to me to be a far-off country, out of my reach. The photos and videos available on the internet were my daily bread, always there to satisfy my hunger for English football. I'd sit and watch the pictures and films of those places, as distant as they were fascinating, in some ways daunting, but always an object of desire. The Burnley hooligans were some of the toughest and most dangerous in the whole country – at least according to the documentary in which I first saw them.

That video was frightening, not just because of the cold and seemingly nasty faces it showed, but most of all in the feeling of desolation emanating from the streets of that Lancashire town. Streets that years later I walked without the slightest fear, day and night, delighted at having seen first-hand one of the most atmospheric and captivating football grounds in the whole of England ...

⚽⚽⚽

It was the summer of 2015 when I first set foot in Burnley. I'll never forget the excitement of the first journeys I made to discover English football. I nearly always travelled alone, after being woken by my alarm at five in the morning on what was supposed to be my day off. In those days I was living and working in Bowness-on-Windermere, a delightful little town in the heart of the Lake District and visited by over a million tourists a year. My working days there lasted 12 or 13 hours, and were sometimes punctuated by episodes of unpleasantness, but I wasn't complaining. Working as a waiter and then as a barman helped me to take a sharper approach to life. It taught me to keep my eyes wide open, and, more than anything else, it gave me an inner strength I didn't know I had.

Working in that job, where I wasn't given the time to eat or even go to the toilet, I have to say that more than once I thought of packing it in, forgetting all my dreams and going back to the village where I grew up. But I decided to tough it out, to be stronger than all the obstacles and the fatigue.

As time went on, my problems were pushed aside by the beauty and the fascination of my trips to the world of English football. To me, those journeys and the grounds I visited seemed to be the best thing in the world. Travelling became the light that kept me going through the long rainy days spent working in that restaurant. It was there that I gave my sweat and robbed myself of time (and, what was worse, of my peace of mind). I regained that peace in my deepest thoughts, immersing myself in those trips before they even started, the better to face the long days of work.

I was just over 20, I'd been living away from home for about four months, and thanks to that job I was learning what it means to make sacrifices for your dreams. Sacrifices that were rewarded week after week, as was the case the first time I fetched up at Turf Moor. I remember everything about that first time, every detail. The lady at the reception was kindness itself. After listening to my story, told in mangled English, she agreed to let me visit the ground. After showing me round that fine old stadium, before I left she gave me a match programme and told me never to stop believing in my deepest desires.

And I never have – desires or dreams. I've worked hard to achieve them, making the most of them whenever possible. By making the most of them, I mean becoming part of the reality I've had the honour and good fortune to experience, mingling with the most fanatical supporters and singing alongside them on the terraces and in the stands.

That's what I did one freezing Monday night in late October 2017, when I went back to Burnley for their Premier League match against Newcastle United.

The seats at Turf Moor, mostly made of wood, exude the charm of times past. Distant times, as hard to imagine as they are to relive, but for the people of Burnley they're unforgettable. A time that saw them crowned as league champions under the guidance of Harry Potts, who went to Turf Moor at the age of 17 as a player and returned to coach the team just over 20 years later. In the 1959/60 season he realised a dream for the people of Burnley, taking the club to the top of English football.

A special kind of manager, he conquered the hearts of those people, who would have given their lives for the colours. Colours that on that late October evening festooned Harry Potts Way, the street leading to the entrance of the old Turf Moor, as the Clarets supporters carried the town's flag high on their way to the match. Burnley has a population of under 90,000 people, but week after week 20,000 crowd into Turf Moor's venerable stands. As kick-off drew closer that evening, those supporters made themselves heard all right, and earned respect, drowning out the voices of the 2,400 or more Newcastle fans who had made the journey.

With their continual chants, songs and mutual insults, the two sets of supporters produced an electric atmosphere, one that you can't find in many Premier League grounds, where sections of fans never stand up and confine themselves to polite applause for a chance just missed. Not in Burnley. At Turf Moor they sing and urge the team on from the first minute to the last, standing – not sitting – in the freezing cold, gritting their teeth and shouting themselves hoarse.

That shouting and cheering threatened to bring the house down in the 74th minute, when Jeff Hendrick gave Burnley the lead and gave me one of the biggest explosions of joy I've ever felt in a football ground. I went mental, finding myself hugging people I'd never seen in my life. It was a night to remember, for me and the people of Burnley, who sang on and on, staying where they were until all the players had left the pitch.

The name most chanted was that of manager Sean Dyche, who for the locals could do no wrong. A tough nut who established a hard-running team able to make life difficult for any side visiting Turf Moor. A fortress of a ground. Not only is it hard to win there, it's impossible to remain indifferent to the unbridled passion of supporters who never say die. People without life's luxuries, who carry on through a host of difficulties, facing life head-on and filling the stands at Turf Moor for every match, dads teaching their kids that being born and raised in Burnley is not a problem – it's something to be proud of.

And that pride has to be shouted out to all the world, because Turf Moor is their home and Burnley is their club. Today, tomorrow and forever.

THE THEATRE OF DREAMS

As soon as the referee signalled the start of the second half, the match ceased to matter. I wasn't even watching any more. I had tears in my eyes. At that moment all I wanted was to go back a few minutes and repair the damage for which I'd never forgive myself. It hurt more than I can say. In a few seconds, that long-dreamed-of photo had vanished, thanks to a little girl who didn't have the sense to get out of the way. My face and Sir Alex's were separated by her arm, evidence of her anxiety to take a selfie with the living legend himself.

I actually managed to embrace that legend after the final whistle, shaking his hand and getting the photo I'd had the audacity to hope for. Such was my excitement, I could barely blurt out a thank you. It had been a long road to get to that theatre ... the stage of legendary victories, and trophy after trophy lifted to the sky. Victories that have gone down in world football history, in the unique setting of Old Trafford and in the name of one of the greatest managers of all time: Sir Alex Ferguson.

❁ ❁ ❁

When I think of Manchester United, to be honest it's hard to be objective. For years the Red Devils were my team. Alex Ferguson as manager, Wayne Rooney and Dimitǎr Berbatov up front. Cristiano Ronaldo and Nani on the wings, in midfield Ryan Giggs and Paul Scholes. A back line of Rio Ferdinand, Nemanja Vidić, Gary Neville and Patrice Evra. And Edwin van der Sar between the sticks. These world-class players, aided and abetted by other great footballers, gave me many wonderful moments but, more than that, they were with me as I grew up. Mine was an adolescence made up of school, hours and hours of football played and hundreds of matches on the PlayStation, held exclusively there, in the renowned arena of Old Trafford.

That stadium, a few years later, I'd have the honour of experiencing first-hand dozens of times, watching matches, admiring its interiors on many guided tours or simply walking around outside it, to get a personal grip on a hundred or more years of history that will live on forever. A history rich in glory and famous victories, with statues of champions and their managers watching over it day and night. Statues, above all, of men whose love of football led them to write indelible pages in the club's storybook.

As well as winning silverware, figures such as Bobby Charlton and Matt Busby endured one of the most awful tragedies ever to befall the club: the Munich air disaster. On 6 February 1958 the Busby Babes were flying back to Manchester after beating Red Star Belgrade in the quarter-finals of the European Cup. That year Matt Busby and his youthful prodigies might have won that cup, but when their plane stopped over in Munich to refuel, the weather took a turn for the worse. After two failed attempts to take off, the third one was fatal, destroying the dreams and the young lives of many of those players.

Despite the thickly falling snow, and although the two pilots had been advised to postpone take-off until the weather improved, they decided to make that third attempt so as not to fall behind schedule. An attempt that turned into tragedy, not only because of the snow but above all the slush covering the runway. Unable to build up the speed needed for a proper take-off, the plane crashed to the ground at 3.04pm. Of the 44 people on board, 23 lost their lives: two crew members, eight journalists, three club directors, eight Manchester United players and two other passengers. Those young players never returned home to their loved ones. The lives of those loved ones were changed forever, irrevocably scarred by a disaster that's still commemorated, on 6 February every year, by thousands of people.

The fortunate survivors of the crash included the young Bobby Charlton and manager Matt Busby. Devastated by the sense of loss, after two months in hospital Busby was convinced he had nothing further to give to football. A few simple words from his wife Jean were enough to change his mind: 'The lads would have wanted you to carry on.' So, following his recovery, Matt Busby returned to his post in the name of the youngsters he'd lost.

And to those lads he dedicated the victories that would have been theirs, taking Manchester United to an FA Cup victory in 1963, league titles in 1965 and 1967 and, above all, the European Cup triumph of 1968, ten years after the tragedy of Munich. The 4-1 victory in that cup was achieved at the expense of Eusébio's much-vaunted Benfica, and it made United the first English club to win the competition. The cup took pride of place in the Old Trafford trophy room, thanks not only to Matt Busby but also to the magical trio of George Best, Denis Law and Bobby Charlton. In those years the three of them wrote the history of the Red Devils, the spectacle of their performances swelling the hearts of United fans. And any of those fans walking outside the majestic East Stand at Old Trafford will be able to relive those distant days of glory.

Indeed, those days seemed close to me when I first found myself in front of the statue of the United Trinity of Best, Law and Charlton, standing right opposite another statue: in honour of club legend Sir Matt Busby. Busby was the United manager for a quarter of a century, carrying the club's reputation to unprecedented heights. But those records were destined to be broken in later years, when Alex Ferguson achieved even greater things. Under his leadership Manchester United won 38 trophies, making him the most successful manager in the history of the game. A success story given particular distinction by the number of players brought through the club's youth system, some of whom made history, not only for the club but on the world stage. A history whose telling would require hundreds of pages, beginning in November 1986 and ending over 26 years later, in May 2013.

Those were seasons of one trophy after another, of boys who became men and men who became heroes. The heroes of my youth, who made me dream, weep and explode with joy, first on my settee at home and then in the stands at Old Trafford. Not just a football stadium, a veritable shrine. The one and only Theatre of Dreams.

In memory of the 23 souls tragically lost on 6 February 1958.

THE RED REBELS

Darlington won 2-1 that autumn afternoon and, hard as that defeat was to swallow, none of the home supporters stopped singing even for a second. Truth be told, after the final whistle the atmosphere actually warmed up further as fans young and old yelled out their encouragement for the boys representing the club they held dear. A club with a special history, one of complex intrigue and outright rebellion. Of trenchant opposition to modern football and chairmen who think of nothing but making money, not giving a damn about the fans and forgetting how much club colours affect people's lives. Colours which, in 2005, a group of Manchester United supporters decided to turn their backs on for good. Not because they no longer cared about their beloved club but to show their disgust at its acquisition by the Glazer family. It was a transaction resisted right to the end, but it went ahead, and many of the supporters opposed to it decided to break away and found a new club. A club based on proper values, one in which every supporter would receive the consideration that Manchester United would no longer give.

Fasten your safety belts; here comes the astonishing story of FC United of Manchester.

⚽ ⚽ ⚽

On the morning of that day in October 2018, I was welcomed back to dear old Manchester by the regulation grey sky. I was living in London at the time, and returning north brought back a lot of memories. I owe Manchester a great deal. Living there, as life handed out its kicks and punches, I'd had the chance to develop a quality I never would have thought I had – resilience.

Developing that invaluable quality has not only made me a better person, it's made me more of a dreamer. I'm ready to face life's challenges, and, above all, I've learned never to take my eye off the targets I set myself. All those objectives, with sacrifice and hard work, I've reached one by one, making them my own and writing them up in my notebook.

More than a notebook, it's an album whose pages contain some of the best and most romantic things that English football has ever graced us with. A reality of passion and defiance, not only against a football establishment ever further removed from the real old values but particularly against the Glazer family, who bought Manchester United for close to £790 million in the summer of 2005.

It's a horrifying sum if you think of the poverty and hunger in the world but, apart from that, the biggest outrage – which precipitated the supporters' revolt – was the £600 million or more that the American family borrowed to finance the purchase, saddling the club with enormous debts and annual interest payments of over £60 million. In one way or another this mountainous debt fell on the shoulders of the fans, who had to put up with price rises for tickets and every single thing connected with Manchester United.

A group of those supporters no longer felt they belonged to such a club, so after the failure of their opposition they decided to found a new club with the aim of reviving the true essence of the game we love. A healthy game, where you can enjoy the match with your friends, sinking the day's umpteenth pint on the terraces, paying much less and getting much better value, not only as a fan but as an individual.

So in the summer of 2005, over 2,000 of them had a meeting and decided to bring their new club into existence. Several clear rules and values were established from the outset. Of the seven core principles, the three most important were:

- The club will develop strong links with the local community and strive to be accessible to all, discriminating against none.

- The club will encourage young, local participation – playing and supporting – whenever possible.

- All decisions will be made after hearing all members' opinions, so that each of them may feel part of one big family.[5]

At the Darlington match that cold autumn afternoon I had the honour of meeting that family in person. Men, women and children, some of them wearing Manchester United shirts, were flocking to the terraces of Broadhurst Park, not for a Premier League fixture but for a sixth-tier league match.

When the club was formed it had to start out well below that level, in the tenth tier, with supporters used to the Theatre of Dreams finding themselves in the tiny – but unfailingly charming – grounds of non-league football. Not watching players like Wayne Rooney and Ryan Giggs, but simple lads who pulled on the club shirts after a long week of work. Not for money, just for the love of it.

In the years since then, the love of those players and supporters has led the club to great things, one of the most outstanding of which was recorded in November 2010, when they went to Rochdale and beat them 3-2 in the first round of the FA Cup – a hard-won victory that players and fans alike will not forget. That was followed in short order by an equally memorable achievement in the second round, when

---

5 The term 'members' refers to fans who support the club with a small annual subscription. Membership confers a range of benefits, from first options on ticket purchases to discounts on merchandise. Members of FC United of Manchester are also entitled to express their opinions on decisions to be made about the club's future.

they travelled to the south coast and drew 1-1 with Brighton & Hove Albion. The replay was played (and unfortunately lost) in front of over 6,500 spectators packed into Gigg Lane, home to the now-defunct Bury.

It wasn't until May 2015, ten years after the club's foundation, and with the help of many supporters and various institutions that the FC United community saw the inauguration of a ground of their own. The great little Broadhurst Park. Their new home.

That October afternoon I was eager to drink in the atmosphere of the 4,400-capacity ground. The 1,900-plus crowd who had turned up weren't there just for the match; they'd come to their meeting place, to spend time together like one big family.

Scarves around necks, colours on display all around the ground, Broadhurst Park is one of the most attractive football venues I've been to, with passion at the centre of everything. A passion that drives supporters to pitch in as volunteers, during the week as well as on matchdays, happy to carry out any task assigned to them.

This is life lived away from the bright lights of the big time, life that fills hearts young and old with real emotions. As does real football, the one that kicks off at three o'clock on a Saturday with shirt numbers from one to 11. The striker wearing No.9, the biggest talent at No.10, and No.4 on the back of the ball winner trading knocks in the middle of the park in honour of the badge sewn on his shirt. In this case, it's a badge that represents every fan of FC United, now far removed from the glories of Manchester United but still bound to them in spirit.

That spirit, no matter how badly wounded, that will never forget its origins, given life in the shadow of Old Trafford and a new lease of it in the heart of Broadhurst Park. All in the name of FC United of Manchester.

THE CLASS OF 92

'You don't just support a team. You belong to it.' Those were the words written on the stands at Moor Lane, home of Salford City Football Club. A simple idea with enormous meaning.

It probably sounds trite to people who still think that football's just a stupid game with 22 players running around after a ball, two coaches yelling like lunatics, and thousands of idiots who pay good money to watch those morons. How many times have you heard people say that? I've heard it so many times, I don't even bother to answer. I just give them a smile and invite them to come with me, to where faces light up with an undying passion that reigns supreme.

Young and old, men and women. Football's not just a game, it's a full-blown modern-day religion. It's being together, feeling you're part of a family, jumping for joy at a last-minute goal. It's leg-pulling with your mates, dreaming of winning a title or resigning yourself to the umpteenth season gone pear-shaped. It's loving your team when they lose, not just when they win.

It's singing your heart out till the last minute, rain or shine, going home with no voice left but as happy as you can be. Football is rising with the lark to get to an away match, heedless of the fatigue and the endless hours of travel. Football is watching the match with those dearest to you, even when you support different teams. Football is this and a whole lot more. It's that famous stupid game that has changed my life and that of countless millions of other people – and in Salford they know that. So well that they wrote it on the stands and then in people's hearts.

Because the people of Salford don't just support a team, they belong to it. It's for reasons like this that football will never be just a stupid game.

An unforgettable moment with Sheffield FC

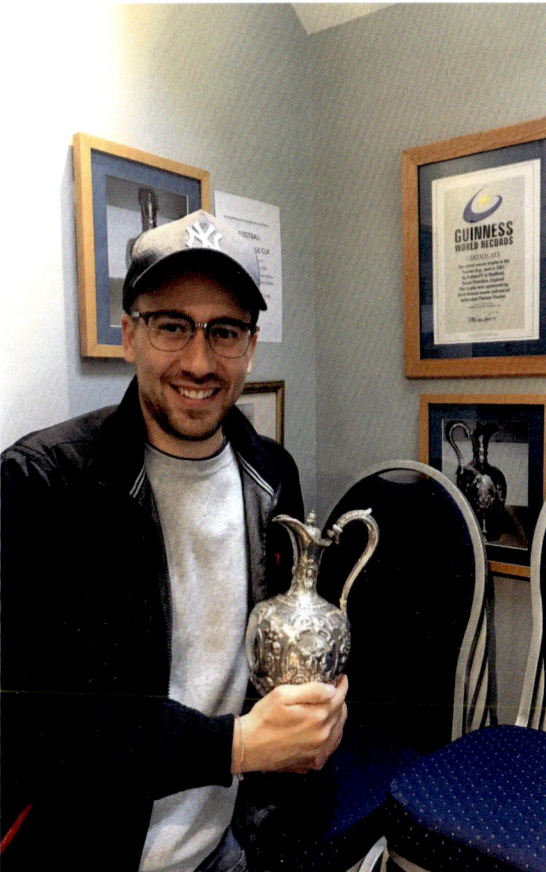

With the historic Youdan Cup

On the pitch of Sandygate with Giuseppe, Sharon, Steve and Fabio. Do you notice the sloping playing surface?

With Alan and some historical relics about North Shields FC

*Me and the goalscorer
Alan Shearer*

With my friend Alan and the statue of Bob Stokoe

Me and Sir Alex Ferguson: an unforgettable moment

Me and Pep Guardiola. That day I went to the stadium with the only aim of meeting him!

With Dave at the Molineux

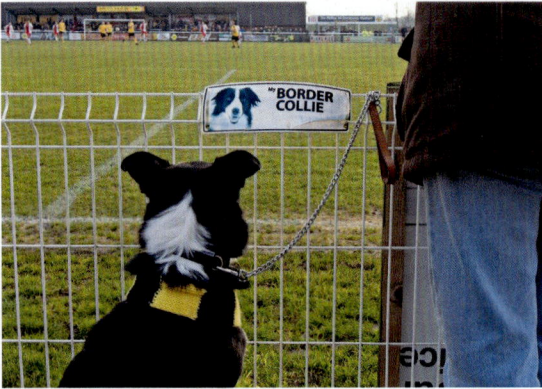

A photo taken by my friend David Bauckham that needs no description

England's oldest and most beautiful grandstand

Me and the mythical Bill

Kenilworth Road: one of the most unique stadiums I've ever visited. Do you see the houses connected to the stadium?

The legendary oak tree, on the terraces of Clarence Park around 1990

Me and John, outside the 'Megastore'

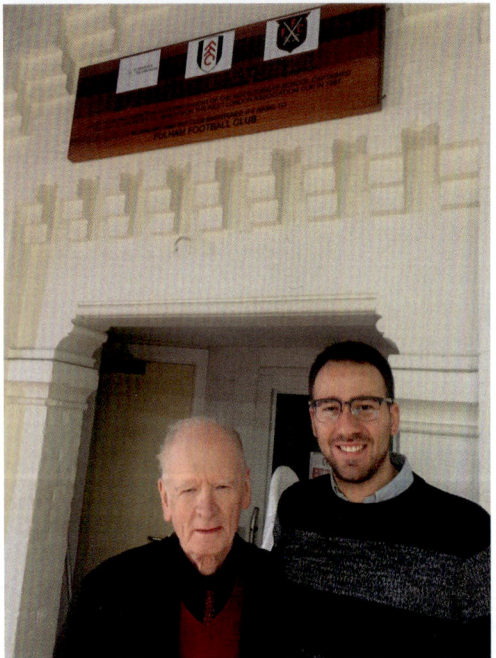

Me and Morgan with the plaque commemorating Fulham's foundation in St Andrew's Church

On that Saturday morning early in September the rain just wouldn't stop. The cold was bone-chilling. September, and it was more like mid-winter. My hair was dripping wet, my jacket as drenched as it had ever been. That was the welcome Manchester usually gave me. Perhaps the fact of having lived there had accustomed me to that, but no matter how annoying and depressing it was to live with that ceaseless rain every day, that morning I was smiling. Sodden but smiling, because of this, my latest journey.

Salford City's journey began in 1940 from English football's 11th tier. To reach the highest point in their history they had to wait something like 70 years. By the highest point, I mean languishing in mid-table in the country's eighth-ranked league, fighting it out with 21 other clubs to gain promotion, not just for the joy of their dear and long-suffering supporters, but to earn enough small change to be able to carry on.

Small change (or, in this case, millions), which in June 2014 was invested by five legendary figures of Manchester United, with the ambition of taking the club into the Championship within 15 years and building a new stadium.

The figures in question were Gary Neville, Phil Neville, Ryan Giggs, Nicky Butt and Paul Scholes. Household names who had won everything there was to win. Between them they'd played over 2,000 matches for Manchester United, the club that had taken them in as boys and made them men, and then champions. Enormously successful men who had grown up in and around Salford, where for years they'd learned their trade at The Cliff training ground and where their latest dreams now lie.[6]

More ambitions than dreams, with the Neville brothers fronting up the operations on the pitch and off it. From day

---

6   The Cliff is a training facility owned by Manchester United since 1938. It was the first team's headquarters until the beginning of this century. Now it's used by the youth teams and women's first team.

one, Phil has been on the pitch, liaising with the coach and striving for excellence across the board, instilling the need for punctuality and making sure training sessions are properly tailored and productive. Gary has been in charge of developing everything to do with the ground – renovating the rickety old stand and refurbishing the changing rooms and clubhouse, previously managed by a dozen or so volunteers. With dedication above and beyond, they'd take care of everything, from ticket sales on matchdays to pitch maintenance.

In November 2015, I too trod that pitch, walking in silence on the terrain where a sensational new page of history would soon be written. On that day, everything at Moor Lane was different to what it is now. There reigned the fascinating air of age and neglect only to be found at non-league grounds. The stand was run-down but unique nonetheless. You could see it had been there for decades, rather like the dugouts – brick-built with breeze blocks supporting the wooden boards the players would sit on.

Players yes, but first and foremost these were simple lads whose life was not just football. In the mornings they'd dirty their hands in their everyday jobs, and of an evening exchange their working clothes for the pride of donning the colours of Salford City. Colours that Gary and company intend to lead to success, taking them to compete on bigger stages and giving their supporters the joys that success brings.

On that rainy Saturday afternoon in September 2018, three years after I'd first set foot in Moor Lane, such exceptional results were already on view, with the construction of a new ground and, more importantly, the club no longer playing the country's eighth tier but the fifth.

Such a quantum leap was achieved through a long and remarkable run of victories, but above all through organisational skills of the highest quality and the priority given to the fans, with ticket prices kept low and a smart new ground as their home. A special home, officially opened on 19 October 2017 by none other than Sir Alex Ferguson, whose name will forever grace the walls of the corridors in the stadium – a state-of-the-art stadium holding about 5,000 spectators and boasting a fine indoor bar open to home and away supporters alike. Not to mention private boxes where food is served on matchdays, a small club shop and the wonderful feeling of belonging visible in the eyes of all the supporters packed into Moor Lane that afternoon.

In the Premier League that feeling is becoming harder to find – rising ticket costs are flying in the face of the devotion supporters feel for their clubs. But at Moor Lane tickets can be bought at the turnstiles until a few minutes before kick-off, while those already in the ground are shouting out the words of 'Dirty Old Town', the Salford song from the 1950s.

Those far-off days are hard to picture – not only was the world a different place then but now there's so much more that we have the opportunity to experience. Opportunities that Manchester United's champions – with the backing of businessman Peter Lim – decided to give to the people of whom they felt part, sparking their dreams and providing the results to go with them. The results would be hard to rack up even on a PlayStation, as they took Salford City to play for promotion to League Two on the mythical pitch of Wembley Stadium and won that promotion at the first time of asking.

For the first time in the little club's history, on 11 May 2019 the Class of 92 took it into big-time football.[7] Behind that club there's more than those household names – there are dozens and dozens of volunteers who have given it their time and their passion. And in February 2019 the club laid

---

7 The Class of 92 refers to the golden generation of Manchester United players who worked their way up from the youth teams to the first team and went on to amass a remarkable collection of trophies in England and abroad.

out the welcome mat for none other than David Beckham, whose arrival reconstituted the Class of 92. Not representing Manchester United this time round, but the great little Salford City.

93:20

In the last few weeks I'd tried everything. Every day after work, no matter what time it was, I'd wait outside his house. At least twice a week at the training ground, outside the Etihad after every home match and even at the station in the hope of intercepting him before he got on a train to London. All in vain.

I'd tried to picture the moment dozens of times, fantasising about what it would be like to shake his hand and tell him about myself, about my dreams and how much I admired him for the genius that he was. Sometimes in my most secret thoughts he even appeared as a friend. One of those you've known your whole life. I imagined myself at his side, talking about football and new dreams to pursue.

Finally, one March afternoon, this dream came true. Pep was there, just a few yards away. After the final whistle he'd gone on to the pitch to greet all the players, and I was waiting for him by the entrance to the players' tunnel. In a minute or two he'd pass by and, one way or another, I was going to grab him. I asked a dear old lady to give me some room; I was in a right state. I couldn't fail; it would be too unbearable.

I'd gone to the ground for him and him alone, not for the match. A few weeks later I was returning to Italy and this was my last chance to meet him. I didn't take my eyes off him for a second, following his every step. My heart was going like the clappers. Pep was coming and he looked in a hurry. Terrified at the prospect of failure, I shouted his name, and then again. The people around me did the same. And they did it for me. Pep stopped, I hugged him tight and for a second looked into his eyes.

All I remember after that is tears of emotion and being hugged by the people around me because I'd done it. I'd done it. Another little big dream had come true. Getting a photo with that living legend. The record breaker. More than a manager. The one and only Pep Guardiola.

❄❄❄

As you know by now, living in Manchester changed my life forever. Living in Moss Side, in the south of the city, taught me not only the importance of learning to live with life's difficulties but also to keep my eyes wide open. At the time, though, all my eyes could do was look beyond the horizon to far-off cities and countries, blinded by my dreams to everything on my doorstep.

The house where I lived on Smalldale Avenue, hard by Alexandra Park, was less than ten minutes' walk from Blue Moon Way, but for all the period I was living in Manchester I'd never made the time to go there. Then, one October morning in 2018, Fabio and I found ourselves walking on that road in complete silence. We passed through a maze of red-brick terraces until we realised we were standing in front of it – the historic location we'd been looking for.

It was in the gardens of a new housing development, obviously with no history. The buildings had risen on the ashes of the famous old Maine Road, Manchester City's home for 80 long years. We were alone, apart from a biting wind and a few curtain twitchers' eyes watching as we inspected the small circular plaque set in the ground. It was there to tell passers-by that on that precise spot there once lay the centre of the pitch at Maine Road.

It was a ground I'd admired only in photographs, wishing I could travel back in time and stand on the terraces, reliving those distant days. A time when City were anything but the footballing superpower we know today, a club fallen from grace, for years yo-yoing between the top two divisions and even spending a season in the third.

Before the arrival of chairman Khaldoon Al Mubarak in the summer of 2008, Manchester City had won just two league titles in over 110 years, leaving their supporters with more bitter memories than sweet. Along with chairman Al Mubarak and the new owner Mansour bin Zayed Al Nahyan, those fans were destined to enjoy one spectacular success after another, celebrating the arrival of world-class players and an unending series of trophies.

But before going into the trophy room, silverware has to be won, and the way the Premier League title was conquered by Roberto Mancini's team on 13 May 2012 was nothing less than historic. The two Manchester clubs went into the last day of the season equal on points, with City in first place on the strength of a superior goal difference. Playing at home, all they had to do was beat relegation-threatened Queens Park Rangers to win the title.

Against all expectations, in the 91st minute that team of stars found themselves trailing 2-1, which would have handed the title to their arch-rivals, who had despatched Sunderland by a single goal. Then the incredible happened. In four short minutes the Red Devils' jubilation was silenced. It was their nightmare and City's dream. First, hope was reignited in the desperate City fans when Edin Džeko headed in the equaliser. The dream came true at minute 93:20 precisely, when Sergio Agüero lashed in the winner. The stadium went wild, the crowd ran on to the pitch and their 44-year wait for another league title was over.

Those five minutes of injury time, the boundless joy of the fans on the pitch and off it – those were things I was only able to experience second-hand, watching them on television with eyes (you know me by now) that were filling with tears. Tears of sadness springing from my great love for England and for those places to which I felt I belonged but at the time seemed too far off, out of reach.

A few years later those same towns and cities would become my home, my daily bread. They'd help me to build the path towards my biggest dreams. Dreams that became clear aims, carefully nurtured despite the difficulties and the many tumbles, which were then remedied by my determination. And the day I met Pep, it was determination that made the difference. Taking that photo confirmed for me that with enough passion and the conviction, you can make it; in this world anything is possible.

It was a passion I cultivated year after year, thinking big and keeping my aim on the objectives in front of me, never on the difficulties to be faced. Objectives that required sacrifices, but I always made them in the name of a promise made on 13 May 2012. On that day, with tears in my eyes (they can be habit-forming), I told my friends that sooner or later I'd go to those distant places and see them and experience them for myself, so that I could tell people, young and old, that dreams exist and that one of them, for Manchester City fans, came true on that afternoon in May 2012.

Minute 93:20, with a goal by Sergio Agüero. Proving to the whole world that when you really want something, nothing is impossible.

THE PEOPLE'S CLUB

There I was, walking past the local houses. There was no one else around, not a soul. Silence reigned supreme. It was seven in the morning, for that matter, one day in May 2015. Liverpool seemed to be fast asleep, and as a pale sun rose slowly into the sky I found myself wandering the streets of that captivating city for the first time in my life.

I'll never forget the sense of wonder that filled me on my first football journeys. And on that day the emotion was particularly strong as I took in the historic setting of Goodison Park. After careful inspection of the statue of legendary goalscorer Dixie Dean, I was in the grip of a childlike curiosity as I explored the vicinity of that famous old ground. Around every corner, step after step, I was breathing football history.

What I wanted then, more than anything else, was to touch that grass and to stand on the terraces that I'd only ever admired on television. I spent at least half an hour looking for some kindly soul who might help me, and then I spotted an open door. Without a thought for the consequences I slipped inside, bounced up some steps and a few seconds later there I was, admiring Goodison Park from the inside. It didn't seem possible, but there I was. As if by magic, I was in one of the most fascinating grounds in the whole of England.

Welcome to Goodison Park, home of Everton Football Club.

❀ ❀ ❀

Liverpool lives for two things – beer and football. Football there is much more than just a sport. The only things standing between its two main grounds, Goodison and Anfield, are the trees of Stanley Park. The distance is as short as the rivalry between their fans is fierce. As is their sense of unity and respect – if need be, Reds and Blues can stand together, as they have done several times in memory of the 97 people who died in the Hillsborough disaster.

On Merseyside, football is the main reason for living. That's hard to explain but wonderful to see, particularly in the environs of Goodison Park. Everton supporters' love for the club involves everyone – great and small, young and old, women and children. Walking in the city streets, whether it's a matchday or not, you see dozens and dozens of kids sporting Everton colours, proudly displayed to all passers-by. It's a love passed down through the generations from grandparents – fans since the days of Dixie Dean – to parents, down to the smallest children.

In the narrow streets around Goodison Park, among the houses just a few yards from the rusty old turnstiles, you can see the club's proud history emblazoned on the stadium walls. Founded in 1878, in their early years the club played their home games in Stanley Park, a venue that Everton soon outgrew as they attracted more supporters.

In 1884 the club moved to Anfield, where they won the first title in their history. With 11 other clubs, in 1888 Everton were founder members of the Football League and went on to win it in 1891, celebrating their triumph in the ground that a few years later would become home to their local rivals – Liverpool Football Club.

Liverpool were founded in June 1892, just a few months after the Blues decided to leave Anfield because of the excessive rent charged by John Houlding, owner of the land on which the stadium stood and the man who founded Liverpool FC. So with the prospect of the new club looming, Everton decided to move to the other side of Stanley Park and put down roots at Goodison, which since 1892 has been their home – and the setting of some epic battles, the stage on which great players have performed.

Still today, despite all the years that have passed, they say that the greatest ever to have trod the Goodison grass was striker Dixie Dean. He was eight years old when his dad first took him to watch Everton, and you can imagine their feelings when he returned to Goodison ten years later to pull on the shirt and play for his club.

In 1928 Everton won the First Division title for the third time in their history, and Dixie – the nickname given to him by his supporters – scored 60 goals in 39 matches, going down in history as the most prolific scorer of all time in terms of goals scored in one season. Epitomising the virtues of the traditional centre-forward, in his 12 years at Goodison Park, Dixie Dean, and his team-mates, won two First Division titles, one FA Cup and two Charity Shields.

With a total of 383 goals, he's Everton's all-time greatest scorer. More than a legend, he was a real footballer, gentleman and Evertonian, as is inscribed on the pedestal of his statue outside Goodison Park. And it was there in the stands, as fate would have it, that at the age of 73 he breathed his last on 1 March 1980, after suffering a heart attack, shortly after the final whistle of a Merseyside derby match against Liverpool. His memory will live on.

On a cold and miserable Saturday afternoon at the beginning of 2017, 18 months after my first visit, I returned to Goodison Park, this time for an FA Cup match against Claudio Ranieri's Leicester City. This was my first chance to taste the atmosphere of that famous old ground with its supporters.

The passionate pride they have in their club was on full display as they began to gather in massed ranks at The People's Pub on Goodison Road, opposite the old-style turnstiles giving access to the Main Stand. As I passed through them I tried to imagine how many others had done the same since 1892, scarves round necks, cloth caps on heads, ready to support their heroes.

Running up the steps, I thought about the first time I'd done that a year and a half before, without asking permission, and then the spectacle of Goodison Park was laid out in front of me. Just like the first time.

The seats were steeped in history, most of them being in old wood with their numbers carefully picked out in white on a blue background – the colour scheme covering every inch of the ground. Such was my feeling of wonder that, even now, every time I think about being there I get goose-pimples. The thought that Dixie Dean and so many other stars had played there, where I stood, is one of the main reasons why I undertook this long and unforgettable journey in the first place.

Whenever anybody asks me about Goodison Park and Everton, I tell them about that May afternoon when, on my first visit to the city, after sneaking into Goodison I found myself walking on the hill in Everton Park. With sunset on the horizon, from up there I had a splendid view of Liverpool, but what caught my eye was a small tower that somehow struck me as familiar. I'd seen it before, but I couldn't remember where.

Then, as I walked on, it came to me – it was the famous tower depicted on the Everton crest. So I ran back to touch that piece of history with my own hand. Everton Lock-Up, or Prince Rupert's Tower, as it's known locally, has stood on Everton Brow since 1787. It was used as a holding cell for drunks and criminals pending their appearance before the magistrates.

Not far from the tower there's said to have stood one of the shops famous for making and selling toffee. It was to them, when Everton still played at Anfield, that supporters would flock before and after matches to satisfy their sweet tooth. This, according to football folklore, is how the club and its supporters came to be known as the Toffeemen (or Toffees), and before the Leicester match I was delighted to see the tradition alive and well in the form of a little girl dressed as a Toffee Lady. I'd already seen her on television and heard mention of it, but to see her in the flesh dressed like that was quite something.

It's one of the most touching of the many traditions in English football. It originated at the end of the 19th century through the good offices of Molly Bushell, owner of Old Ma Bushell's Toffee Shop. The story goes that in order to beat the competition of the nearby Mother Noblett's Toffee Shop, she had the idea of sending her daughter to Everton's home matches dressed in her Sunday best to sell toffees and mints at the side of the pitch.

In and around Goodison Park there are traditions and rituals repeated week after week, which I had the chance, once at least, to experience for myself: a pint at The People's Pub and then watching the match, without forgetting to pop into the little church of St Luke's, on the corner between the Main Stand and the Gwladys Street End. It's a unique spot where, with hundreds of supporters before every home match, you can drink a cup of hot tea and enjoy every moment of an atmosphere whose days are numbered.

Work is underway on a new stadium. Although the project is an exciting one and the area around Goodison Park will be completely redeveloped, local history and traditions can never be replaced. But they'll leave an indelible mark on my heart and the hearts of everyone who has experienced, at least once, the charm and the glory of Goodison Park.

THIS IS ANFIELD

Steven was there, just a few yards from me. That living legend, who until then I'd only ever been able to admire on television, was finally ready to pull on his No.8 shirt and take the pitch before my awestruck eyes. This was my chance to experience new sensations and excitement, feeling first-hand the warmth and passion of Anfield and feeling part of that community, which is able to transmit an intense, vital enthusiasm that everybody should live through at least once in a lifetime. It's a community of people who live just for those colours, living their lives waiting for the next match and going from day to day with Liverpool FC in their hearts and on their skin.

At Anfield, on that sunny afternoon in March 2017, those hearts sang with devotion for their captain in the hope of seeing him score and celebrate with them once again. That duly came 20 minutes before the final whistle as supporters leapt from their seats, knowing that they'd written another small page in a romantic story.

The boy had come home, the captain's armband on his sleeve and No.8 on his back, and scored in front of the Kop, even though his playing days were over. There he was, in that charity match against the greats of Real Madrid, in his red shirt, fighting for every ball, as he'd always done.

Tears came to my eyes as I saw Steven's goal, grateful to life for yet another story I'd soon be able to tell. A story set in the heart of Liverpool, in the spectacular arena of Anfield. All in the name of Liverpool Football Club and Steven Gerrard.

⚽⚽⚽

When I think of everything I've lived through, I'm conscious of my good fortune. When I say lived through, I don't just mean excitement felt and experiences accumulated, I mean what I've had to overcome, difficulties and failures included.

Setting foot in the grounds I'd always admired from afar, going to dozens and dozens of towns and cities was something more than the realisation of my little big dream. In those years of travelling, I grew up, my thinking evolved, my character was strengthened and my determination increased beyond recognition. Taking on challenges that seemed insuperable, which people said were impossible, made me a better man, giving me strength and greater wisdom – which I'm still trying to improve and develop, in the knowledge that life is by far the greatest gift you can ever receive. It's a gift offered only once, and one that we should try to appreciate every day, come what may.

By appreciate, I mean counting your blessings, especially in small things, such as the embrace of a parent or a brother's open smile. Too often, in my teenage years, I appreciated none of these things, convinced that they'd always be there. That conviction gradually faded as my journeys unfolded, because I could feel the need for the embraces that my mum, my dad and my brother would silently send me. The love and kisses that won't be there forever, which is why we should appreciate them above all else, leaving aside all the bad feelings life brings and wrapping ourselves in the best thing in the world – Love.

Love, with a capital L, is the feeling that ties the Anfield club to its huge body of supporters in a unique, indissoluble bond. A bond of undying passion that unites fans, players and coach in the spirit of 'You'll Never Walk Alone'. A hymn to life, the anthem that best expresses the fans' visceral love for the Reds. And on the Kop they're always there – singing their hearts out, holding up their old scarves and waving their famous banners bearing the club's history and the faces of the players and managers who have brought so much success.

Under the legendary Bill Shankly, success was certainly achieved on the field of play, but mostly off it, when he won the hearts of the community to which he felt he belonged. He came to Anfield in December 1959, and it was thanks to him that the club enjoyed one of the most memorable stories English football has ever told. It began with the club in the Second Division, but in a few seasons Liverpool were back at the top, winning the First Division title in April 1964 (for the sixth time) and their first-ever FA Cup in May 1965. In the following seasons they won another league title and three Community Shields, going on to collect the first of many European trophies when they brought home the UEFA Cup in May 1973. That succession of triumphs engraved Shankly's name on Liverpool hearts forever. When, on 12 July 1974, he unexpectedly resigned, those hearts were engulfed with sadness.

His successor was Bob Paisley, a former Liverpool player and for years his right-hand man. And he outdid Shankly. In just nine years Paisley added 20 pieces of silverware to the Anfield trophy room, including three European Cups and six league titles, earning his own glorious place in the club's history.

That March afternoon at Anfield, as I walked through the Paisley Gateway and found myself in front of the statue of Bill Shankly, it was like going back to relive the times when those two giants made Liverpool great.

On matchdays Liverpool fans converge on Anfield in massed ranks. Before passing through the turnstiles and plunging into the extraordinary atmosphere of their home ground, many of them pause for a minute's thought at the memorial to the 97 victims of the Hillsborough disaster. A tragedy I've already discussed, it struck on 15 April 1989, and every year is still commemorated with silent tears. A silence that I also honoured as I stood on that spot. And when the words of 'You'll Never Walk Alone' resound around Anfield, as they do on every matchday, they're also being sent to those no longer with us.

On that sunny March afternoon I was welcomed with open arms into that historic home, not for just another match but for the big charity game between Liverpool Legends and Real Madrid Legends, with all those champions to remind us of their illustrious history.

What stayed with me most from that day, though, was the Anfield anthem. As ever, to the strains of 'You'll Never Walk Alone', the fans raised their scarves to the sky and sang with a passion, giving me one of the most moving football moments I can remember. Moments and feelings that will always make me proud to have set foot in that hallowed ground and happy to have witnessed a tiny piece of history. To the notes of 'You'll Never Walk Alone' and in the name of Steven, Bill and Bob – besides winning trophies, they won their people's hearts. People who, a hundred years from now, will still be shouting to the rest of the world: 'This Is Anfield' and 'We Are Liverpool'.

For them, that's as good as it gets.

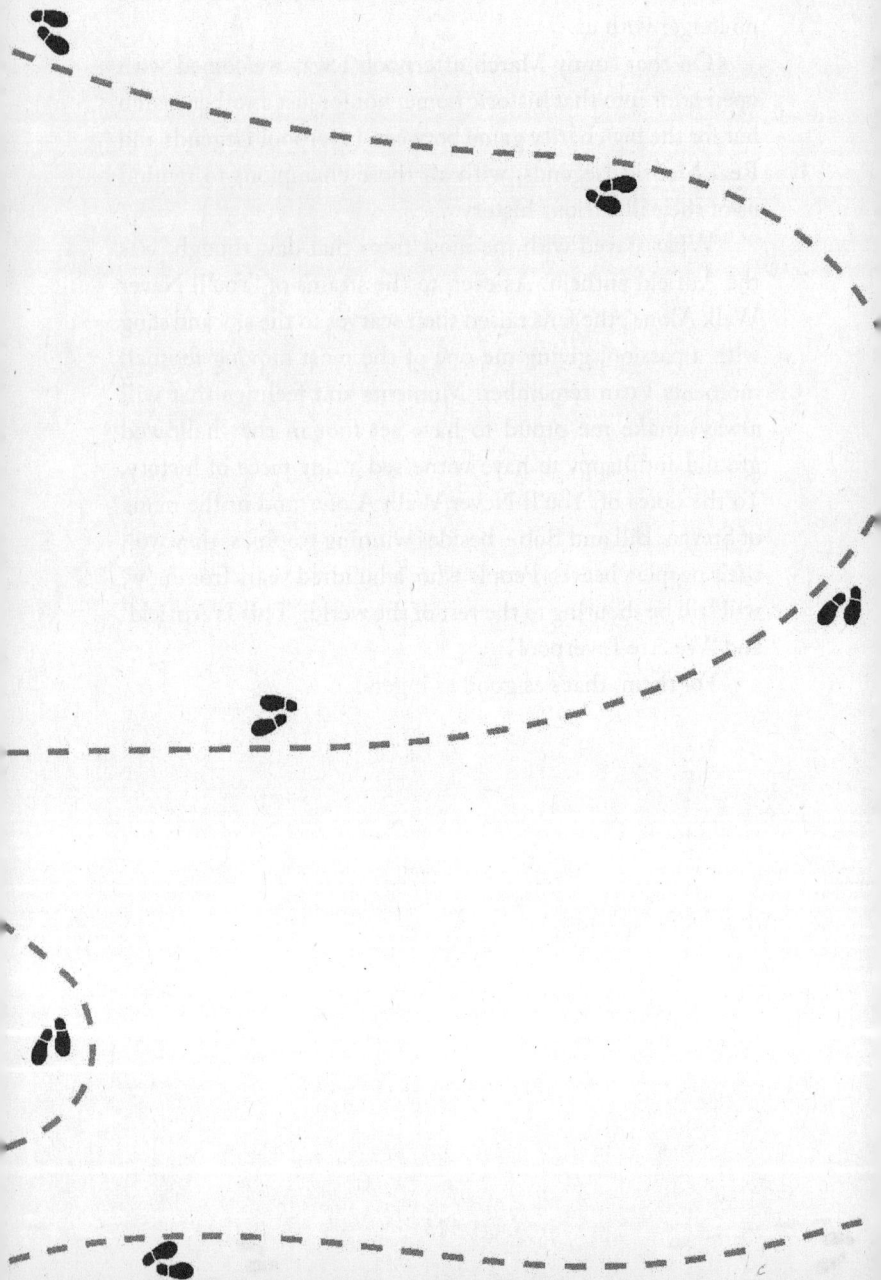

CHAPTER 4

STAY PATIENT AND TRUST YOUR JOURNEY

Good things take time ...

BEING BORN and growing up in a village just outside Naples taught me two things. First, keep your eyes open, everywhere and with everybody. The second is the art of getting by and carrying on, no matter what, because – as the local saying goes – the darkness will pass. This expression, and the deep-rooted mindset it reflects, is one that I've carried with me around England, in the conviction that moments of difficulty are challenges that life throws at us to test our resolve.

It's all very well to have dreams and believe strongly in something, but remember that you can never achieve anything without sacrifice and patience. I've always thought that sacrifice and patience are two essential requirements for every dreamer. Without them you'll never get anywhere. Sacrifice helps us to grow, gives us strength, improves who we are and tells us whether the path we're following is really the right one. Patience is the hardest quality to develop, complicated to manage and hated by almost everyone. Being patient requires optimism, consistency, determination, conviction and many other qualities, but rest assured that once you've developed these gifts, nothing and no one can stop you.

However, being patient doesn't mean waiting for our dreams to fall into our lap without doing anything – far from it. To my way of thinking, being patient means working hard until the right moment comes, and then being ready when opportunity knocks, never losing hope, and – more than anything else – facing life in the conviction that, step by step, you'll get to where you want to be.

When I talk to people, I've often concluded that the main reason for their failures and unhappiness lies in their lack of patience and willingness to make sacrifices. I'd like to have it all now too, but that's not how life works. Realising a dream takes sweat. You have to get busy, get your hands dirty and face life's challenges head-on, with courage and grit.

Being convinced that you've got what it takes, in my view, is the first and most important step in achieving something, be it great or small.

More than once I've had to make more sacrifices than I thought I would, adapting to circumstances that I certainly didn't like; but to achieve my aims I persisted, and will continue to do so. I've always thought that the difference between those who achieve their ambitions and those who don't lies in their approach to life.

Be mad, be hungry. You've only got one life and its leading player is you.

London, 13 December 2019

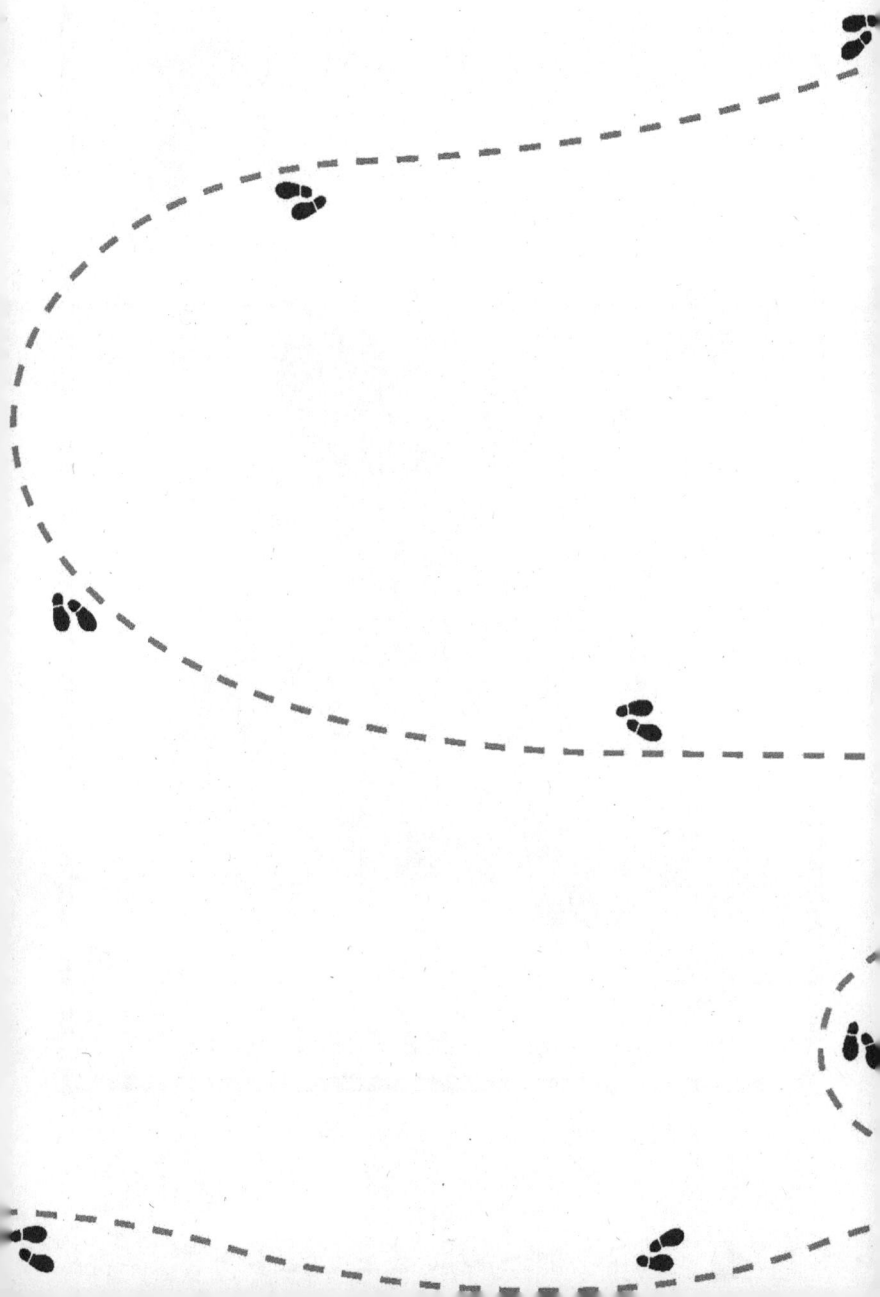

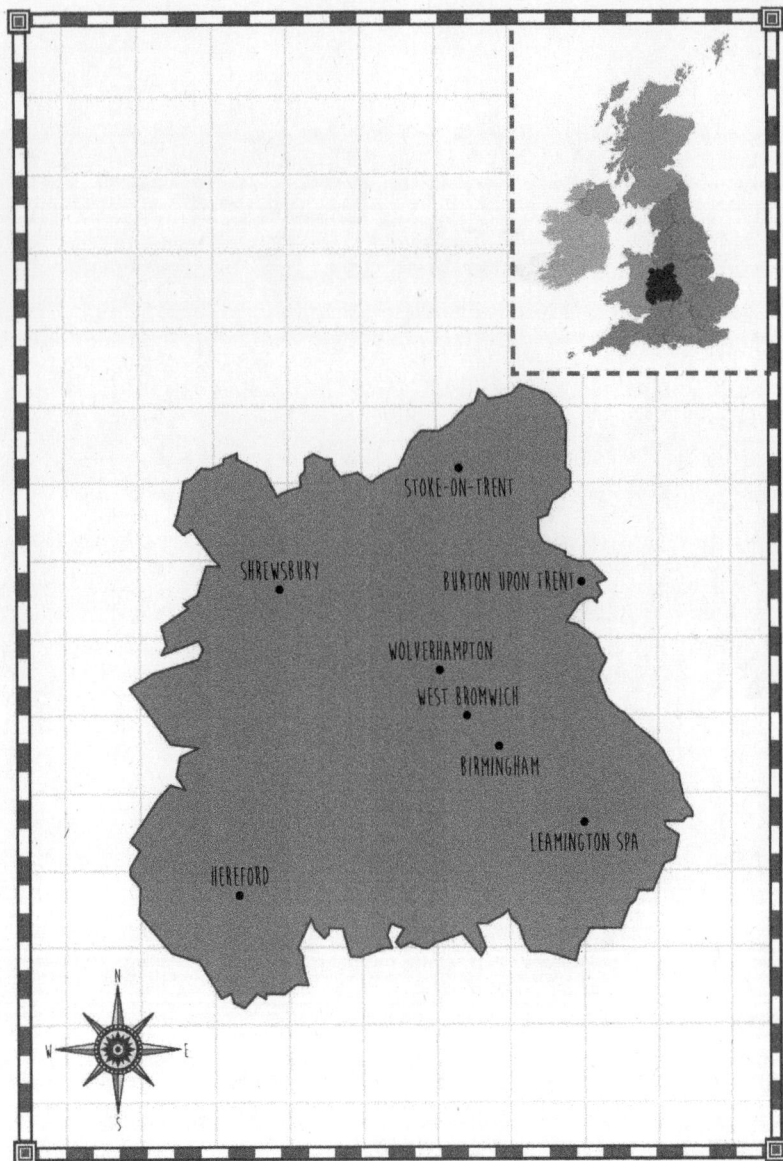

STOKE-ON-TRENT

SHREWSBURY

BURTON UPON TRENT

WOLVERHAMPTON

WEST BROMWICH

BIRMINGHAM

LEAMINGTON SPA

HEREFORD

N
W — E
S

WEST MIDLANDS

I have a vivid memory of the first time I set foot in Birmingham. It was the summer of 2016; the sky was dismal and rain kept me company for most of the day. Since then, though, having visited Villa Park and then St Andrew's, home to Birmingham City, I've been back at least 15 times, discovering something new each time. With its old canal network, the city has always fascinated me, often reminding me of a bygone age.

Beyond Birmingham, hub of the West Midlands, are other big clubs and their grounds that I've been able to experience. From the Wolves of Molineux to The Hawthorns to see West Bromwich Albion play Arsenal on the cold and rainy afternoon of 31 December 2017, taking in the much-vaunted atmosphere at Stoke City, where the wind rules the roost. From Stoke-on-Trent a compulsory visit is to Burton upon Trent, renowned for its production of beer.

Jumping from one train to another and walking for hundreds of miles, I've had the pleasure of investigating a series of non-league grounds, treading their pitches, often kicking a ball that I happened to find in the back of a net or tucked away in a stand.

Another journey is about to start, and although I'd have liked to tell you a whole lot more, I can promise that the next stories will take you to magical places, historic places, from the majestic setting of Villa Park to a little non-league ground where even man's best friend has a place of his own …

WELCOME TO STOKE-ON-TRENT: CITY OF RAIN AND WIND

A sullen, threatening sky was visible through the freezing windows of Manchester Airport. There was hardly anyone around. Just silence and a poor vagrant slumped on the ground near the coffee machines so as to get warm a bit more quickly and postpone the cold and solitude of the city streets till tomorrow.

My head was crowded with a host of thoughts as I made my bed on the cold and uncomfortable airport seats that night early in February 2016. I'd spent a carefree evening wining and dining with honest friendly faces – until they told me that they had nowhere to put me up. When they asked me where I'd spend the night, I mustered an ironic grin and said, 'Maybe the airport.'

So that's where they took me. I could hardly believe it. Before we went out to dinner I'd told them that the last train to take me back to Bowness-on-Windermere would be leaving in half an hour and I had nowhere to sleep in Manchester. They assured me I had nothing to worry about. But their words were carried off by the wind.

All I needed was a space on someone's floor, at the end of their bed or beside a sofa. A simple gesture would have been enough.

No one could be bothered; the girl I was seeing at the time, who was there with all of us, watched me get out of the car and said, 'Night, love.' Other than that, she said nothing. She didn't speak to any of those people who were so important to her. She didn't protest that somewhere could surely be found for me and that I shouldn't stay all alone in the airport. When it came down to it, no one was bothered about me. When they dumped me at a roundabout a few hundred yards from the airport entrance and the sound of the car was fading into the distance, I remembered one thing: Love, the one with a capital L, is for a select few ...

⚽ ⚽ ⚽

That night was interminable. The hands on my watch seemed frozen. Fed up with the whole situation and chilled to the bone, instead of getting on the first train to go back to my friends in Bowness, as I'd planned the day before, I decided to do something else. At that time I was living in Italy but had come on a trip to England for ten days with those honest friendly faces. They stopped in Manchester, where some of them had work commitments, whereas I went on to Bowness-on-Windermere, where I'd lived a few months before and where all my friends were. But in those days I went to Manchester several times. First, to spend some time with all of them, and also to get to know the city that would become my home a few months later. I never imagined I'd be spending one of those nights in the airport.

After reaching Manchester Piccadilly from the airport, just before five o'clock in the morning I boarded one of the first trains of the day and set off to discover some new football grounds. As luck would have it, the train I was on would pass through a place I'd wanted to see for a long time: Stoke-on-Trent.

I don't remember much about the journey because as soon as I sat down in the warm and cosy Virgin train I fell into a deep sleep. Then I awoke with a jolt and saw that the train was sitting in the station of ... Stoke-on-Trent. I grabbed my rucksack, pulled open the nearest door and jumped off the train five seconds before it left for the next stop down the line. I was in a complete daze. Trying to rub some life into my face, I focused my sleep-filled eyes and made my way towards the exit. I looked around me for a few seconds. Such was the silence that for a moment I thought I could hear my heart beating.

Above me was the arch of a dark but clear sky as I started walking towards another adventure; all I could hear was my own footsteps. I strode past the houses on the approach to the station and, having looked behind me to check that no one else was there, I was suddenly confronted by a fork that was none too enticing ...

The A500 trunk road was highly dangerous. As cars and lorries sped past me, the only 'safe' area to walk was the narrow roadside, just inside the guard rail. No two ways about it, I was frightened. In some places, trees blown down by a recent storm blocked my way along the grass verge and I was forced to walk on the carriageway, a few inches from the unbroken stream of speeding traffic. Daunting though it was, following that road was much better than taking the towpath of the Trent and Mersey Canal, which that morning looked like the perfect setting for a horror film.

After walking for about 40 minutes I found myself on Stanley Matthews Way, and the stadium I'd wanted to see for so long was finally in sight. I explored the area all around it and, predictably enough at that time of day, there wasn't a soul to be seen. The imposing statue of the legendary Stanley Matthews seemed to be twitching into life, but then I realised that it was just fatigue that was playing tricks on me.

Squinting into a fierce wind, I saw that, although it was only 7.30 in the morning, light was coming from some office windows near one of the entrances to the ground. The sky was brightening. Despite the hour and the thought that I might be bothering the individual I'd glimpsed through the blinds in the office windows, I approached the door. Knock knock ... The astonished face of a man of about 50 peered round the door; he looked at me for a few seconds and said, 'Well, my lad, what brings you to Stoke-on-Trent at half past seven in the morning?' I couldn't help laughing. To be honest, I thought he was perfectly right to look at me like that, and I replied, 'It's a long story! I've wanted to visit this ground for years, and here I am.'

Wayne had no more questions. All he said was: 'I still don't know what brings you here, but you're welcome! Your eyes speak for you. Come in.' A familiar feeling of excitement came over me and my heart began to race.

Wayne had been working at Stoke City for over 20 years. He showed me the dressing rooms and all the locations where interviews were held. Then, after passing through the tunnel used by the players on every matchday, we got to the place I'd dreamed of – the pitch itself. As soon as we left the players' tunnel and climbed the last steps, that wind blasted into our faces. The same wind that has always found out the weaknesses in the many teams that have come unstuck at the Britannia, the wind I'd only ever seen on television and wanted so much to feel. As I did that February morning, thanks to Wayne's good offices, and as I did again more than a year later.

It was a Saturday in October 2017 when I went back to Stoke to see a match. This time with Uncle Umberto and my cousin, Alfonso. And this time the towpath of the Trent and Mersey Canal, which had looked so forbidding on that first day, was the route we took to get there, now free of fear but with a vivid memory of that first day.

Wind and rain, needless to say, gave us an unceremonious welcome. It was bitterly cold, and as we reached the Britannia Stadium the weather only got worse.

The statues of past champions such as Gordon Banks (dubbed the greatest English goalkeeper of all time and World Cup winner in 1966) and John Ritchie (Stoke City's all-time top scorer) sported the scarves and shirts of the club that had made them great.

As the skies grew even more ominous, it was finally time to pass through the turnstiles and immerse ourselves in the stadium and the atmosphere that had fascinated me for so long. A stadium different to all the others. What makes it so special is that two of its corners are completely open, allowing the wind to blow in as it pleases and dump sheets of rain on to the fans inside. As it happened, right where I was positioned, next to an old lady sitting in the seat beside me. Margaret, who had been supporting the team of her hometown since the age of eight, asked me where I was from, given that Stoke is not exactly a tourist destination, especially on a day like that.

I told her about myself, my plans and my travels, and she told me about her life. She talked about supporting the club in the old Victoria Ground, and how she wept as she watched it being demolished, piece by piece. She spoke of her love for her city, even though the weather was almost always wind and rain. She said she'd never, but never, swap her home for anywhere else in the world because, if she did, she wouldn't be able to support the club she loved. There was a break in her voice when she spoke of Stanley Matthews at the official opening of the Britannia Stadium in August 1997 and his death at 85 years of age in February 2000.

And then, as Stoke proceeded to lose 2-1 to Bournemouth and the rain continued to pour, she told me how 100,000 people took to the streets of the city to mark Stanley Matthews's passing. To pay tribute to him and remember him in the best way possible, making him an indelible part of Stoke City's history. His ashes are buried beneath the centre circle of the Britannia so that he'll always be where he loved to be for his whole life – on a football pitch.

I was moved by what she told me. As I left the Britannia on my way to whatever adventure came next, happy to have experienced such a memorable rainy day, I understood that for Margaret and all the fans like her there was nothing, nor would there ever be anything, better than Stoke City. A club that plays in a ground I'd always yearned to visit, where I'd met Wayne and then Margaret. Two people who didn't even know my name but immediately struck me as a hundred times more genuine and honest than the faces who had dumped me on a cold night at an airport roundabout ...

OUT OF DARKNESS COMETH LIGHT

On that cold February evening the eyes of the Wolverhampton supporters exuded nothing but sadness and disappointment. A 2-1 defeat at the hands of their rivals Birmingham City had left them closer to the relegation zone than to the play-offs they'd been dreaming of. A position those fans didn't deserve, since over 27,000 had turned up to Molineux on a freezing Friday night. There were lots of other things they could have been doing after a long working week, but their club was more important. They could have stayed at home wrapped in a duvet and watched the match on the sofa with a beer or a hot cup of tea. But nothing would have matched being there in their home ground to support the colours to which they belong.

Support that never flagged, songs and chants to lift the team and every player in it. Not even defeat could quell their passion. For 90 minutes they swirled their scarves and shouted out to the world that they were Wolves. Wolves who have never abandoned the pack, always solid behind the club no matter what division they play in, devoted to the old gold and black.

Then, just over two years after that cold February night in the lower reaches of the Championship, they found themselves playing against Torino to qualify for the group stage of the Europa League. It was 39 years since Molineux had seen European football, a result achieved with hard work to match the dreams of an entire community. A community I've had the honour of meeting twice. First on that freezing February night in 2017, but particularly against Torino in August 2019, when the Italians had no answer to the hunger and strength of will of the wolf pack.

Pack your bags and come with me now, because that's where we're going. Next stop Molineux, the Wolves' lair.

❋ ❋ ❋

It seemed as if I'd known Dave for years, such was the warmth of his welcome. As soon as he saw me he gave me a hug and pressed a Wolves scarf into my hands before taking me on a guided tour of the historic Molineux ground. In the next two hours he recounted the club's history and his passion for the colours. Love actually, rather than passion, because it started on his fourth birthday, when his dad took him on his first visit to the ground. Ever since that day in September 1989, Molineux has been his favourite place. As the years went by, his feeling for Wolverhampton Wanderers steadily grew and he got the chance to live the dream, working for his town and the club he has always supported.

It's a club with an enviable history, one of the 12 founder members of the Football League in 1888, a club whose greatest glories go back to the 1950s. That was when Wolverhampton, led by England captain Billy Wright and managed by the legendary Stan Cullis – both of whom have statues outside Molineux – won three league titles and, perhaps more importantly, made the name of the club resonate the world over.

It was a name that captured the imagination of an 11-year-old George Best, who was inspired by the stories of the club's triumphs. Triumphs that enabled the wolves from the Black Country to change the history of European football. At that time the European Cup had yet to be instituted, so the only way to organise international club matches was through friendlies. One friendly remembered to this day was played on 13 December 1954 in the atmospheric setting of Molineux, where 55,000 spectators were privileged to witness one of the most important encounters in Wolves' history, watching their club win 3-2 against the mighty Hungarians of Budapest Honvéd.

Honvéd were led by their legendary striker Ferenc Puskás, but also included five of his team-mates who just a few months earlier had played in the Hungary team that not only humiliated England but managed to do it twice – first at Wembley, 6-3, and then in Budapest by no less than 7-1. Those defeats had knocked the whole country sideways, but on that evening in December 1954 Wolverhampton Wanderers sent the Hungarians home empty-handed.

The next day the newspapers were full of nothing else, praising Stan Cullis's men to the heavens and anointing Wolves with the unofficial title of world champions. But in the following days, since some journalists were unimpressed by all the fuss, convinced that clubs such as AC Milan and Real Madrid were far superior, the proposal emerged to set up a new competition to establish which club side was actually the best in Europe. This led a few months later to the creation of what rapidly established itself as the continent's most sought-after trophy – the European Cup.

For the first five years of its life, from 1956 to 1960, the cup was won by Alfredo Di Stefano's legendary Real Madrid. On 17 October 1957, Wolverhampton played the European champions in a friendly and beat them 3-2, writing another heroic page in the club's history. A history that, on that late August morning, thanks to Dave, I had a chance to see up close, discovering the treasures of the Molineux museum, which conserves all the silverware and shirts from the past, not forgetting the myriad photographs celebrating the most memorable events in the club's history.

One of these took place in 1990, when Sir Jack Hayward decided to buy the club to which he felt he belonged. Not just because he was born a stone's throw from Molineux but, above all, on the strength of his attachment to the Wolves. As soon as the transaction was completed, Sir Jack – supporter first and chairman second – began his stewardship by paying off all the debts accumulated by the previous owner. He followed that by rebuilding most of the stadium, proving his unconditional love for the club and the community of its fans.

The community loved him back from day one – when Dave told me the story of him and his feeling for the club, I was almost speechless. All the more so when I heard that in May 2007 Sir Jack sold Wolves to Steve Morgan for the symbolic sum of £10, on the undertaking that the new owner would continue to invest in the colours he loved so much.

Those colours were his second skin. Sir Jack was given pride of place in the club's Hall of Fame and received the tribute of a stand at Molineux named after him and a statue of him placed between that one and the Steve Bull Stand.

On that historic night of European football at the end of August, it was there that I spent some time sitting a few yards from the statue of Sir Jack Hayward, watching the fans make their way to the ground as their anticipation grew for the kick-off against Torino. And as the two teams filed on to the pitch I was swept up by their feverish enthusiasm, singing out their devotion to the club and willing them to win. Which they did – that night they beat Torino 2-1 and wrote another page in the club's history. After 39 long years Wolverhampton Wanderers were back in Europe.

It was a qualification meticulously managed by Nuno Espírito Santo and doggedly fought for on the pitch by players ever ready to chase down every ball, to the delight of the 29,000 there that night, fans who have proved their loyalty irrespective of the club's fortunes.

Their club is as important to them as their own lives, a tradition passed down from father to son, a focal point in the famous old Molineux. A home more than a stadium. The lair of the Wolves.

THIS IS VILLA PARK

It was the 20th day of April 1895 when in the heart of Crystal Palace Park, in front of over 42,000 spectators, Aston Villa won the second FA Cup of their history with a 1-0 victory over local rivals West Bromwich Albion. To reward the commitment of the supporters who had travelled to London for the final, about five months later the club had the idea of displaying the famous trophy in the window of a shop on Newtown Row, a road connecting Birmingham city centre with Witton, the suburb where Villa Park stands.

As luck would have it, on the night of 11 September the FA Cup was stolen, never to be found. Mr William Shillcock, owner of the shop and maker of footballs and football boots, offered a reward of £10, no small sum for the time, for the recovery of the cup. But the thieves were never identified and the cup had disappeared without trace. The blame was officially ascribed to Aston Villa, who were fined £25 by the Football Association for failing to take proper care of the trophy.

Decades later, in February 1958, an 83-year-old man by the name of Harry Burge stated that he and two accomplices had stolen the cup and melted it down to make half-crown coins. But nobody knows the truth of the matter. Since then, more than a century after the crime, other claims have emerged, but only one thing is certain – since 1871 a host of clubs have won the FA Cup but just one has managed to lose it – Aston Villa.

⚽⚽⚽

'It's great, but hard to explain. It's something everyone should experience personally, otherwise there's a risk of perceiving just a small part of it. The one thing I know is that this country has changed my life, and every day gives me another reason to be grateful for everything I'm going through.' I wrote those lines on 24 February 2017, a day that was one of the most exciting of all.

As I walked into the reception at Villa Park in the hope of finding a kindly soul who would help me discover the legendary home of Aston Villa, I was expecting nothing but the day's umpteenth 'no', but that's not how it turned out …

'Hi, I'm Ivan and I come from Italy. I'm writing a book about English football and I've been in many stadiums around the UK. Please, is it possible to visit the stadium inside? Can you please help me?'

That was my usual refrain. Everywhere I went, with my limping English, I presented the same introduction, hoping to convince people that I was doing something unique, not only to realise my dream but above all to give some meaning to my life. And it worked. When it comes down to it, everyone is chasing a dream. And when they're presented with someone who's trying to make his dream real, they always seem to feel obliged to help.

So it was that Mick Dale, in charge of guided tours at Villa Park, regaled me with a big smile: 'You've got a lucky face, my lad. Come on then, I'll show you round Villa Park!'

There it was – yet again, the kind heart of someone I'd only just met was giving me a day to write home about. Moments later, as I found myself touching the grass of Villa Park, I was so moved that Mick put his arm around me: 'I can see the emotion in your eyes, Ivan, it's great! In all the years I've been working here I've never seen anyone get into such a state.' Mick didn't know what else to say, but how could I explain my feelings to him?

At that moment my heart was full, my eyes sated and my mind free of unpleasant thoughts. The smell of the grass went deep into my lungs and the majesty of the Holte End left me spellbound. Villa Park is one of the few grounds in the world to have hosted international matches in three different centuries, but above all a place that jealously conserves stories and legends going back as far as 1897.

Those stories Mick knew by heart – and I asked him to tell me some of them so that I could do the same in turn. In love with his job and happy to share his knowledge, Mick stopped by the corner flag between the North Stand and the Trinity Road Stand and began to tell me about himself:

> I owe my love for this club to my dad. I'll never forget the day he brought me here for the first time – I was nine years old. It was 15 March 1969, and we were playing Blackburn Rovers. At the time we were bouncing between the Second Division and the Third, but I was so overwhelmed by the atmosphere of Villa Park that I became a fan no matter what division we were in. And now, working for the club, I can say that I've realised my dream. Representing the Villa makes me so proud.

Hearing Mick's words as they hung in the morning quiet of Villa Park, I could feel the strength of his devotion to the club. A club with the prestige of being one of the 12 founder members of the Football League thanks to the foresightedness of William McGregor, club director and founder of the world's first football league.

A true-blooded Scotsman and respected textile merchant in Birmingham, Mr McGregor grew tired of seeing friendly matches cancelled because of other teams crying off, so he proposed to other clubs in the Midlands and north of England that they organise a competition with regular matches. This led in September 1888 to the foundation of the first football championship in the world – the Football League. On the strength of this historic innovation, in November 2009, almost a century after his death, a statue of William McGregor was unveiled outside the ground that Mick was now helping me to explore.

With his permission, having admired the pitch, I sat for a minute in the manager's seat on the bench, and as we turned back towards the players' tunnel, he asked me a question: 'Ivan, do you know what happened on 26 May 1982?' I had to confess that the date meant nothing to me. So he asked me to close my eyes until he told me to open them. He placed his hands on my shoulders and guided me down the tunnel, until we reached a point where he told me to stop and open my eyes.

'See that, Ivan? That's our most important trophy. We keep it here, where the players' tunnel is, to remind them that nothing is impossible, and to make it clear to our opponents that we're not just anybody, we're Aston Villa. A big club with a big history.'

I was flabbergasted. I'd never thought that Aston Villa could have won a European Cup, and there it shone, right before my eyes. Won against Bayern Munich, with the only goal of the match scored by striker Peter Withe. Alongside the European Cup, exhibited in a special cabinet, were the FA Cup and the old First Division trophy.

I stood there for at least a minute gaping incredulously at that silverware, and when we got to the home dressing room Mick turned round and said, 'You told me your great ambition is to be a professional coach, right? Here's what we'll do. I'm going off to pick up a few things and I'll be back in about ten minutes. You go in and make yourself at home. See you in a bit.'

At first I thought he was joking, but when the dressing-room door closed behind me and I found myself alone in the club's inner sanctum, I realised that reality had far outstripped my wildest dreams. I sat on the floor, right in the middle of the room. The silence was a sound I could hear, and when I closed my eyes I found I was in a new dimension. I seemed to have made a leap in time as my mind began to delve into its deepest memories. Distant memories, from when I was a boy and would lose myself in photographs of English football grounds. Obsessing over details, spending hours down that rabbit hole. I'd covered my bedroom walls with pictures so as to feel closer to a world that I felt was mine but in those days was far away. So far away but always dreamed of, longed for and now finally experienced.

Mick opened the door and found me sitting on the floor. There were plenty of benches, what was I doing there? 'I'll sit on the bench when I come back here as a coach,' I said. The voice of hope. Mick said nothing, just looked me in the eye. Then he smiled and said it was time to go. Before seeing me out, he gave me some match programmes, wished me luck and said, 'Don't forget me, Ivan, and come back soon. For you Villa Park will always be open.'

I'd never have forgotten that morning with Mick, and when I returned there seven months later, for a Championship match against Bolton, it felt like a homecoming. With the difference that this time I had to share the day with 30,000 other people. Women, children and men of all ages crowded into the ground, proudly wearing the scarves and shirts of the club they loved. Ready to support their team, and just as ready to raise their voices when the away fans tried to sing, reminding them that Villa Park was not a good place for opponents. A bit like all dreamers – to realise their aims they summon their courage, strength and determination, silence their fears and life's insecurities and convince themselves that sooner or later their desires will find fulfilment.

MY BORDER COLLIE

Adventures – on my travels around the English countryside I've had quite a few. Footslogged miles, enlivened by wind and rain, especially in the wicked British winters, have been my daily bread. My dear old backpack, as heavy as ever, and the long black jacket that keeps me warm were wet through on that freezing January afternoon, as were my face and hair. I can't remember a day as cold and exhausting as that one. The four miles or so from Leamington station to the ground I was heading for had to be walked – there wasn't a bus to be seen.

It wasn't easy to get to, but it was worth the trouble. Not just because of the incredible story I'd soon find myself telling, but because of one of the warmest welcomes I've ever been given ...

❂ ❂ ❂

The grey sky promised nothing but another day of rain. As I tried to warm my hands, aching in the pitiless freezing wind, a fond childhood memory came to me. It was 6 January 1999, Epiphany, not long after my fifth birthday. In those days, to keep me warm I had no long black jacket, but I had the soft duvet on my parents' bed.

On the night of every Epiphany I was afraid that the Old Witch would come and wake me up and give me the traditional nagging. So as not to spend the night alone in my room, I'd creep into their big bed, which I felt was my safe place. As the years went by, I stopped going to that big bed, but the stocking full of chocolate was always there. Except on that cold morning on 6 January, 18 years later.

It wasn't the gentle voices of Mum and Dad that woke me that morning, it was the first grey light of dawn over Manchester, letting me know that the cosy old duvet was just a memory and it was time to slide out of bed and get going again …

No tarmac, unless it was for the traffic. No shelter, only my long jacket. I walked for an hour along Tachbrook Road and then Harbury Lane, swearing at every car that shot by and missed me by inches. There was no one around me, just miles and miles of fields. The wind and the rain just kept on coming and Harbury Lane didn't do pavements. The only place to walk was its grass verge, reduced by the rain to a treacherous mud track.

The miles still left to get to the ground seemed unending, and as the light of the day began to fade I couldn't help wondering what it would be like trying to retrace my steps in the dark, with nothing to show me the way but the headlights of the speeding traffic. But I kept on going.

These thoughts were interrupted by the distant sight of floodlights – those of the New Windmill Ground, home of Leamington Football Club. The main gate was ajar. Without a second thought I slipped through it. Looking out to see whether I was being watched, I crept towards the little gate between the players' dressing rooms and the pitch. A few seconds later I was standing on the sacred green carpet, whose magic made me forget the miles I'd walked to reach it. As I always did in such moments, I imagined being a footballer playing on it.

Staring at the pitch, I saw the child inside me running towards the goal and scoring, celebrating in front of the North Bank – alongside the special supporter who was the only reason for my presence in a town hitherto unknown to me. By special supporter, I mean man's best friend. A dog with a place all of his own made that moment unique, leaving me wondering at another story I'd soon be able to tell. A moment and a story that I captured with my camera before hurrying away to the exit.

A long walk back to the station awaited me, and darkness was descending. As I was thinking about that impending ordeal, I saw two old men, each holding a rake, who were looking at me. 'Oi, who are you? What do you think you're doing here?'

My first reaction was an embarrassed laugh, since I'd neglected to ask for permission to go in. But to mollify them I immediately raised my hands and said, 'Don't worry, I'm just an Italian boy in love with your country. I came to take a photo of the home of the dog.'

I wish you could have seen their faces. They looked at me in bewilderment for a few seconds, began to nod, and one of them said, 'Since the car park's empty, would you mind explaining how you got here? There are no buses running today ...'

Hoping that my smile didn't mark me down as a nutter, I told them I'd walked, and for someone who visited one ground or another every week, walking all that distance was nothing unusual. Neither of them knew what to say, but I could see that they were curious to know more. So much so that one of them, Idris, asked me if I wanted some hot tea and a biscuit or two in the nearby clubhouse.

Leamington was a long trip for me. One on which I was able to see first-hand the little place where Jack – the dog – and his owner spend entire afternoons watching a ball roll on the grass in that little football ground. Grass that Idris and Barry nurture every day, keeping it in perfect condition for the players and for people like me who turn up, heart in hand, on their trips round England in search of stories. It's not just to put them in books, but to tell to people who are sensitive to the feelings aroused by a journey.

People like Idris, with whom I enjoyed a long chat over tea and biscuits. When we finished I could see the emotion in his eyes as he told me to get into his car so he could give me a lift to the station, where he wished me the best of luck with all my dreams.

Dreams that I'm sure I'll fulfil. And if I haven't got a car, I'll go after them on foot, despite the cold, despite the rain, despite the solitude, despite everything. Because when you really want something you can always find a path to get to it. What counts is to trust in life, which in the long run will always reward our efforts, great and small ...

CHAPTER 5

BE THE FARMER OF YOUR LIFE

*Keep on sowing your seed, for you
never know which will grow –
perhaps it all will.*

Albert Einstein

IF I close my eyes, I can see myself back there, in the fields with my dear granddad Alfonso. I was eight years old, perhaps nine. Before me, in those very fields, my father grew up with his two brothers, Giuseppe and Umberto. I've never lived there, but I went to my grandparents' place almost every afternoon after school.

In cold weather or hot, my granddad was always working those fields, from the first light of dawn till nightfall. When I saw him, I'd greet him with a kiss on the cheek, mindless of the dirt on his face; when he hugged me with his work-worn hands I breathed the life and the smells of the fields and the earth on which he'd always lived. A life of sacrifice and patience, waiting for the seeds he'd sown to bring the harvest he hoped for. A harvest that fed his whole family, loading their table with tomatoes, lettuces, peas, beans and many other good things.

I can still remember him teaching me that every harvest is preceded by the careful and loving act of sowing. That was the secret of his inner peace. Sowing today to reap tomorrow, learning to have patience and to appreciate everything you have.

Perhaps, now that I think of it, it was through him that I learned the importance of patience, facing and overcoming the hardest obstacles that life has put in my path. Those challenges have formed my character, made me stronger and taught me the art of being the farmer of my life. An art that's with me on the wonderful journey of life, made up of careful sowing and confidence in the harvest soon to be reaped ...

Remember to sow love whenever you can. The rainy days will pass and the sun's rays will come to warm you again. That's the time when your sacrifices will be rewarded. Sow today so as to reap tomorrow. Everything will come – in its own time.

What about you, what have you sown?

London, 4 February 2020

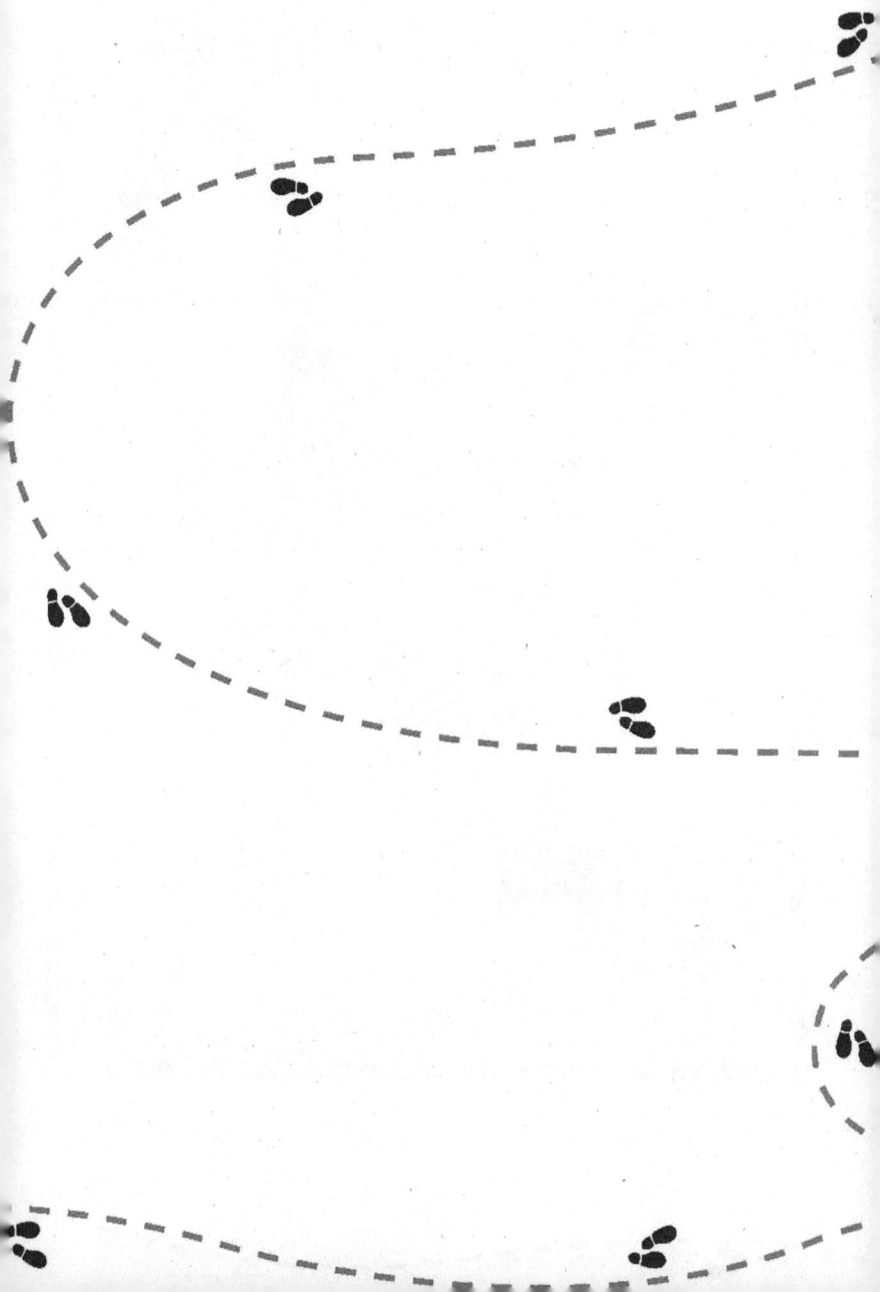

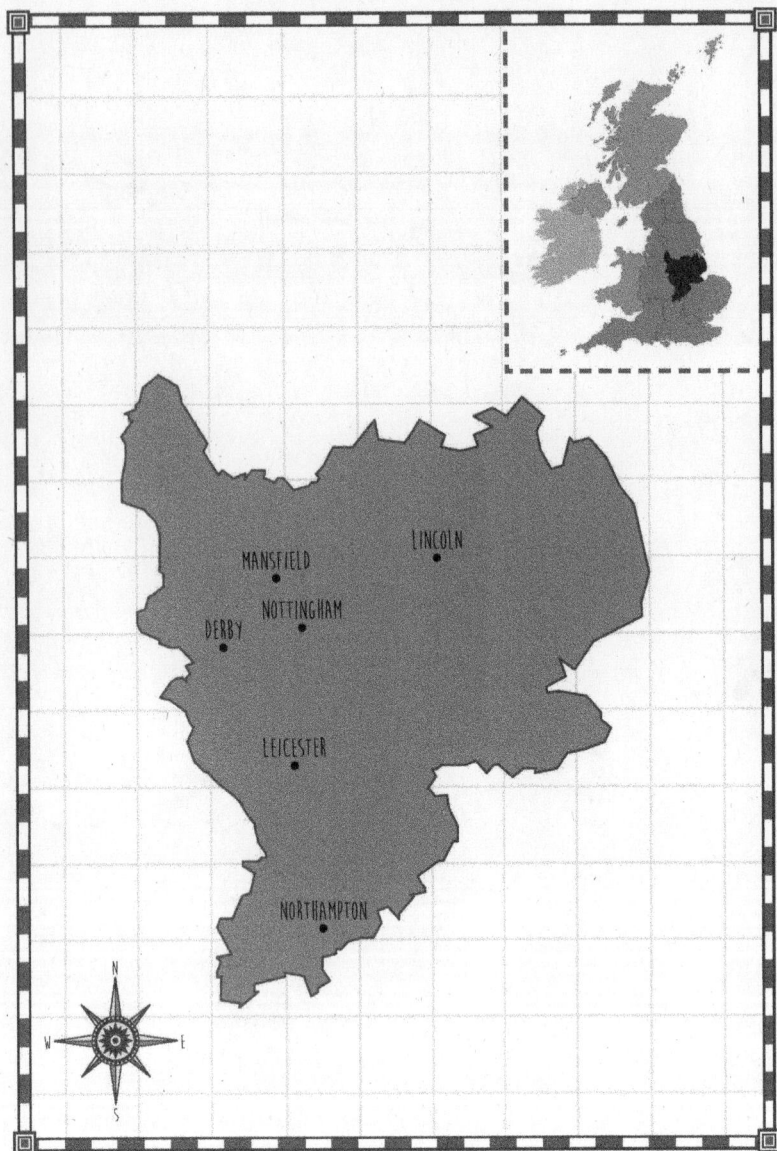

EAST MIDLANDS

Derby, Nottingham, Leicester, Lincoln, Sherwood Forest, the Peak District and much more. The East Midlands is one of the country's most fascinating regions, both because of the magical places within its borders and for the legendary figures who have passed through it. Not just the much-loved Robin Hood, but the more recent arrivals Brian Clough and Claudio Ranieri, whose unforgettable victories have assured their place in football history.

Walking through the city of Lincoln I pictured myself in a fairy tale as its winding streets took me and a host of other travellers towards the majestic cathedral. With the legend of the imps sent by the devil to smash up the minster, in the 14th century the city became famous in the whole of England. One of those imps not only remains in the form of a stone statue in the cathedral but is the symbol of Lincoln City Football Club – nicknamed the Imps – who have been playing at Sincil Bank since 1895.

A short way to the south, the streets of Nottingham feature three statues of historic importance: one of Robin Hood, one of the much-lamented Brian Clough and, close to Meadow Lane, one of Jimmy Sirrel and Jack Wheeler, legendary players of Notts County Football Club, famous as the world's oldest professional club.

Leaving Nottingham by route of Brian Clough Way, it's about a half-hour drive to Derby. One town where he made history wasn't enough for Brian Clough: he did it in Derby too. And the next stop on our journey is Leicester, the city that wrote one of football's most incredible stories, where the impossible became possible. Make yourselves comfortable, as we're about to set off. Brian Clough and other legends await.

THE STORY OF A DREAM

My heart started racing as the emotion swept through me. I couldn't believe my eyes. I'd waited for that moment for months, perhaps years. I'd imagined it over and over again, and when I found myself face to face with the lads who had made football history, it was a confirmation that dreams exist for a reason and nothing in life is impossible. What follows is the greatest football story ever told.

It's the fairy tale of a group of down-to-earth blokes who fought their way to an unrepeatable series of victories and worldwide fame. It's the story of an Italian manager who made the impossible possible. It's simply the unbelievable feat of Leicester City Football Club. The no-hopers who were crowned English champions ...

⚽⚽⚽

A light breeze caressed my face as I stood transfixed before the finest mural I'd ever seen. Painted on the wall were 11 young men, and Claudio Ranieri, who had led them to triumph. The man who rewrote the textbooks. Who fulfilled a dream not just for the people of Leicester but for the whole world. A born dreamer, I stood enchanted in front of his portrait. I sat down between him and the Leicester City colours, rested my back against the wall, closed my eyes and for a few seconds sank into my deepest thoughts.

I was immediately cast back to my old classroom, with my gaze, as usual, directed out of the window. I've got a clear memory of that day – I must have been nine or ten. As we all walked out of school, the maths teacher, Annarosa, took my mum to one side and told her that my head was always in the clouds and I never paid attention. Even back then I'd lose myself in some dream or other, completely disconnected from the world around me. Perhaps that's how I learned to dream.

Shying away from the real world and losing myself among the photographs in our English textbook. Big Ben, Tower Bridge, Stonehenge, Sherwood Forest and a host of other pictures led me to a discovery of those far-off places. I loved those photos. I used to stroke them gently, putting my face as close up to them as I could, almost hoping that someone could take me into them – rather like Alan Parrish in *Jumanji*, who was transported into the game.

And yet, although nobody ever took me into those photos, ten years later the places I admired in the textbook actually became my home, proving that dreams exist to be realised – if you believe enough and strive enough.

In the streets of Leicester those dreams were there to be seen in people's eyes, irrespective of their age, enamoured as they were of those lads in the enchanting mural. Young and old alike, they seemed to have a fire within them, burning with pride for the players who had taken them in two incredible years from the Championship to the pinnacle of English football. The people of Leicester know what it means to live and fulfil a dream. As soon as I reached their stadium I saw proof that the main quality needed to achieve something special is to face life without fear, just as is written everywhere inside the ground: #fearless.

That implies courage and determination – the qualities Claudio Ranieri and his players produced to win the coveted Premier League trophy, lifted high in May 2016 against all predictions, against all the odds.

Those qualities were exemplified by goal machine Jamie Vardy, one of the key players in that sporting miracle. At the age of 15 he was told he had no future at Sheffield Wednesday, the club he supported, and the world collapsed around his ears. At which point he could have given up and abandoned his dreams, but he didn't. He picked himself up and started again, finding a place with Stocksbridge Park Steels FC, who were then playing in the eighth tier. And it was there, at one of the humblest levels of English football, that he took back control of his life, dividing his time between training, playing league matches and working in a factory, which provided him with a living for several years.

His speed, grit and consistently high goalscoring record took him from Stocksbridge Park Steels, who paid him £30 a week and now have a stand named after him, to reach the heights of the Premier League, and the Champions League, and then the highest honour of all – pulling on an England shirt.

Fighting against everything and everybody, on the pitch and off it, Jamie Vardy succeeded in realising his greatest dreams. Not only that: match after match, goal after goal, he broke a whole series of records, putting his name in the history books and – more importantly – together with his team-mates he presented a gift to the people of Leicester, who will never forget his name. Not so much because of the triumph he achieved as his refusal of multimillion-pound contracts so as to stay with the supporters who were so dear to him.

I had the honour of seeing those supporters up close one Sunday afternoon late in October 2017, when I watched Leicester at home to Wayne Rooney's Everton. It was a day memorable not only for their 2-0 victory, and the goal that I saw Jamie Vardy score but for the lesson in life imparted a few minutes before kick-off. In reverent silence, the 30,000-plus spectators in the ground paid tribute to the soldiers killed in the First World War in an enormous poppy display covering the stands.[8]

---

8 In Britain and the Commonwealth, poppies are worn in the period up to Remembrance Day to mark the end of the First World War. Poppy fields were common on the battlefields of the Western Front, as witnessed by Canadian Lieutenant-Colonel John McCrae in his famous poem 'In Flanders Fields'. The revenue from the sale of paper poppies by volunteers representing the Royal British Legion is donated to numerous worthy causes.

Years later, I can confirm that my trip to Leicester was indeed unforgettable and full of excitement. I felt it well before that journey began, as I followed their ride to the top of the Premier League.

Having made the impossible possible, Claudio Ranieri's Leicester City will remain forever in the Olympus of world football, and when your life feels flat and your dreams seem out of reach, get on a train and go to Leicester. When you're there, walk around the city centre and look at people's eyes – to be honest, there's not much else to admire. Which is why I'd advise you to walk along St Augustine Road and cross the River Soar over West Bridge. From there it's not far to Kate Street, on the right, where until May 2019 there stood the finest mural I've ever seen. Once you're there, I'd like to be able to tell you to stand in silence and immerse yourselves in the rustling of the wind, but unhappily there's nothing left of the mural but a fond memory.

The building on which those legendary faces were painted has been sold, and the new owner – a property developer – decided to remove the mural with the promise that sooner or later he'd set it up in another part of the city. Be that as it may, if you ever happen to be near Kate Street, close your eyes and try to imagine the faces of those lads. And if you do, you'll realise that in life anything is possible. So all you have to do is fight for your dreams. Just like Jamie Vardy and Claudio Ranieri. Who started from nothing and shot to the top of English football, proving to the world that dreams are there for a reason and nothing is impossible.

In memory of Vichai Srivaddhanaprabha, chair–man of Leicester City, who tragically died after a helicopter crash on 27 October 2018.

WELCOME TO DERBY

At The Neptune, an old pub and meeting place for Rams supporters, the atmosphere was a blast. Derby County's 4-1 win over Barnsley on the last day of the season had ushered them into the play-offs, and the chance of a return to the Premier League had set the fans alight. Joining in with the chants, the pints and repeated hand-clapping, my Derby-supporting friend Gianpiero and I became one with the people cramming the pub. Their signature song, 'Don't Take Me Home', belted out by every soul in the place, made us feel we belonged to them.

It's a fanbase that deserves better, not just because of their ineffable love for the colours but for the club's glorious achievements. Their success story started in 1967, with Derby County languishing in the basement of the Second Division – five years was all it took for them to be crowned Football League champions. And the man who took them to those heights was a young manager who became a legend: Brian Clough.

⚽⚽⚽

We'd been up at dawn that morning, and later, even though the kick-off for the Barnsley match was still six hours away, Gianpiero could hardly contain himself. Such is his madness for Derby County that we found ourselves near the ground at eight in the morning. I was pleased to see him so happy, and we just wandered aimlessly around the city streets. He fell in love with the club when he was ten years old, playing Subbuteo with the black-and-white English team he'd been given. Everything started there, with that unexpected present from his dad. Since that day, Gianpiero has come to know a great many stories about that club located in the heart of England.

He did so first of all through the book and the film *The Damned United*, and then with a group of friends in 2014 he breathed new life into Italy's first Derby County fan club. This earned him the respect of the people of Derby, as he showed his devotion to the colours by travelling to matches at home and away, each time as excited as if it was his first.

That's how he was on that late May morning in 2018 – his thick beard seemed to conceal the delight that infused him, but his eyes revealed how happy he was. When we stood in front of the statue of Brian Clough and Peter Taylor, surrounded by hundreds of Derby fans, I was caught up in it. For five minutes I stood there, drinking in the figure of the two men celebrating the First Division title they won in 1972. The following year Brian Clough's giant killers had to be content with seventh place, but they stood tall in Europe, playing a European Cup semi-final against Juventus, a tie that they controversially lost.

Looking at the history books almost 50 years later, now it's easy to see that those were Derby County's glory years, set in the atmospheric environs of the Baseball Ground, home to the Rams from 1895 to 1997. Not only under the light of Brian Clough but in the popular memory of another historic figure. Not a manager, but a player. One who at the turn of the 20th century found the net more than 330 times, making him Derby's all-time top scorer. Over a century later he remains a club legend, with a bust of him gazing, arms folded, across the pitch at Pride Park. His name? Steve Bloomer. A striker from another time, when football was different, and supporters were different. Football with no logo-branded boots or sponsor-festooned shirts – just mud, heavy lace-up leather balls and a few, very few, black-and-white photographs.

Those same colours were proudly worn on that sunny May afternoon by more than 30,000 fans filling Pride Park with spine-tingling anticipation, especially in the South

Stand, the supporters' most hallowed ground. Flags flying, drums, hand-claps, impassioned shouts, non-stop chanting and unbridled love for the colours etched on the skin of every supporter as a sign of undying devotion, which gathers young and old into a single faith. With no distinction for age or skin colour, tied by an invisible thread that's pulled, a few seconds before kick-off, by the notes of 'Steve Bloomer's Watching', and Pride Park is filled with decibels.

Children of seven or eight, Derby shirts on their backs and scarves held high, all eyes on the pitch in front of them, yelled out every word of their anthem, words indelibly engraved in their heads and on their hearts. Their love burst out with every goal their heroes scored on that beautiful sunny day as they fought their way into the play-offs, from which they were unfortunately eliminated a few weeks later. A defeat for the club and above all for those fans. But their passion and loyalty for the colours will remain undimmed.

Those colours have left an indelible mark on the hearts of those people and on the history of English football. Their club history goes back more than a hundred years, starting at the Baseball Ground and continuing in the heart of Pride Park. More than a stadium, a place of worship. Consecrated to the names of Steve Bloomer and Brian Clough.

IN MEMORY OF BRIAN

Travelling around England, I've visited and experienced my share of football grounds. Of football stories, the sort that make your heart race and your spirit soar, I've heard even more. When you first hear them, they seem anything but real. More like the fairy tales our mum would tell us when we were little, as her voice took us on a journey to discover faraway places and characters, who always triumphed in the end and whose exploits sparked our daydreams. Exactly as happened at Nottingham Forest between 1977 and 1980, years that changed the club's history forever, regaling their fans with trophies nobody dreamed they could ever win. Nobody except him – Brian Clough.

⚽ ⚽ ⚽

That late September morning the sky over Nottingham had no pity for anyone. My watch told me it was 9am and the welcome back I was receiving had nothing but a cold wind and driving rain. The cold stayed with me and Eleonora, my partner in life and its adventures, for the whole day, first in the captivating streets of the city centre and then in the heart of the historic City Ground, home to Nottingham Forest since 1898.

Those streets breathed an air replete with history and legends. First of all, of course, that of Robin Hood, commemorated by a statue at the foot of Nottingham Castle – one of the biggest points of attraction in the county of Nottinghamshire. However, the county and the city of Nottingham owe their worldwide renown not only to the above-mentioned gentleman thief but above all to the man who arrived there in 1975, exuding his customary brash confidence. To understand the importance of Brian Clough to the people of Nottingham, all you have to do is go to King Street and admire his fine statue.

It's a monument he earned with triumph after unexpected triumph. He came to the City Ground when Forest were flirting with relegation from the Second Division. From there he took them to English football's highest pinnacle and immediately afterwards to the highest European honours, making Nottingham Forest a club of world standing. Fame that he and his stalwart right-hand man Peter Taylor achieved in just five years, bringing home a First Division title, two League Cups, a Community Shield and a European Super Cup. And the European Cup. Twice.

On that freezing September morning I had the opportunity of admiring those two cups in person. I was so close to them that I had the impression of being with Brian and Peter as they made football history. As they lived through moments that would last forever. Even today, walking around outside the City Ground, with the Trent flowing nearby, you'll seem to merge into the photographs on display behind the Peter Taylor Stand. They form a pictorial record of the two victorious European Cup campaigns with Brian Clough and Peter Taylor and the players lined up behind them. Men first, footballers second. In taking their names and the name of the club to the top of European football, those red-shirted heroes regaled Forest fans with one of the greatest football stories ever told.

Sadly, even the best stories must come to an end. Brian Clough's ended on 20 September 2004, when he died at the age of 69. His old friend Peter Taylor had passed away on 4 October 1990. Despite some flaming rows they had, Brian and Peter formed a unique pair in the history of football management and left a legacy of unforgettable times to the people of Nottingham. As witnessed by the naming of the two biggest stands in the City Ground: the Brian Clough Stand and the Peter Taylor Stand.

Those stands, seething with passion, were part of a cold and windswept crowd of 27,000 on that rainy September afternoon, waiting impatiently for the match to start. The action on the pitch paled into insignificance in the 14th minute when Brian Clough's smiling face appeared on the City Ground's maxi-screen. Whereupon every man, woman and child in the ground got to their feet and burst into applause. A long round of warm, affectionate applause commemorated the 14 years elapsed since his passing, as did many a teary eye.

The tears were for the remarkable man in whose remembrance they were shed, but for more than that – what he'd given them: unconditional commitment, which then brought success. He came to Nottingham with a head full of dreams and an iron determination to win trophies. And became one of the greatest managers football has ever known.

From the lower reaches of the Second Division to the highest European honours in five years – that's one of football's greatest stories. A story that no football fan can ever forget, no matter what his stripe. Written by a man who never stopped believing in his dreams. A man who became a legend. A man who, alongside Robin Hood, will always be a symbol of the city of Nottingham: the one and only Brian Clough.

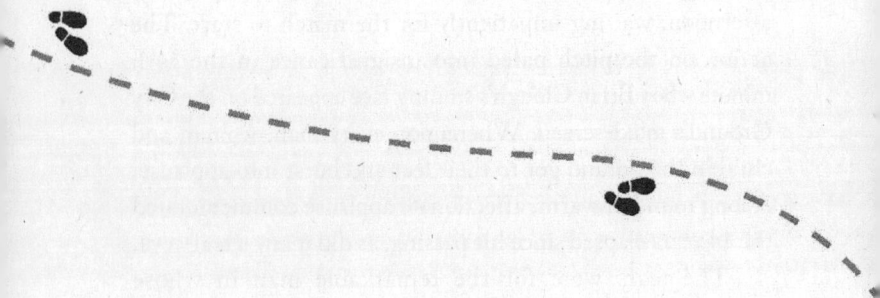

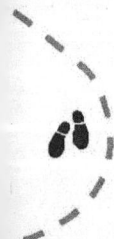

CHAPTER 6

THE IMPORTANCE OF
THE LITTLE THINGS

*Enjoy the little things in life because
one day you'll look back and realize
they were the big things.*

Kurt Vonnegut Jr.

TRAVELLING CHANGED my life. It really did. Discovering distant locations, getting to know different people and cultures, eating different food and interacting in another language made me a better person. Placing more importance on being myself than on my appearance has made me happier, more confident and more grateful to life. Travelling around for four years with the same rucksack on my back taught me that you don't find happiness in material things but in experiences. I've always thought it was better to have a story to tell than an object to show, because that's the essence of life.

In recent years I've had the chance to meet hundreds and hundreds of people, and the only ones who had a big impact on my life were those who had the courage to chase their dreams, against everything and everyone. In chasing my own dreams I realised that life is too short not to appreciate the little things. That's why I've learned to be happy every day and take the best from every thing that happens to me.

Travelling around England I realised that you can't only be happy when the sun is out. You have to be happy with rain too. When it rains, you grow and move ever closer to happiness.

I've always believed that happiness is a choice. Our choice. Happiness is eating a sandwich in the park. It's enjoying the sunset with the person you love. It's walking along the seafront. It's organising a trip. Above all, it's learning to give people a hand. Happiness is seeing others smile. It's giving your time to the people you love. It's learning to love life for what it is, doing everything you can to achieve your dreams and always smiling, despite all the difficulties we face.

Happiness is all this and much more, and I believe we all have to work to achieve it. Happiness is doing what you love and what makes you feel good, because life is love and love is happiness. With love in your heart and joy in your eyes, all the little things become big things and you'll see that life is the best journey you can ever take.

London, 19 December 2019

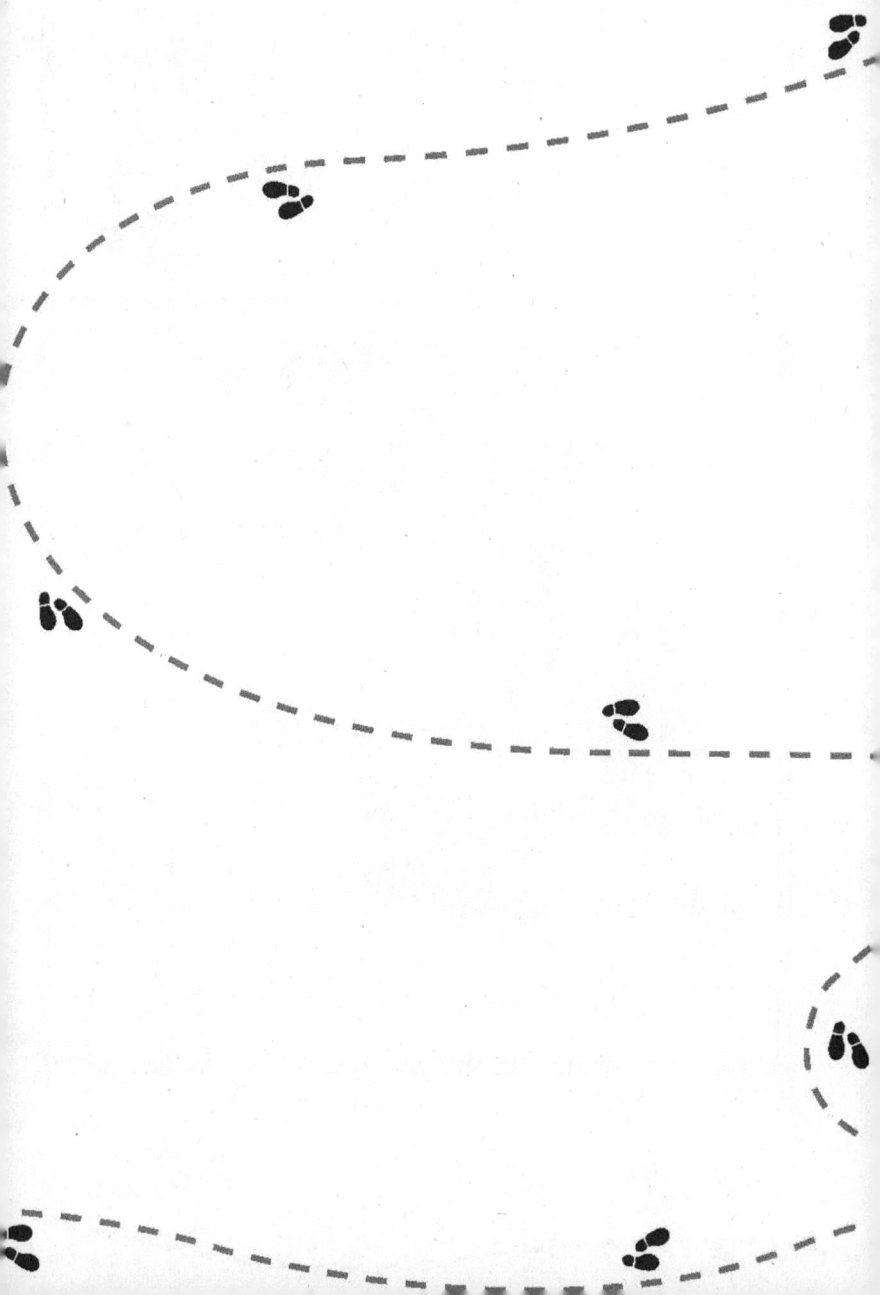

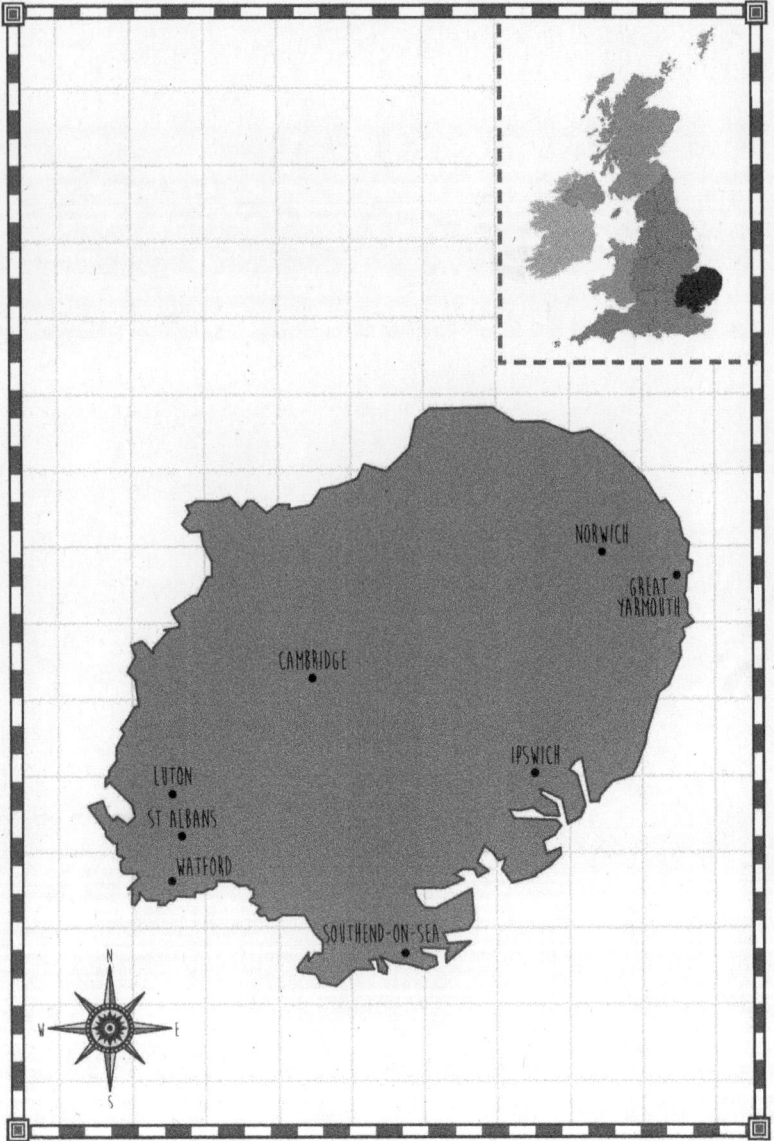

NORWICH

GREAT YARMOUTH

CAMBRIDGE

IPSWICH

LUTON
ST ALBANS
WATFORD

SOUTHEND-ON-SEA

EAST OF ENGLAND

I don't remember where I was on 12 May 2013, but what I'll always remember is Watford striker Troy Deeney, in the 97th minute of their match against Leicester City, smashing the ball into the back of the net to seal a 3-1 win, just a few seconds after Leicester had missed a penalty. In the years since then I've seen the video clip of that goal dozens of times, but the excitement never wears off. A goal that drove the Watford supporters to burst on to the pitch, galvanised by one of the most stunning moments English football has ever produced. A few years later I too had the honour of running delightedly on that same pitch. Not to celebrate a last-minute goal, but to savour a moment of complete freedom, with my heart beating like a hammer for fear of being spotted.

I've had similar experiences at Cambridge United and Norwich City, treading the grass in grounds that I'd only been able to admire on television. As a matter of fact, in Cambridge's Abbey Stadium I was able to have some fun with a ball I found nestling in one of the goals. But after half an hour of freely fantasising with the ball, I remember having to leg it because the groundsman saw me and started berating me in terms ill-suited to the varsity surroundings.

Thinking back, as I write and relive times past, I'd do it all again, every single thing, and although none of the above-mentioned clubs will appear in these pages, I can highly recommend a trip to that neck of the woods.

In England, irrespective of a club's division and status, spectacle and excitement are never lacking. Which is why in the following pages I'll take you to places full of atmosphere, rich in history and with the unique charm of times gone by. Take your seats, the next stop is a pebble's throw from the sea. The town of Great Yarmouth awaits.

THE FINEST STAND IN ENGLAND

The first impression was dazzling. I was stunned as soon as I saw it. It had the magnetic attraction of a painting. All I wanted to do was touch it and hear its ancient wood creaking under the weight of my tread.

It was opened on 11 June 1892, and 125 years later it was still standing there, a few yards from the sea, as neat and graceful as any small stand to be found in English football. The location is Wellesley Recreation Ground, home to Great Yarmouth Town Football Club. Which happens to have the finest little stand in the land.

❂❂❂

My alarm went off at a quarter to five that morning, and when the train left Liverpool Street station for East Anglia just over an hour later I fell back into a deep sleep. I woke up a few seconds before leaving the warm comfort of the train, happy to be on a new adventure but only too well aware of the cold rain waiting for me outside.

On that late December morning, the sky over Great Yarmouth, on the windy Norfolk coast, was a leaden grey, releasing a steady supply of drizzle to accompany me on my walk towards that particular holy grail.

I don't remember where or when I first saw the photo, but it was certainly love at first sight. Years later, what I do remember is the first time I saw it with my own eyes, rising behind a small gate on Sandown Road. I savoured the moment. I was finally there, just a few steps away from it.

A glance was enough to give you a feel of the history it emanated. Not to mention its architecture, perfect in every tiny detail. I'd explored a good many English football grounds by then, but I'd never seen anything like this. So … although the gate was closed and a sign forbade entry, I went through it, as was my wont, without a second thought. As I reverently approached the stand, it grew in size with each slow step.

Fixed to the red bricks of the stand, a small blue plaque informs visitors that in all probability they're standing before the oldest stand in an English football ground. To me those words were a confirmation that, in the realm of England, football is not just a sport – it's a religion.

It looked as though it had been built with posterity in mind, and I wonder whether its builder, John William Cockrill, had ever imagined that it would take its place in history. On 2 May 2000 it was officially announced that the stand had been designated as a listed building, so nothing and nobody would ever be able to demolish or modify it without the permission of the relevant authorities.

I'd known it straight away – I was in a special place. As was confirmed by a small plaque hanging from a thin metal chain, forbidding entry beyond that point to prevent any damage to the stand. I reluctantly complied with the order, and after inspecting that architectural gem from all possible angles, with a touch of sadness I made my way towards the nearby seashore.

Dozens of seagulls flapped overhead as a frail-looking old man walked his little dog slowly along the calm and silent beach. It was cold, no one else was near me and the only warm and inviting place was a small brightly coloured shack, located at the entrance to the broad deserted beach.

To warm up a bit I ordered a cup of tea. As I sipped it I began to think it was time to go back to the ground and find a way of getting into that historic stand. When I got there I saw a young goalkeeper going through a training routine on the muddy turf. I watched him for a while, thinking how nice it would be to join in, maybe giving him a few shots to save, until I heard voices coming from the tea hut in the ground.

Affecting an air of candid innocence, I sauntered quietly towards the hut. When I saw that the door was ajar, I summoned my customary cheek, knocked a couple of times and walked in. A man of about 60 who was there chatting to a friend looked up in no small surprise and said, 'Hello, son, what brings you here in this rotten weather?'

That's how Ronnie welcomed me, with his soft voice and his hands around a cup of steaming tea. 'I'm from Naples and I've come all this way just to see your magnificent stand,' I hazarded with a confident smile.

'That's nice. It's been months since anyone showed up here. I'm glad you've come. Shut the door, it's cold. Come and join us for a nice hot drink.'

In just a few minutes Ronnie made me feel at home. After drinking my second tea of the day and nibbling a chocolate biscuit or two, I was delighted to find myself wandering with him around the changing rooms. I couldn't believe my luck. I was in the heart of the oldest stand in England.

Life had regaled me with yet another splendid surprise. All I wanted was to make the most of that priceless moment. One of those moments when I'd never felt happier, not just because of where I was but because of the warmth of the welcome Ronnie had given me in the shadow of that historic stand.

The stand has been there since 1892, lived through two world wars and innumerable historic events, playing host to supporters in three centuries, taking its place in the history books with a charm that put it up there with the best-known and best-loved football stands in the world.

A bit later, when Ronnie had gone, the goalkeeper had finished training and there was no one around to see me, I took off my shoes and stepped over the chain with the sign forbidding entry. With the reverence due to a shrine, I walked delicately on that ancient wood and heard it creaking under my careful tread. My heart racing, partly out of excitement and partly for fear of being caught, I sat down where the seat numbers had been painted by hand and everything seemed even more romantic.

To remind anyone who has been there that the stand in question was not only the oldest in England but also – and above all – the finest ever ...

THE FAMILY CLUB

I stood there until the last second before the London train left. Simone, Claudio, Frank and Giusy said goodbye as if we'd been lifelong friends, wishing me the best of luck and hugging me close. I'd have loved to stay in Ipswich that night but the next day I had to go to work.

A few hours later, alone in my little room in London in the dead of night, I opened the wardrobe and took out my box of souvenirs. Another trip had reached its end, so before closing my eyes and heading into dreamland, I opened my dear old box and stashed away the mementoes from that remarkable day. All except one. I kept the scarf beside me for the whole night, so that when I woke up I'd be reminded that fairy tales can be real, and one of them had been written at Portman Road …

⚽⚽⚽

The first time I set foot on the historic Portman Road pitch was in March 2017. My companions, as usual, were the wind and the rain. A gate left open had given me my chance. I tip-toed silently through it, reached the playing surface and walked slowly towards the centre circle.

I've always loved being in grounds as they stand in silence; I find it romantic. At the time I didn't know the club's history, but a banner across the top of the Sir Bobby Robson Stand made it clear that Portman Road was a very special place.

'What is a club? It's the noise, the passion, the feeling of belonging.' That's Ipswich Town Football Club. When I returned to Portman Road two years later for a match against Hull City, I realised that supporting that club meant being part of a family. A big family. It may seem strange, but after visiting over 300 football grounds and watching hundreds of matches, I found Ipswich to be one of the few places where I was made to feel really at home. I'd met Simone and Claudio, fanatical Ipswich-supporting brothers, in June 2017 at the fifth Italian Connection tournament in Milan. Their warmth and affection for me was evident from the word go. To start with they gave me a precious club shirt. Then, almost two years later, they invited me to Ipswich for a Championship match against Hull City, and welcomed me with open arms.

Having completed our hugs of greeting, the three of us walked happily off in the direction of Portman Road, not far from the station. Once we'd crossed the River Orwell and left Princes Street, Simone and Claudio began to fill me in on Ipswich lore, telling me that the town was one of the oldest in England. Their love for the town and the club knows no bounds. Although I greatly enjoyed listening to them, and discovering the history of a town is fascinating and important, my thoughts were totally wrapped up in football.

Claudio, the elder brother, fell in love with Ipswich Town in 1981, when he saw the club win the UEFA Cup. Simone, born a year and a half after that triumph, became a fan as he listened to the football stories told by his big brother, who would proudly show him the pages of *Guerin Sportivo* (the world's longest-living sports monthly) whenever they featured Ipswich Town.

Then one December evening in 2001, Simone's interest in the Tractor Boys flowered into love. From the county of Suffolk, over 10,000 Ipswich supporters crowded into San Siro for their UEFA Cup tie against Inter Milan. After watching the match among the away fans, despite their 4-1 defeat at the hands of Inter (thanks to a Christian Vieri hat-trick), he went home happy as a sandboy because he'd been able to admire the great little Ipswich Town first-hand.

About a decade later, in 2011, Simone was elected president of Ipswich Town Italian Branch, intensifying his involvement with the club. An involvement – and a passion – that has taken him to the Suffolk town more than 20 times. When I had the opportunity to go back to Portman Road with him and his brother Claudio, I was caught up in that passion.

Sir Bobby Robson's statue stands on Portman Road itself, right outside the ground. It was ten o'clock in the morning, and unexpected sunshine would keep us company for most of the day. The club shop was still deserted, and as Claudio and I enjoyed surveying the stadium from the floor above, through a picture window giving a view of the Sir Bobby Robson Stand, Simone appeared beside me. To make sure I knew where I was, he presented me with the day's match programme and a club scarf. I put it proudly round my neck and we set off on a tour of the town.

Each step took us deeper into the historical atmosphere of the place, especially as we approached Ipswich market, an institution going back to 1317. But as we walked among the stalls, the air of history gave way to a host of inviting smells. Freshly caught fish, bread just out of the oven, a staggering array of pies, all sorts of cheese, greengrocers and flower sellers. You name it, they had it.

The mere thought of strolling through a market that went back over 700 years was something unique. No different was the sensation when we reached the highest point in Christchurch Park, hard by Ipswich School, which has stood there since 1399. On 16 October 1878, a group of Ipswich School old boys had the idea of forming Ipswich AFC – renamed Ipswich Town FC in 1888. The club started life playing in Broomhill Park, in the north-east of the town. Portman Road was built a few years later, in 1884.

As we left Ipswich School behind us, our pace quickened as we made our way to the ground, and the adrenaline in our veins increased in proportion. Former players and hundreds of supporters were eating, drinking and chattering happily in the stadium's fan zone, the habitual meeting place for most home fans. Terry Butcher, Russell Osman, Ray Crawford and other footballing names were there spending time with the supporters, telling stories and reliving matches they all remembered. Simone and Claudio were in their element. Shaking hands with Russell Osman and Terry Butcher, legendary figures for club and country, they were overcome with emotion, and it was no different for me. I'd defy anyone to remain unmoved in such company.

As I looked at them I pictured myself there in May 1981, when Bobby Robson's Ipswich Town astonished Europe by lifting the UEFA Cup. The Dutchmen of AZ Alkmaar, beaten 5-4 over the two legs of the final, were up against the central defence of Butcher and Osman. Although the two were a model of politeness with the fans that day, I've no doubt that in defence of their colours in Europe their approach was entirely different …

For Ray Crawford, whose glory days came earlier, there were no attackers to stop – his trade was scoring goals. In the club archives his name stands at the top of the list of goalscorers in the history of Ipswich Town. Of the 200-plus goals he amassed in his time at Portman Road, the ones that took him and the club to greatness came in the 1961/62 season; 33 goals, the First Division title (straight after promotion from the second) and top scorer of the season.

History had been made and Ipswich Town's first big – huge – piece of silverware was put on display. Two years later manager Alf Ramsey left the club to take charge of the England team – that's right, the one that won the World Cup in 1966. And his statue stands at the corner of Portman Road and Sir Alf Ramsey Way.

Leaving the fan zone behind us, we made our way towards the Cobbold Stand through the blue-shirted crowd milling in the streets around the ground. In view of the club's position at the foot of the table and the imminence of relegation to League One, the atmosphere was far from ideal, but the passion of the fans remained undimmed.

A 2-0 defeat didn't help matters but, all the same, most of the fans spent the last few minutes of the match singing Bob Marley's 'Three Little Birds' in the hope that sooner or later things would turn out for the best.

After the final whistle there were no boos, no protests, just applause and chants of loyal support – unbelievable when you think about it. At Ipswich, football is much more than a sport. For those people, who have lived through good times and bad, football is happiness, togetherness and belonging.

Football is spending time together, before the match and after, no matter whether you're a simple supporter or a player who has made football history. What counts is feeling part of the same family, laughing and crying, winning and losing. Always together, regardless of the level. At Ipswich they understand that you never get anywhere on your own, and only by pulling together, just like a family, will you make your dreams come true.

MYTHICAL BILL

The first time I ever set foot in Luton, I was afraid. It was in July 2016, close to midnight, and the flight that would take me to Naples for a few days was scheduled to leave about dawn. Nights spent in airports are always interminable, so I was looking for a way to pass the time without wasting it in malodorous slumber on the uncomfortable seats of a departure lounge.

The old and atmospheric ground of Kenilworth Road was about 20 minutes' walk from the station. Going there and seeing it up close in the dead of night seemed to offer the most interesting prospect – until that is, I changed my mind ...

Never before had I seen such desolation and neglect. Even the darkness hid from itself, frightened by the grinning faces giving me the once-over. They watched my every move, planning who knows what. They were hanging around outside the station, right where I'd have to pass on my way out.

A sixth sense made me step back, keeping a watchful eye out. Nothing but darkness and silence surrounded me. Scared half to death, when I saw them heading towards the footbridge leading to the platform I stood rooted to, with their hands in their pockets and hoodies up, the airport seats suddenly seemed particularly inviting.

The airport, as it miraculously happened, is where the train now approaching my platform was going. Its headlights glared in my eyes, which were stricken with fear of what might happen but alert to the movements of those shadowy faces, which then broke into a sprint, coming right for me.

I leapt on to the train. Seconds later, as the doors closed just in time and the faces saluted my departure with fists brandished, V-signs pumping and oaths flying in who knows what language, I breathed a huge sigh of relief and vowed never again to come to Luton at night ...

✪ ✪ ✪

In the bright morning sunshine of that day in December, the green grass of Hyde Park was as pretty as a picture. It was two days after Christmas, and my family and most of my friends were miles away. In those days I was living in Manchester. Solitude and my dear old rucksack were my only faithful travelling companions. My dear friends Gianni and Caterina, who were spending the Christmas holidays in London, had chased away my loneliness, at least for those important days. As I said my goodbyes to go to Luton, my eyes filled with tears.

At that time I had to count the pennies, lived in a tiny room in a particularly run-down part of Manchester and worked as a dishwasher in a McDonald's kitchen, but my dreams were more important than any hardship.

The empty sandwiches I'd eat after a hard day's work didn't bother me; on the contrary, they reminded me that those are the challenges that make you grow. My mum and dad kept asking me to come home, but I insisted that what I was doing would make me stronger. Only a few weeks earlier, Giuseppe, someone I hold in the highest esteem, had told me that if you want to grow stronger you'll have to eat a lot of dung. The secret lay in being prepared to pay what it took. Hungry for the realisation of my dreams, I was ready to pay that price. Ready and willing.

When I found myself wandering around the streets surrounding Kenilworth Road, I began to appreciate everything about my tiny room in Manchester, including the difficulties I had to grapple with day after day. Dirt, degradation, self-neglect. My first impression of Luton was pity for the people living in those houses, without for a second imagining that it was from those very houses that my saviour would emerge.

170

That December morning I spent over half an hour walking around Luton Town's home ground, looking for an open gate or a wall I could scale. The long alley connecting the two ends of the ground, passing alongside dozens of those silent decrepit houses, was distinctly uninviting. Especially when I thought of those faces I'd met at Luton station a few months before.

There was no one in sight; the streets were completely deserted. I was at a loss and was about to leave. Then, on Oak Road, tucked away by the away fans' entrance among the mass of houses around the ground, I spotted a door with a bell. Unconcerned by what day or what time it was, with barefaced abandon I rang the bell – and then leaned on it. I waited for well over a minute, to no avail, until a kindly face popped out from behind the door.

Bill, the caretaker, unwrapped a smile and asked me what brought me there. Having listened to an abbreviated version of my personal story, he explained that he couldn't let me in, but a few yards down the road there were some blokes working, and I could ask them. I said goodbye to Bill with fulsome thanks, and as soon as he'd disappeared behind the door I ran off in the direction indicated.

Perhaps I missed them, but I saw nobody working anywhere. Be that as it may, I had no intention of leaving empty-handed, so I went back to Bill's door. This time, his smile even broader, he opened the door to Kenilworth Road – 'Come in!' he laughed.

I didn't need asking twice. I followed his shuffling steps as he led me into every corner of his den. He showed me old photos and cups commemorating the history of Luton Town. Walking within those walls I remembered that we were literally surrounded by people's houses, and the question came to me – what was built first, the stadium or the houses?

Peering through the windows on the staircase inside the ground, I could see mothers with their children in the pokey rooms of the adjacent houses. There was a surreal atmosphere about the whole scene, but Bill's smile and unhurried gait had a calming effect.

When he told me I could climb the stairs leading to the Kenilworth Road terraces, I hugged him as if he'd been my granddad.

'I'll wait here for you, but don't be too long,' he sighed. I ran up the stairs to the terraces two at a time. When I saw the ground spread out before me, all I could do was gape. It was old, that was obvious enough. An aura of history enveloped its every corner, and although it was showing its age and frankly pretty shabby, every nook and cranny had its charm.

Silence was all around me – the sort of reassuring fairy-tale silence that only an empty stadium can harbour. Most of the pitch was bathed in sunshine, and after scrutinising every inch of the old stand I made no effort to resist the temptation to touch that grass.

Happy as a little boy in a sweetshop, I rushed on to the pitch and ran around, stroking the wet grass and breathing in every moment. It was like a dream. Years and years of history followed in the wake of my joyful romp, as I pictured myself in a Luton Town shirt and heard the fans chanting my name. The dream I'd nurtured since childhood seemed to have come true, until Bill's voice brought me back to earth.

'Oi! I told you to be quick and there you are right on the pitch! Give you an inch …'

He sounded cross all right, but when he saw how happy I was he dissolved into laughter. I made my profuse apologies, and before showing me out he gave me a little book about the club's history, recommending a return to Kenilworth Road, if possible, to see a match. I later did. Not once, but twice.

The first time was in December 2017, for a League Two encounter with Grimsby Town. The second was in February 2020 for a Championship match against Stoke City, which I watched with Giò, Gianluca and Giovanni, my mates from Ischia. Both times there was a great atmosphere, but the Stoke match had something special.

For my friend Giò, being in Kenilworth Road was a dream, a moment he'd awaited for years. He'd often told me that he'd fallen in love with that ground in January 2006. Watching Luton's FA Cup tie against Liverpool, he saw Xabi Alonso shoot and score from over 60 yards. You can imagine his delight when, through the good offices of John, we found ourselves walking on the Kenilworth Road pitch.

John, the club's Supporters' Liaison Officer, heard my story and was good enough to offer us a tour of the ground a few hours before the match. He was happy to show us every detail, from the players' tunnel to the little trophy room, from the VIP stand to the dressing rooms. We were taken to places not everybody can see, and little did we know that the best was yet to come.

At the end of the tour we thanked John for his kindness and returned to the outside world. After we'd knocked back a beer or two, it was time to go back in through the turnstiles. It was just over an hour before kick-off, and our day couldn't have begun better. There were three old chaps checking tickets, and they let us through the narrow turnstiles, painted in the club's colours of orange, navy blue and white. When the hallowed grass pitch came into view once more, we felt we'd come home.

John had given us a memorable tour, but now, when he invited us to sit on the bench to watch the warm-up, it was like touching the sky.

By that time I'd visited 300 football grounds and watched over 100 matches, but the experience of sitting on the bench at Kenilworth Road watching a pre-match routine was up there with the best.

We sat there taking our photos and enjoying the experience until the players trooped back towards the dressing room, when I noticed that John was rounding up a group of children. They were going to wave Luton Town flags as the teams came on to the pitch. Thrusting my embarrassment aside, I went up and asked him if we could join in. In less than two minutes John came back wreathed in smiles, presented us with a flag each and put us in the centre circle to wait for the players.

I'll never forget fits of giggles from Giò, Gianluca and Giovanni as they bashfully joined the 12-year-olds in waving their Hatters flags in front of the crowd, whose 10,000 voices made themselves heard in fine style as the players of Luton Town and Stoke City made their entrance – an experience to treasure.

Then, as the home crowd ratcheted up the noise, we vacated the pitch, thanked John again, gave him a quick hug and ran off to take our seats in the Kenilworth Stand. On that cold late February afternoon, the match, as you can imagine, felt less important just then than what had preceded it.

Just eight minutes into the first half, Stoke took the lead. For a few moments the Kenilworth Road support was stunned into silence. Then with a series of hand-claps, chants for the home side and a barrage of insults for the opposition goalkeeper, the celebrations of the away fans were drowned out.

Only a few seconds of the match were remaining when Luton equalised. A roar of liberation rose from the terraces as all the home fans, old people and children included, looked to the skies and shouted their love for the colours. The colours of a club that has played at Kenilworth Road for over a century, but is destined to leave for pastures new.

The new stadium will lack nothing. It will have brand-new seats and mildew-free walls. No more pensioners checking tickets – the turnstiles will be automatic. No longer will entry to the away end pass through the local houses but be rationally planned, as with all new stadiums. There will be a new club shop, new bars and sweet-scented toilets. The dilapidated charm of Kenilworth Road will be gone for ever, but it will live on in people's memories.

Special memories, times to talk about by the fire on a December evening. Perhaps two days before Christmas, the very day when I had the luck to meet mythical Bill, the man with the winning smile and a heart as big as a stadium.

THE OLD AND GLORIOUS OAK TREE

Travelling around England, I've had more than my share of adventures. Stories, the ones mixing legend and reality, I haven't heard so many. I don't mean the stories found in school textbooks, but tales that only the people in them can tell. Stories that make your heart beat faster, for the listeners more than the tellers. As I found out in the pretty little city of St Albans. A city that stole my heart, with its ancient charm but above all with its compact little stadium a stone's throw from the railway station.

The stadium boasts more than a century of history, taking pride of place in the heart of the park in which it was built, the bearer of stories and legends that are passed down from one generation to the next. The first time I heard one particular story, it touched my heart. It made me feel part of those distant times, when an old oak tree stood in the middle of the terrace at one end of the Clarence Park pitch, an integral part of the ground. That tree is at the centre of one of the most touching stories in English football.

⚽⚽⚽

The first time I set foot in St Albans I was smitten. It was a late December morning in 2016 when I entered Clarence Park, surrounding the stadium of the same name, and was overtaken by a sense of profound peace. Squirrels were cavorting in the trees to the tune of the birdsong around them. The magic of the scene was enhanced by the tenderness of a young mother, stroking her baby's face as she held him close. For a few minutes I observed and reflected on that tableau of maternal devotion, sitting on a tree trunk in the middle of the park, afraid to break the spell.

Shortly afterwards I approached the little football stadium, and its charm was immediate. Built mostly in wood, it was carefully painted in the club colours of yellow and blue. I'd fallen in love with the place and the ground. They'd entered my heart, making me feel part of the history I could see silently unfolding before me. A history comprising over a century of non-league football, row upon row of wooden seats and the smell of beer with which the old wooden stand had been impregnated down the years.

On that freezing December morning, unseen and with only birdsong for company, I was able to savour the ancient wooden stand undisturbed. I lovingly touched every seat, seeing my hands black with grime with eyes full of joy. For a few minutes I sat on one of the seats, taking in everything around me. I've always loved being in empty stadiums; it's the best way to soak up their atmosphere.

As I was making my way out, three old fellows in the clubhouse spotted me, interrupted their chat and asked me where I'd come from. They hardly gave me the time to begin my story before they invited me to sit down and have some tea, asking only that I tell them about my best adventures.

Fourteen months later I was back in St Albans, not just to see the ground but to watch a match played by the club that had won my heart. The feeling of that February morning was the same as the first time – the peace and calm of strolling in the park where children and dogs played happily with their families. I'd rub shoulders with them a short time later on the Clarence Park terraces, wrapped up head to foot against the cold, with club hats and scarves, ready to cheer on St Albans City.

It's a club with few successes behind it but a beguiling sense of togetherness in the spirit of all those who follow it. A feeling of community I could feel on my skin as soon as I passed through the old turnstile, its charm by no means eroded by the rust on it.

Travelling around the country, I'd experienced that charm dozens of times, but this ground had something special. As did the beauty of its setting in Clarence Park. The terraces were full of fans of all ages, savouring the occasion as they looked forward to another afternoon of football. Real football, represented by a ticket costing little more than a pint, and by the pensioner on the turnstile who for years without number has welcomed every spectator, wishing them a pleasant day. Football whose excitement needs no television cameras, no millions of pounds, just passion and love for the colours. Yellow and blue, colours passed down from father to son, from granddad to grandson, rooted in the values of supporting your local team and enjoying the true essence of football.

As in many grounds in non-league football, in Clarence Park spectators aren't stuck in their seats, as they are in all Premier League stadiums, but are free to enjoy the match a yard or two behind the goals, leaning on a railing as they nurse their pints.

On that cold February afternoon, the pints in question were fuel for the excitement and passion of that great little community of fans. They sang and chanted for their lads on the pitch, going wild when they took the lead shortly before the final whistle.

When that whistle sounded, Chippenham Town had been beaten 2-0, both goals coming in the final seconds. The joy of victory was a common joy, as the players shared high fives with many of the locals close to the pitch.

A quarter of an hour later I went into the clubhouse, where I found a group of supporters and the lads who had been doing battle on the field of play. Thanks to Felix, the club secretary, I got to spend some time with those lads and their manager, telling them of my travels and hearing one of the stories only England can tell.

It's not a story of victories against the odds or intrepid feats, but of an old and glorious tree, the oak tree that for more than a hundred years was an integral part of the ground at which I'd immediately felt at home.

From the day of its inauguration, 23 July 1894, the tree was part of the stadium. Located on the terracing behind one of the goals, it was as treasured by the locals as it was feared by visiting teams, bombarded by the acorns that fell from its branches and were chucked at them by local fans. The tree and its acorns created no end of problems for the club, repeatedly criticised in the local paper and called to account by the Football Association, which demanded an immediate solution to the issue.

A century later the oak tree was still there. And in the early 1990s it was because of 'that tree' that St Albans City were denied promotion to the Conference League. Not because of any flying acorns but the safety risk represented by a tree in the middle of a terrace. Acorns and safety requirements notwithstanding, the oak was protected by a Tree Preservation Order, which meant that it could never be felled. So the club had to relinquish any prospects of promotion and content itself with its indissoluble bond with the old oak tree.

Alas, on 25 August 1998, that long love story was brought to a brutal end. Having been officially found to be diseased, the tree was cut down. On that day dozens of supporters went to the park to pay their last respects to their treasured totem. Many of them gathered little pieces of the old oak to take home as mementoes. Since that day, the trunk has lain in the heart of the park, laid to rest and carefully preserved so that it can remain in its home forever. In the heart of Clarence Park, home to St Albans City and its old and glorious oak tree.

In memory of Clive Churchhouse, supporter and volunteer assistant of St Albans City. Clive tragically died at the age of 71 on 18 July 2017 while carrying out maintenance work on the roof of the East Stand. He fell from the roof and died of his injuries a few hours later. A section of the ground now bears his name: The Clive Churchhouse Terrace.

CHAPTER 7

WATCHWORD: SACRIFICE

*Believe in something. Even if it
means sacrificing everything.*

Nike

THE GREATEST lesson the school of life has ever given me came from living in Manchester. That city gave me a good few kickings, and never asked afterwards if I was all right. I think my time there was the hardest I've ever had to face, forcing me to make one sacrifice after another. I can remember everything about my stay there. And when I think back, I can hardly believe how I managed to stand it. The tiny room I lived in, slaving in the kitchen at McDonald's and the five miles I had to walk there and back every day for six months because I didn't have the bus fare. Eating dry bread rolls and dragging myself out of bed before dawn to answer the siren call of another football ground I'd yet to visit.

Tears and solitude. Missing home and my loved ones. The hands of the clock standing obstinately still during working hours. My thoughts fixated on my greatest dreams, then still a long way off.

Manchester was this and much more, for better or worse. That place never gave a damn about me; it treated me like dirt – but I'll never be able to thank it enough, or express how much I love it. Manchester taught me to appreciate the little things in life, to live on bare necessities and, more than anything else, never to give up in adversity, never to lose sight of a better tomorrow.

That place changed my life, pointing me in the right direction, but it never warned me of the difficulties I'd come up against. Manchester made me a better man. Ready to do anything to realise my dreams, because if it's true that only dreamers can fly, it's also true that before you can fly you've got to learn how to fall.

What about you – are you ready to fly?

London, 2 December 2019

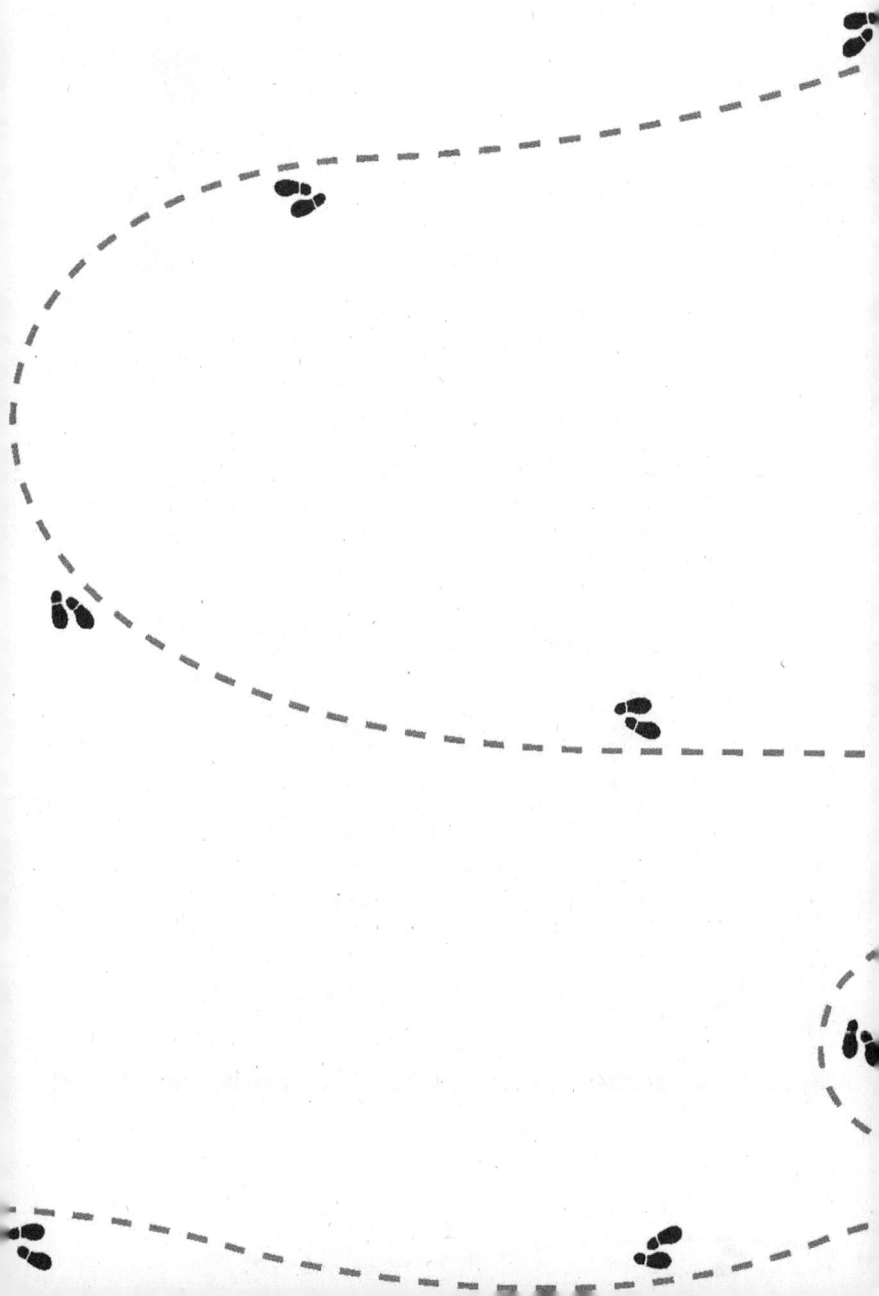

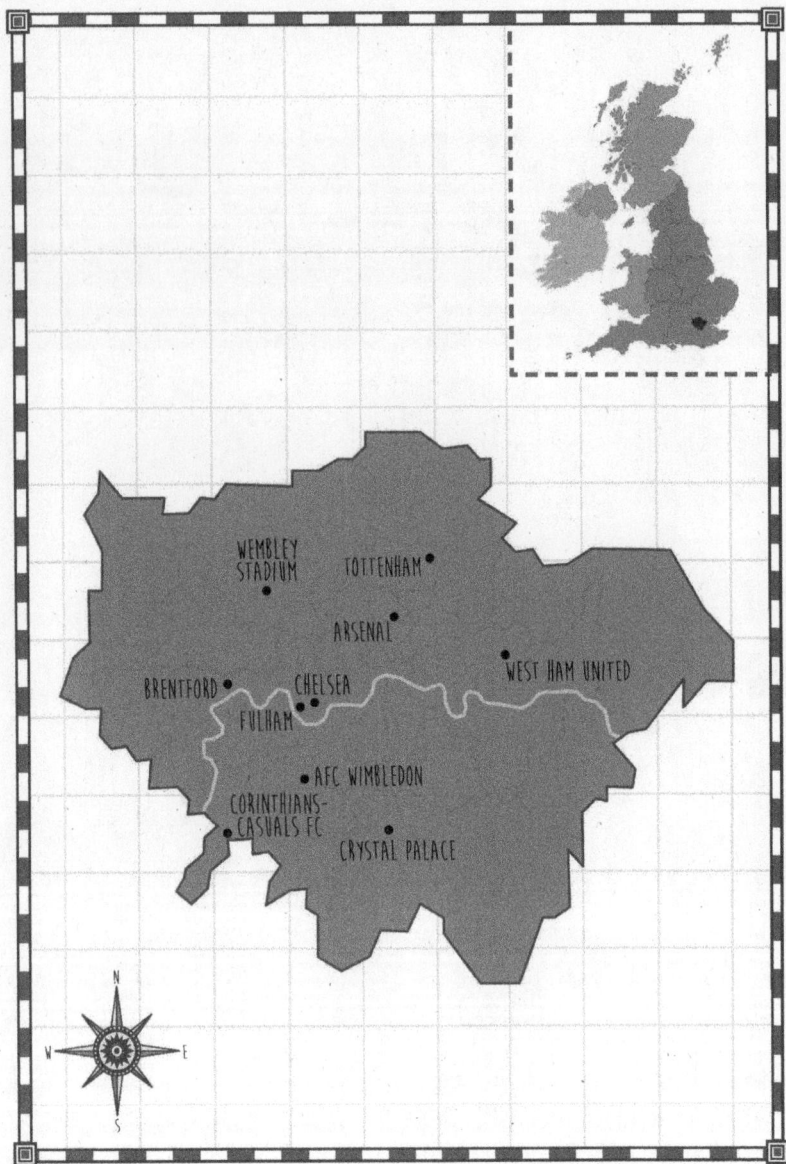

WEMBLEY STADIUM

TOTTENHAM

ARSENAL

WEST HAM UNITED

BRENTFORD

CHELSEA

FULHAM

AFC WIMBLEDON

CORINTHIANS-CASUALS FC

CRYSTAL PALACE

LONDON

Calling London home for over two years of my life was one of the best experiences I'll ever have. It's a remarkable place – unique, difficult to do justice to in words. You've got to live in it to believe it, walk its streets and explore its boroughs, some rich, others anything but …

Strolling through the streets of London is one of the best adventures you can have – modernity rubs shoulders with history, and dozens of smells mix in the air. The whole world is there; hundreds of nationalities and cultures learn to share the same space, enjoying the cuisines of every corner of the world.

London skies are often grey, sometimes too grey, but when a timid sun peeps out and lights up everyone's eyes, or a blue sky reigns for a while, London takes on a charm all of its own.

Stories and legends are the denizens of its streets, streets that are alive day and night. London is life – its green parks and imposing squares the stage for street artists and performers who attract thousands of people every day.

Living London first-hand means jumping from one train to another on the Underground, from the District line to the Central line, the Piccadilly line to the Jubilee line. And it doesn't matter if you get lost – on the Tube, that's part of the fun.

London lives 365 days a year. It offers something to everybody. And there, football is a religion. From the Premier to non-league football, the capital boasts about a hundred grounds, from the majestic Wembley Stadium to the smallest and most beguiling amateur homes.

London is an enchanted land of football, with stadiums over a century old that are still the theatres of epic battles, drawing millions of people from all over the globe. London is this and much more besides. In the following pages I'll be telling you about a small part of its world, but my advice is to pack your rucksack and go and discover it for yourself. Nothing will amaze you as London does – if you see it with your own eyes.

LIBERTÉ, ÉGALITÉ, FRATERNITÉ WEMBLEY STADIUM, 17 NOVEMBER 2015

Words gave way to silence. The only sound to be heard was the sighing of the wind, whose cold, insistent caresses flowed over the faces of all those present at Wembley. Fear did not daunt us. Despite the feeling that another attack was in the air, we were there to show the whole world that the French were not alone. Fear would not get the better of us.

The attacks that had plunged Paris into panic a few days earlier would not bend us; they'd bring us closer together. Like brothers, singing 'La Marseillaise' with tears in our eyes. In memory of the victims who will never be forgotten …

⚽⚽⚽

The regulation drizzle – dense and irksome – of the long Lake District winters showed no signs of giving up. That night I wasn't able to go to the pub to enjoy the friendly between France and Germany, so I calmly set about packing for my journey to London.

I was brought to a halt by a phone call from my mother. 'Ivan, where are you? Have you seen what happened in Paris? There's been an attack. So many people killed.'

Her voice was worried and frightened. I thought she was going to ask me to go home to Italy. When I saw the news and the pictures on television, I froze. More than 120 people were dead. Some of them had gone to the Bataclan for an Eagles of Death Metal concert. Others were out in bars and restaurants, unaware that on that evening, that terrible evening, some of them wouldn't be going home.

I did go home. By home I mean Bowness-on-Windermere, a town in north-west England where I was living at the time. I travelled in silence, still shocked by what had happened a few days previously but no less moved by having taken part in the remarkable spectacle staged the night before in the majestic setting of Wembley Stadium. With over 71,000 people in attendance.

Determined to make a show of solidarity, only four days after the Paris attacks, we'd all assembled for the friendly between France and England, forming one of the most memorable gatherings I've ever had the chance to admire. The atmosphere outside the stadium was surreal, unlike anything I'd felt before. There was an inevitable undercurrent of tension and fear, but prevailing over it was a feeling of brotherhood – which the whole world witnessed a few minutes before kick-off, when we looked to the heavens and belted out 'God Save the Queen'. After which, in honour of those who had so tragically died, we all sang 'La Marseillaise'.

Like those of most people there, my eyes filled with tears, shivers ran down my spine and I went weak at the knees before such a spectacle. Impossible to do justice to it in the telling, equally impossible to forget. Players and supporters were one. Nothing could divide us. We were all brothers and sisters, even more united when a long applause and a splendid choreography featuring the French tricolour accompanied the final notes of 'La Marseillaise'. Then the most moving minute's silence. I'd never imagined that one solitary minute could express such emotion. Some people's eyes were turned heavenwards. Others around me continued to wipe away the tears. Still others stood in silent remembrance, heads bowed.

The only sounds to be heard were the soughing of the wind and beating of the helicopters monitoring Wembley from above. As the tears continued to fall, the whistle for the kick-off signalled another demonstration of courage and solidarity.

For fear of further attacks, there had been thoughts of calling the match off, but going ahead with it was the right thing to do. To show the world that when we stand together, any achievement is within our reach.

Football took a back seat that night. Although the youngster Dele Alli scored a superb goal and Wayne Rooney made it 2-0 with a fine volley, the most lasting impression struck me when I'd left the stadium. Olympic Way, leading from the stadium to Wembley Park tube station, was full of supporters proudly waving their scarves and flags in the cold night air. I stopped, a few yards outside the turnstiles leading into sector H. At the foot of the statue of the mighty Bobby Moore, I watched the river of people flow past me.

Half an hour I stood there, silently reflecting on how far I'd come. I was at Wembley, a legendary football venue. It was there, on 30 July 1966 in the splendid setting of the old Wembley Stadium, that Bobby Moore's England team were crowned world champions.

There I was, under the landmark Wembley arch, lit up in red, white and blue in France's honour. I'd come from a village near Naples, a place you've got to leave behind you to achieve your ambitions. To do that, I'd packed my rucksack and started out on a journey to discover myself and realise my dreams. To explore English football and its fabled stadiums, from the smallest and humblest non-league grounds to the famous Wembley.

And my first time there was on that November night, singing 'La Marseillaise'. For the victims who will never be forgotten ...

In memory of the victims of the Paris attack of 13 November 2015.

WE ARE TOTTENHAM FROM THE LANE

It seems only yesterday that Gareth Bale stunned the world of football with an unforgettable exhibition of youthful pyrotechnics. It was a Champions League night in October 2010. In front of a capacity crowd in San Siro he used his blistering speed to shred the Inter Milan defence and score three goals with almost embarrassing ease. Tottenham lost that match 4-3, but in the reverse fixture at White Hart Lane, Inter had nowhere to hide. They lost 3-1 to the Londoners, and Gareth Bale reappeared as the architect of their downfall. Wearing the No.3 shirt, he was faced by Inter's much-vaunted Brazilian right-back, whom he sprinted past time and time again ('Taxi for Maicon!'), setting up two goals and sending White Hart Lane into delirium. As I watched his devastating runs and pinpoint crosses on our little television at home, the spectacle of that match and the atmosphere in the stadium took my breath away.

About six years later, in August 2016, I experienced that ground for myself. So that I could tell people that at least once in my life I'd breathed the inebriating air of the historic venue of White Hart Lane.

⚽ ⚽ ⚽

I approached the ground from the south, and walking in the environs of Park Lane was unsettling, to say the least. There wasn't a soul to be seen. As dusk closed in around the South Stand, the evening was as silent as the grave. It was one of those silences that make you want to turn and run, but when I saw one of the gates to the ground standing open, I left my fear in the dark street behind me and went through it.

My heart was going nineteen to the dozen, partly out of excitement and partly for fear of being seen, but a few steps later all the wonder of White Hart Lane was laid out before me, and that first view is one I'll never forget. After standing in rapt silence as I took in the scene, I began to approach the pitch. I was just about to step on to that mesmerising green sward when I was stopped in my tracks by a thundering shout.

One of the security guards had caught me in the act. A bruising six-footer sporting a thick, unkempt beard, he demanded to know what the hell I was doing. 'My dad works here and I was trying to find him,' I blurted out.

Somewhat taken aback, he looked me up and down. 'What's his name then?'

'His name's Mario and he's just started here. I can call him if you like, or I can wait outside, it's not a problem.' I stuffed conviction into my voice in the hope of getting out of there in short order. It seemed to have the desired effect and the big man relaxed a bit. So I introduced myself, said thank you and goodbye and beat a hasty retreat, trying not to laugh about my barefaced lie, and congratulating myself on getting away with it.

For a few seconds I'd admired all the splendour of White Hart Lane. But that wasn't enough, I wanted to go back there and get a proper experience of the stadium that had cast a spell on me on that Champions League night. So it was that ten months after my encounter with the security hulk, I managed to return.

I'd tried everything to see a match there, but tickets were impossible to get hold of. So if I wanted to get a first-hand grip of the history Tottenham made inside White Hart Lane, there was nothing for it but to book a tour of the ground.

In my fevered imagination the tour started before I even got to London, as I travelled back in time to discover that hallowed ground. Tottenham Hotspur had been playing there for over a century. It had been their home since September 1899, and every time I saw it on television I was transfixed. The rush of expectation that ran through the fans with every Tottenham attack. The electrifying atmosphere before and during the big matches. Supporters just a few feet from the pitch. All the eyes on the tunnel as the players came on to the pitch, within touching distance of the fans, striking fear into the hearts of the away team before a ball had been kicked. White Hart Lane was unique – its fascination immediately recognisable even on television, unlike most of the new stadiums, which all look the same.

So my longed-for tour finally got under way. The players' route from the dressing rooms to the tunnel to the pitch, which I'd only been able to admire on television or in photographs, was one I could walk down myself. I trod the same path as legendary figures such as Alf Ramsey, Jimmy Greaves, Teddy Sheringham, Robbie Keane, Gareth Bale, Luka Modrić and Harry Kane. Players whose exploits had brought joy to generations of fans.

Before I left, I lifted my gaze to take in all the fascination of White Hart Lane one last time. And it was to be the last time – my heart sank at the thought that that fine old ground was about to be demolished. Work had already started on a new stadium and, despite the imminent loss of all that history, everyone seemed happy with the prospect of its shiny modern replacement. Which made me curious. I wanted to see what it was like.

So it was with a heavy heart that in January 2020 I found a way to see Tottenham's new ground. To get there I took the exact same route I'd followed three and a half years earlier, with the one difference that I was no longer living in Bowness-on-Windermere, but in London.

The White Hart Lane Overground station, completely refurbished, shone with its own light, as did the new stadium, standing majestically before me as I glumly gaped at it. It grew in size as I approached, dominating the whole area – it generated work for thousands of people more than the old ground had.

As I looked around me I had the impression of being in another dimension. The stadium was beautiful, years ahead of its time, but completely alien to the football I love. My football is made of simple things, with a ground sewn into the fabric of the local houses, where a club's history can be experienced by looking at the old turnstiles, perhaps with the regulation old gent who welcomes you into the ground where he grew up.

I was there on a cold and windy January evening for an FA Cup replay against Middlesbrough. I was welcomed into the ground, not by the friendly old man of my imagination but by a world far removed from what football should be. Cutting-edge bars, swanky restaurants, ultra-giant screens, lifts and escalators between floors, a club shop the size of a supermarket, a retractable pitch – to accommodate American football matches – and even a microbrewery.

To put it briefly, going to the billion-pound Tottenham Hotspur Stadium is like a journey into the future. But for all its stunning appearance and the customer comforts on offer, that night I left the ground 20 minutes before the final whistle. Tottenham won the match 2-1, much to the satisfaction of the hordes of home fans who saw it, and as I made my way home I was driven to the conclusion that everything I'd seen was to be expected and, at the end of the day, as it should be.

Times change, the world evolves and football is more and more of a business, no longer the people's game. What does it matter if White Hart Lane had been there for over a century and the club's entire history was contained within its walls? Nothing at all, and those things will never matter to people who think like entrepreneurs. When it comes down to it, all you can do is respect their decisions and carry on with your life. Looking to the future and accepting change, but never forgetting history, because White Hart Lane can never be replaced. White Hart Lane was Tottenham's real home, and in all our hearts – whatever our loyalties – it always will be.

THE INVINCIBLES

I was nine years old, perhaps ten, when I stood staring shiny-eyed through the window of a sports shop a few yards from the seafront. I'll never forget that day and that moment. It was in Portici, where I was staying with my Grandma Anna. Every summer, while she was still of an age to keep up with me, she had me to stay, spoiling me with affection and letting me run around town like an urchin. Shirtless, as brown as a nut and always with a football under my arm.

Any old ball, until one afternoon on our way back from the park when my gaze was captured by a mini-football displayed in a shop window on Corso Umberto I. My eyes were full of longing and, although I knew that what little money Grandma had would be needed for food, I let her know that I'd happily forgo my ice cream to get my hands on that ball.

It was a special ball, embellished with the Arsenal crest – I'd carry it in my heart for the rest of my days. At first I put it next to my pillow. Then on the shelf in my room, so I could always admire it. Not only in memory of Grandma Anna but, above all, to bring back that afternoon of childhood enchantment. Love at first sight. For that ball and that country. For football and for England.

❁ ❁ ❁

It seems only yesterday that Thierry Henry's Arsenal outclassed Juventus in the magnificent venue that was Highbury. It was 28 March 2006, and I can remember everything about that night too. Juventus were my boyhood heroes but I was also enamoured of the star-studded north Londoners – they were my PlayStation regulars. And on that Tuesday night I sat enthralled by the sight of them as the match played out on television.

Highbury looked its usual splendid self, but what captivated me was the roofs of the typical English houses that appeared behind a corner of the ground, sending me off into fantasies of walking round the local streets.

Ten years later, as if by magic, I was able to get as much direct experience as I wanted of those streets, those houses, those districts. Not only before and after a match but also in their habitual quiet, which is just how I like it.

In that area the new Emirates Stadium has replaced dear old Highbury. It's all it's cracked up to be, don't get me wrong, but it's got nothing like the charm and the atmosphere generated by the Highbury I admired on the small screen as a boy. More a salon than a stadium, Highbury was sadly demolished a few months after the Juventus match. But the façades of the two stands are still there, preserved as a mark of respect for the history and the old times they represent.

I remember the first time I saw them, marvelling at their classical English style, breathing in the history emanating from them. And today the fine façade of the old East Stand still looks down over Avenell Road, with the difference that dozens of new luxury flats have taken the place of the stands themselves, occupying what used to be the playing pitch. A pitch with so much glorious history, the stage on which Arsène Wenger marshalled one of the strongest and most prolific teams English football has ever produced.

That strength and those goals took the Gunners to the Premier League title in 2004 without losing a single match, equalling the record of an unbeaten season set by Preston North End as long ago as 1889. Thierry Henry and his team-mates not only gave their supporters the double satisfaction of winning the title and clinching it at White Hart Lane, just to rub it in for the Tottenham fans, they earned the moniker of the Invincibles, going straight into the annals of football. As if that wasn't enough, a few months later that Arsenal side accumulated 49 consecutive league matches without defeat, beating the old record of 42 matches set by Brian Clough's legendary Nottingham Forest.

I had the opportunity of immersing myself in this fame and fortune on the evening of 7 March 2017 when, shortly before the kick-off of Arsenal's return leg against Bayern Munich for a place in the Champions League quarter-finals, I walked into The Gunners pub for the first time.

It was there, not far from their old Highbury home, that I enjoyed the match. The place was a gem – the air was full of the smell of beer impregnated in the floor, the colourful walls were covered with old photos, signed shirts, drawings of the Invincibles and other memorabilia documenting Arsenal's victorious history. More than a hundred years of it, bookended by the stewardship of Herbert Chapman and Arsène Wenger, with most of the club's successes achieved in the irreplaceable setting of Highbury.

I felt almost as if I was in the ground itself as I lost myself among the photographs so lovingly arranged on the walls of the pub, which by that time had been plunged into a stunned silence by Bayern's umpteenth goal – in the 85th minute of the match the Germans racked up an aggregate score of 10-2.

The glazed eyes of the fans in the pub were oblivious to me as I slipped quietly out and made my way towards the Emirates Stadium, to get a taste of the bitterness and dismay. The pain was all too evident on the faces of the fans as they hurried towards the nearest Underground station, to go home and try to expunge the memory of that terrible night.

It was a night I observed from up close, not on the terraces but first in the pub and then outside the Emirates, looking for another story to tell. I'd just about given up on the idea and was about to go when a young lad appeared and knelt in front of the statue of Thierry Henry. He crossed himself, bowed his head and remained for at least a minute in silent prayer to his god, kissing his head before walking away. I never thought I'd see anything like it. It was an act of love, impossible to comprehend and wonderfully mad. Its image stayed with me as I made my way towards the place where Highbury used to stand.

In the silence of the night and with nothing but the moon lighting my way, I reached the historic façade of the old East Stand. Lost in my thoughts and somewhat overwhelmed by the place itself, I stood for a couple of minutes and stared at the beauty of the structure. Then I sat down on the steps where Wenger's men would enter the ground, cheered on by their supporters.

In the silence of the evening I pictured the scene, imagining myself among those fans. With a scarf round my neck and my grandma's ball under my arm, ready to celebrate yet another goal scored by the champions whose class and determination made them the Invincibles, which they always will be …

In memory of José Antonio Reyes, one of the Invincibles.
Tragically killed in a road accident on 1 June 2019.

LONG LIVE THE BOLEYN

Silence filled the air. Around us there was nobody left. Only dark streets and an area that was fading with each day that passed. Wrapped around Matteo's shoulders, the flag in memory of Enrico flapped in the dark of the night. A sad night, not just because of the stadium that was no more, but above all for the premature death of Enrico, a young father and passionate Hammers fan. I never met him personally, but being present at his funeral made it feel a bit like I'd always known him. The grief was writ large on the faces of his wife and children, warmly comforted by all the friends who chanted his name with passion and love, to make it feel like he was there with them. A passion suddenly cut down, but one that will remain in the hearts of all those who loved him.

That late September evening we went to bed downcast and disconsolate, leaving behind us the streets that had meant so much. Green Street was deserted and the iconic Boleyn Ground was a thing of the past. A home more than a stadium, an identity more than a district. One that I've had the honour of experiencing in person, as now, with tears in my eyes, I'll begin to relate ...

⚽⚽⚽

History, tradition, the pubs around the ground. Thousands of fans thronging Green Street before and after matches, the historic Upton Park Underground station. The bubbles flying so high before the match as the renowned Irons anthem rang around the stadium. The striking sight of the towers facing Green Street and the charged atmosphere in the Bobby Moore Stand behind them. The hordes of youngsters proudly wearing the shirts of their idols, and the not-so-young who can remember the exploits of the legendary Bobby Moore with the No.6 on his back. The unconditional love of that community, hard to explain and now impossible to relive.

West Ham United was all this and much more besides, and although times change and the old has to make way for the new, it's hard to swallow what was done to the Boleyn Ground. A slap in the face for an entire community. Over a hundred years of history bulldozed into the ground, replaced by a stadium that – no matter how much bigger, new and warmed by the devotion of long-suffering fans – will never be anything like the old, unique Boleyn Ground.

I had the pleasure and the honour of experiencing that ground on 14 September 2015. Also visiting were Newcastle United, for a Premier League Monday night match.

Caught up in the emotion of singing 'I'm Forever Blowing Bubbles' with the West Ham faithful, I looked up at the darkening sky; I was to learn that it was then that my dear Grandma Anna said her last goodbye and left us forever.

I have so many memories of her, and when my mum gave me the sad news, my determination was redoubled. Raising my tearful eyes to the heavens, I promised myself that I'd realise my dreams for her too. Hers had been a hard life, one of tremendous sacrifices built on a bedrock of sound values, which I shall always carry with me. Values based on love and the belief that tomorrow will be better, that you must face things with a smile and count your blessings – exactly what I felt as walked along the streets surrounding the Boleyn Ground, which showed signs of poverty but were rich in history and atmosphere.

In the case of West Ham United, that history goes back to 1895, not in the area of Upton Park but in Canning Town, a couple of miles closer to the Thames. The river gave a livelihood to the many men employed at the Thames Ironworks and Shipbuilding Co. Ltd, managed by Arnold

Hills, which operated a foundry and specialised in the construction of warships.

A few years later the hammers characteristic of shipyard work was adopted as the symbol of West Ham United, founded in 1900 on the ashes of the Thames Ironworks Football Club, which had been set up to provide healthy recreation for the company's workers. From 1897 to 1900 Mr Hills's ironworkers played their matches at the local Memorial Ground, as did their heirs West Ham United before moving to the Boleyn Ground in 1904. The stadium was located on the site of Boleyn Castle, a stately home believed to have been given to Anne Boleyn as part of a love pact with Henry VIII, who had set his sights on her as a replacement for his first wife. The pact reached fruition in 1532, with all the political turmoil and personal tragedy that history has recorded.

It's a story long past, but one that in my own small way I felt around me on that rainy mid-September morning as I stood for the first time outside the main entrance to the ground, gaping in admiration at the most striking football stand façade I'd ever seen. Behind it were years and years of illustrious history, symbolised by the two imposing towers. I was overcome by the power of the place. Words wouldn't come to me. I stood in silent wonder. And in happiness that I find hard to render on paper but I think you can appreciate if you picture yourself alongside me on that unforgettable occasion. It was a day on which I realised another great little dream, achieved through sacrifice and made to come true with all the love I had in my heart.

And it was the heart of the West Ham support that I experienced in the hours before kick-off. First by enjoying the traditional pie and mash with parsley liquor at the one and only Nathan's and then immersing myself in the East End pub atmosphere of The Boleyn; as the pints crossed the counter by the handful, I felt part of those supporters, as impatient as they were to go through the old turnstiles and enter their unique inner sanctum.

The Boleyn Ground was a magical place, and I could feel that magic working on me as I first saw it from the inside, left speechless once again. I've always been intrigued by places steeped in history. I was excited by the mere thought of having trod on the same ground as champions who have written the history of English football. Champions who not only made their name in claret and blue, winning the FA Cup in 1964 and the Cup Winners' Cup the following year but, more importantly, took the England team to the top of the world in 1966 – Martin Peters, Geoff Hurst and legendary captain Bobby Moore, who still live in the hearts of the West Ham fans. These are legends carefully cultivated in the club's youth academy, which over the years has produced stars such as Frank Lampard and Rio Ferdinand, whose brilliant careers started on the grass of the Boleyn Ground.

Floodlit grass that was a treat for the eyes as I gazed upon it that Monday night to the tune of 'I'm Forever Blowing Bubbles', words of passion tinged with fatalism that summed up a memorable night. By the end the Hammers ran out 2-0 winners, but I have to say that I had other things on my mind ...

At least 20 more minutes had gone by when I finally walked out of the Boleyn Ground, asked by the stewards to leave the terraces that in all probability I'd never see again. The thrill of experiencing a night match in that ground had been tempered by pain and sorrow. The pain that the fans had to endure at the prospect of the demolition of the place that had been their home for over a century, the symbol of a whole community.

And the sorrow was laced with anger when I returned there a couple of years later, and found that the home was gone. Leaving only rubble and pain – for the district itself, for the faithful supporters and for everyone who had grown up on the terraces of that legendary stadium: the irreplaceable Boleyn Ground.

In memory of my Grandma Anna and Enrico Lutzu. No matter how far away, you're always in my thoughts.

A FRIENDSHIP IN THE NAME OF CRYSTAL PALACE

The excitement was there to see in my eyes and theirs, filled with wonder in a special moment, a moment to capture. It began with my face set in a smile for a souvenir snapshot, not in a football ground but in the unique historic setting of Stonehenge.

The first photo wasn't up to much, so I swallowed my embarrassment and asked Matt to take another one, saying that I'd like to put it in the book I was about to write. His interest aroused by the mention of the book, he told me that his son was a Crystal Palace supporter, whereupon I took off the bracelet that I'd been given the day before at Selhurst Park and gave it to him. I said it would be of more use to him than to me, and said goodbye, with the promise that we'd meet again. In memory of that April day that none of us will forget.

✦✦✦

I can still remember the first time I set foot in Hyde Park. It was 20 February 2013 when I walked through a little gate on Bayswater Road. At the sight of the first squirrels and the perfectly manicured grass I was filled with a feeling of happiness and release. I'd longed for that moment for months, leaving behind the problems and insecurity of the life I'd been leading. A life of monotony and resignation that left no room for the dreams and desires that many people thought were unachievable. But then, working hard and concentrating my energy on positive thoughts, I understood that anything is possible.

Having a positive spirit is a great thing, but there's no hiding the fact that you've got to work hard to develop that quality. You don't just wake up one morning and find yourself all positive, far from it. Sometimes you feel your whole world collapsing, everything looks at its blackest, but it's precisely then that you have to fight back. In my darkest moments, personally I go for a walk. It's something I love, it makes me feel better. Walking has always helped me see things more clearly. And walking in Hyde Park has always led me to picture myself in a time far removed from our everyday life, when there was no football as we know it, when a palace was built in the heart of the park.

It was a monumental palace, destined to write a new page in British history. An enormous structure, made for the most part of cast iron and glass, it was the brainchild of Prince Albert, designed to house the Great Exhibition, which was held in 1851 in Hyde Park. The event was a huge national novelty, and the majestic beauty of the Crystal Palace – so it was dubbed by a contemporary commentator – attracted millions of visitors. Despite this spectacular success, to conserve the quality of Hyde Park, Prince Albert and Queen Victoria decided that the whole building should be dismantled and re-erected in another part of London. The place they chose, together with the palace's architect Joseph Paxton, was one of London's highest points: Sydenham Hill.

In just over two years after the Great Exhibition in Hyde Park, the entire Crystal Palace had been rebuilt on the hill in London's southern suburbs, giving the area a higher profile, continuing to attract huge numbers of visitors from all over the country and playing host to all manner of exhibitions and events, within it and in the surrounding park. These included theatre performances, concerts and festivals, innumerable cricket matches and, of particular interest, no fewer than 20 FA Cup finals. The first final to be held at the Crystal Palace ground was in 1895, and the series continued until 1914, bringing thousands of fans to London every year for matches whose attendances sometimes exceeded 100,000 – even then the FA Cup Final was a national event with tremendous pulling power.

Even before the FA Cup came into being, enthusiasm for football had led a group of men in the palace staff, together with some members of the Crystal Palace Cricket Club, to form a new club in order to keep the cricketers active during the winter months. So the first Crystal Palace Football Club was founded in 1861, with colours of blue and white stripes.[9] Having taken part in the first-ever FA Cup competition, held in 1872, a few years later the club ran into financial trouble and disbanded, disappearing almost without trace.

That was a history that felt close to me as I walked in Crystal Palace Park in the quiet of a November morning, trying in my mind's eye to travel back in time once again, picturing myself in the early years of the last century. Times so long past that they can't be relived, but they can be researched through photographs and a few books that relate the foundation, on 10 September 1905, of the club we know today: Crystal Palace Football Club.

It took the name of the proud palace, and of the park where I was walking, and indeed of the entire surrounding district. The park soon became the new club's headquarters, attracting thousands of supporters and writing the first pages of its history in the park made famous as the regular venue of the FA Cup finals of the period. After the outbreak of the First World War, in 1915 the park was used as a military base, so Crystal Palace FC had to find a new home.

---

9 Founded in 1861, the first Crystal Palace Football Club is considered by some sources to have no connection with the Crystal Palace we know today. On 21 April 2020 Crystal Palace FC wrote to the Football Association, claiming to have found direct links with the original Crystal Palace (1861). According to historian Peter Manning, on the strength of this, Crystal Palace should be recognised as the oldest professional football club in the world. Will the claim ever be recognised?

They finally did so in Selhurst Park, where the club settled in 1924. The ground had a singular setting, in a hilly area close to the park itself and surrounded on all sides by the typical English suburban houses that give the area its distinctive old-time feel.

On a cold April evening in 1962 the club welcomed European Cup giants Real Madrid, who had come to London to mark the inauguration of the new floodlights at Selhurst Park in a specially arranged night match. Almost 25,000 spectators crowded into the ground to watch Ferenc Puskás, Alfredo Di Stéfano and the other masters work their magic – the likes of which were hitherto unseen, since Palace were playing in the Third Division at the time. Despite the enormous difference between the two sides, the hosts left the pitch with heads held high after a defeat by the odd goal in seven, leaving their fans with a memory to treasure.

Almost 60 years after that royal friendly, I had the pleasure of experiencing that ground and the Palace support for myself. It was an early November afternoon and I was in the company of Matt and his son Leo, whom I'd met two and a half years before at Stonehenge.

It seemed like no time at all when we met again. After drinking a toast to our first encounter in one of the many pubs around the ground, we made our way to Selhurst Park. To celebrate our friendship Matt had given me a ticket for a seat in the middle of the Arthur Wait Stand.

He told me all about little Leo's ambitions and his devotion to Crystal Palace. Like many other boys, he dreamed of becoming a professional footballer, playing – naturally – for Crystal Palace. He was six years old when he went to his first Palace game, not at Selhurst Park but in the splendid setting of Wembley, for the 2016 FA Cup semi-final against Watford. Palace won the match 2-1, which made it one of the most exciting events of Leo's life – he asked his dad to buy him a shirt with the name of Connor Wickham, scorer of the winning goal. Matt was doubly delighted, not only by his son's enthusiasm but because from then on he, a Liverpool supporter, no longer had to put up with hearing about Chelsea, the club that all Leo's friends supported and so was tempting Leo too. In the end Palace won him over, and he asked his dad to get them season tickets at Selhurst Park.

As I watched Leo, I could see all his commitment, especially when the Palace signature song rose over the ground, with the fans singing the whole match long despite their 2-0 defeat at the hands of Jamie Vardy's Leicester City. As we filed out of Selhurst Park, Leo was understandably a bit down, but it was clear that nothing had dented his pride in the colours and his love for the badge. A badge that represents the history not only of the club but of a whole area, with an eagle proudly surmounting the monumental palace. Sadly, the palace's end was as spectacular as its life had been: on the night of 30 November 1936, it burned to the ground as the result of an electrical fire, leaving a huge void in the park and the district it had come to symbolise.

Now that symbol is proudly sewn on to the Crystal Palace shirts, showing the whole world the club's origins and encapsulating a remarkable history. That history began within the walls of a palace, for me it touched on Stonehenge, and it continues on the terraces of Selhurst Park, in the name of football and my friendship with a boy called Leo.

THE LEGEND OF
CORINTHIAN FOOTBALL CLUB

'Ivan, here we're a proper family. Come back whenever you like. You're one of us now. The doors of this house will always be open.'

That's how John and the boys said their goodbyes, warm embraces all round. The welcome I'd been given in Tolworth was a special one, and when it was time to leave I was overtaken by a feeling of sadness. I could have stayed there forever, but I had a train home to catch.

As I walked away, and the neat little ground of King George's Field shrank gradually into the distance and the sun began to sink, my thoughts returned to the wondrous story I'd just discovered. The story of a journey that began in London and passed through various countries, with stops in Madrid and finally in São Paulo, in Brazil. A journey replete with records and victories. A unique story the like of which I'd never heard, the like of which only football 'Made in England' can produce. This is the incredible story of Corinthian Football Club.

❁ ❁ ❁

The second half of the 1881/82 season was underway when Nicholas Lane ('Pa') Jackson, assistant secretary of the Football Association, decided it was time to put a stop to the series of defeats being suffered by the England team at the hands of the Scots. At a meeting he organised in a small room on the third floor of 28 Paternoster Row, next to St Paul's Cathedral, the initial ideas about the foundation of a new team were put down in writing.

Jackson's idea, recorded today in a picture in the clubhouse at King George's Field, was to form an amateur superteam made up of the best footballers then playing in the various clubs, schools and universities around the country.

The innovative feature was to allow them to play together regularly, so that when they pulled on an England jersey they'd be more prepared to face their opponents from north of the border. The first problem was when. Saturday, the day traditionally devoted in England to the worship of football, was obviously out. The other question was what name to give to the new team. The first idea that came up was the Wednesday Club, but on the advice of Harry Albemarle Swepstone, one of its founder members, the meeting agreed on the name of Corinthian Football Club.

It wasn't long before the new club was playing its first match. On 1 November 1882, Corinthian FC turned out in Lambeth to meet St Thomas' Hospital, winning 2-1. That season they played 13 more times, beating high-flyers such as Royal Engineers AFC and Upton Park FC along the way.

After the end of their first season, in autumn 1883, Jackson and the other founders organised a meeting to ponder the club's future. Of the many subjects discussed, two decisions stood out: the first regarded the club's colours and the second was that they'd take part in no official league or cup competition except the Sheriff of London's Shield, a trophy awarded to the winner of the match between the best professional team and the best amateurs, the proceeds to go to charity.

In the following months, wearing a white jersey with the club's initials sewn on the chest, the redoubtable Jackson led his team to the north of England, to challenge the big clubs in their industrial heartlands. There the Londoners took on Preston North End, Darwen, Bolton Wanderers, Blackpool, Derby County, Aston Villa, Blackburn Rovers and Blackburn Olympic, northern England's first team to win the FA Cup.

You win some, you lose some, and that's what Corinthian did, but their most astounding result was an 8-1 thrashing of FA Cup winners Blackburn Rovers in front of 10,000 spectators. Jackson could barely contain his delight.

As the years passed and the club went back and forth from England to Scotland in search of fresh adversaries, Jackson's plan was slowly coming to fruition. First by establishing English pre-eminence over the Scots and then by packing the England team with Corinthian players. So it was that after several victories over Scotland, on the afternoon of 12 March 1894 the England team faced Wales on their home turf at Wrexham's Racecourse Ground. In front of a crowd of 5,500 they beat the Welsh 5-1. That day, all 11 England players were Corinthians.

Although the scoreline was different, history repeated itself exactly a year later when England – again fielding 11 Corinthian players – beat Wales, this time in the sumptuous setting of their home, the prestigious Queen's Club in West Kensington.

It was there that the boys in white challenged the biggest teams of the period. One match that stands out in history took place on 5 March 1904. Bury had travelled down from Lancashire having just trounced Derby County 6-0 in the FA Cup Final. In the Sheriff of London's Shield Final, Corinthian were all over them, winning 10-3.

Another illustrious scalp was that of Manchester United, and this time Corinthian went one better. The 11-3 defeat inflicted on the northerners remains to this day their worst-ever result. To honour that occasion, in July 2004 the Red Devils went down to Tolworth to play Corinthian a century later, running out 3-1 winners. The Manchester United shirt and club pennant from that match are still on display in the Tolworth clubhouse, which is run by down-to-earth people with a deep passion.

A passion I could see in John's eyes when he spotted me from inside the ground's 'megastore': 'Hello, mate, if you need help with anything, I'm here.' I'd just set foot in the place, and John, a club volunteer, stood a few yards away, a Guinness in his hand.

Scarves, shirts, caps, badges and hundreds of match programmes formed the colourful décor of that little wooden hut – the impression was somewhat surreal. It was all very basic, with prices written on scraps of cardboard that were sellotaped to each item on sale.

Time seemed to stand still. I felt the material as I browsed through the rows of shirts. Then, as I turned the pages of a book about the club's glorious history, John – wearing an S.C. Corinthians Paulista shirt – walked towards the door and proclaimed, 'You can find all our history in that book, and if you read it, you'll feel like you're living those times, those victories, those journeys. You can find everything on the internet, but the book's much better!'

I'd read something about the club's history, but not all that much. I've always preferred to hear the best stories from people in the know rather than reading about them online. So, Brazilian club shirt on his back, Guinness in hand, John took me back to that glorious past …

That incredible win over Manchester United was just one of the many records established by the boys in white. After going down in history as the club that has provided most players to the England team (86) – no other club could live with the amount of talent we had – Corinthian decided it was time to make themselves known in the rest of the world. So they organised tours and matches taking in South Africa, Austria, Hungary, Sweden, Denmark, Canada, the United States, Germany, Holland, France, Czechoslovakia and Switzerland. Then, on 5 August 1910 they set sail from Southampton, bound for Brazil.

The voyage to Rio de Janeiro took a little over two weeks. The Brazilian tour was inaugurated with a match against Fluminense, which the Londoners won 10-1. Almost all of the other matches followed suit. When the team arrived in São Paulo to take on the local sides, the story was the same.

This string of performances by the English club made a deep impression on local football fans, and it so happened that a group of them was just in the process of founding their own club. That's how Corinthians Paulista came into being, named after the Englishmen they had just seen play. Which is a bit like what Real Madrid did – it was in our honour that they decided their shirts would be white!

John was in love with the story he told, I could see it in his eyes. And I listened to him like a child with a dreamy gaze, picturing each episode from those years. After a short interruption as he greeted some of his friends, I asked him what happened to Corinthian following their return from Brazil.

The years rolled by and we played other matches around the world. In fact, in 1914 the club went back to Brazil for another tour, but the outbreak of war put a stop to everything. The players had to return home immediately.

Some of them were killed in the fighting and others never returned to a football field. The post-war years were difficult, and a new club was formed when Corinthian joined forces with their fellow amateurs in the Casuals Football Club. That's how Corinthian-

Casuals Football Club came into being. But it was 1939, and another world war was about to begin.

John's words transported me back to another era. As I touched every picture and every piece of memorabilia in that clubhouse I realised how lucky I was to be able to discover another treasure – of the sort that only England can give you.

Shortly afterwards, the whistle blew for kick-off in the FA Cup tie between Corinthian-Casuals and Croydon FC. My eyes began to wander and get lost in the faces of the fans who gather week after week in Tolworth on the terraces of King George's Field, home of Corinthian-Casuals since 1988. That was the year the Londoners were invited to Brazil by Corinthians Paulista to play a father-and-son exhibition match between the two clubs; the legendary Sócrates played one half wearing the shirt, now chocolate and pink, of the parent club.

On the August afternoon when I watched them, the home team cantered to a 6-0 win over local rivals Croydon, progressing to the next round of the glorious, never-tarnished FA Cup. After the final whistle, John and his friends welcomed me back into the clubhouse, where they made me feel one of them, telling me stories I never thought I'd hear.

We're all volunteers here. No one pays us, we do everything we do out of love for this incredible club.

We're proud of our history and work every day to get to the next level. Everything you see around you has been built and carried forward by the love these people have for our community. When the club moved to this ground, around us there was nothing. Now we've got a proper stadium!

We're a family, you see, and we like to communicate sound values, particularly to the kids in our youth academy. That's what the great Corinthian spirit teaches us; knowing that many of those youngsters will never be professional players, it's a good idea to teach them honesty, teamwork, respect for others and belief in their dreams. Football should be played for the love of the game, and here everyone plays out of passion, getting nothing in return. Except our love.

That afternoon I could feel all the love John talked about, and the simple warmth of those people. Just before leaving, I had a last walk around the ground, touching the flags that give even more colour to the terraces of that little stadium in the southwest suburbs of London. It confirmed my conviction that the real essence of football is to be found there, in its humblest institutions. There, in the non-league grounds of England, where the dogs walk free and the beer flows untrammelled by restrictions. Where the trees are taller than the stands, and roofs of the local houses can always be seen, making the whole scene more romantic, just as I'd always imagined it.

Non-league football is that magical place where you're not just one among many, you're one of them. The place where you turn up as a stranger and go away knowing you've found a family with a great history behind it. So when I walked out of Barons Court tube station, instead of taking my usual route home, I went down Palliser Road. It would take me to where I lived all the same, but with a difference. That day I passed in front of the world-famous Queen's Club, the Corinthian headquarters of old. So that I could stand there, shut my eyes for a minute and relive the legend of Corinthian Football Club.

THE REAL DONS ARE HERE

Stop for a second, wherever you are. You know the team you fell in love with when you were a kid discovering football? The one you support now and always will, rain or shine. Now picture yourself in the ground you grew up in, proudly wearing the scarf and the shirt that mean so much, sometimes everything. Colours you'd make any sacrifice for – you already have and will do so again, because your love for your club is the greatest love there is. It's impossible to explain, it defies all logic, but it's in your thoughts every day.

Now picture something else. You've got to leave the ground you grew up in. For good. And worse than that, your beloved club is moving to another town, 60 miles away, and its name is being changed. Not possible, I hear you say. But it is possible, and it's happened. Hold on to your hats, this is the story of Wimbledon Football Club ...

❁ ❁ ❁

It was a Saturday afternoon in November 2017 when I stood for the first time on the terraces at Kingsmeadow, in Kingston. The air was crackling with enthusiasm. An FA Cup tie between AFC Wimbledon and Lincoln City had attracted over 3,000 fans of all ages, full of passion and ready to get behind their team. Looking into those people's eyes, you could see the love that bound them to Wimbledon. A club driven forward by immense passion and innumerable sacrifices.

I think these are the essential prerequisites for any project and ambition you want to achieve in life. Passion is at the basis of everything, but what counts more than anything is willingness to pay the price demanded by that ambition. I mean the sacrifices to be made, the difficulties to overcome, constancy in pursuit of your aim and, above all else, the right attitude. A positive attitude and belief in eventual success are the qualities that will help us climb any mountain.

Especially the steepest ones. Which is rather like what Wimbledon fans were faced with in May 2002. In order not to lose their football club and all its traditions, they decided to join forces and surprise the world with one of the most admirable acts of love ever exhibited – they decided to re-found the team that belonged to them. A team that millionaires devoid of values and feelings had decided to uproot from south London and move to Milton Keynes, over 60 miles from the borough of Merton, where Wimbledon FC had always been. The dear old Plough Lane ground was home to Wimbledon FC from 1912 to May 1991.

Only three years before leaving it, Wimbledon had performed the astonishing feat of bringing the FA Cup to Plough Lane after beating Kenny Dalglish's mighty Liverpool team in the final. The Crazy Gang earned the respect of the whole country, but were blissfully unaware that everything was about to change for their little club.

In the wake of the Hillsborough tragedy, in January 1990 the Taylor Report laid down that for the safety of spectators every First Division club had to play in an all-seater stadium. Since Plough Lane was made up mostly of terracing, complying with that obligation would have required millions of pounds and reduced its capacity from 16,000 to 6,000 people – not a viable number for a top-flight club.

In light of this, club chairman Sam Hammam came up with the brilliant idea of leaving Plough Lane for good and having 'his club' play at Selhurst Park, home of local rivals Crystal Palace. Wimbledon supporters found his decision pretty hard to swallow, but some of them were prepared to go along with it on the understanding that it was a temporary arrangement only, pending the construction of a new ground of their own.

That new ground never materialised, and on the strength of the millions by that time being poured by television companies into Premier League clubs, little Wimbledon included, Mr Hammam and his partners decided to squeeze even more cash out of the English football cow.

Their idea was to take the Premier League beyond the borders of England by transferring Wimbledon FC, lock, stock and barrel, to Dublin. Not just to find a new home for the club, but also to make the Premier League more saleable – an even more attractive commercial product. When this ludicrous idea came to light, the 1996/97 season was already in progress. But in the face of increasingly bitter protests from fans incensed by the prospect of seeing their club play 'home' matches in the Irish capital, Mr Hammam elected to sell his majority shareholding in the club for £25 million pounds. He tried to pass it off to the supporters as an act of love for Wimbledon, assuring them that the new owners would take the club to the top of English football.

The new owners were Kjell Inge Røkke and Bjørn Rune Gjelsten, Norwegians whose considerable wealth was matched by their lack of experience in English football. The first thing they did was put all their efforts into completing Wimbledon FC's move to Ireland. Unwilling to see an English team playing in their country, the Football Association of Ireland intervened to block the move, leaving Wimbledon adrift in a sea of uncertainty.

This did nothing but intensify the pain and resentment of the supporters, who wished only to see the club back in their home borough. Since the old Plough Lane ground was slated for demolition, the Norwegian duo came up with promises of a new stadium and a quick return to the Premier League – in 2000 the club had been relegated to the First Division after 14 years in the top flight. That relegation induced Sam Hammam to sell his remaining shares in the club to Charles

Koppel, who was immediately appointed chairman by the Norwegian owners. Unsurprisingly, he too weighed in with a series of promises for a return to success.

But all the promises made, including the remote possibility of building a new ground in Merton, vanished into nothing when a call arrived from Pete Winkelman, a businessman heading the Milton Keynes Stadium Consortium, suggesting that the London club transfer its base to the Buckinghamshire new town. This proposal, highly abnormal whichever way you look at it, would not only give Wimbledon a ground of their own (60 miles from their London home), but would provide Milton Keynes with something the town had never had – a professional football team.

Needless to say, Koppel and the club's unscrupulous owners fell over themselves to accept, giving not a damn for the club's history and traditions, and blithely ignoring the impact such a move would have on its supporters and the whole local community. That community was to be deprived of the thing it held dearest, so when it was officially announced that the shameful transfer would go ahead, on 30 May 2002 a group of fans got together and decided to do something about it. A new club was about to be founded.

As a result of the Wimbledon fans' irrepressible passion, two weeks later AFC Wimbledon came into existence. But the club had to start from scratch. Instead of rubbing shoulders with the game's top professionals, they began life in the ninth tier of English football. Little did it matter to the supporters. What counted was that they'd regained their club and could really call it their own, without having to deal with the harebrained schemes of grasping chairmen who wouldn't know a principle if it hit them on the head.

The new Wimbledon had finally got back its heart and soul, even though the team could no longer play at Plough Lane. More than just a football ground, it was demolished to make way for new flats, built in six blocks, each named after a club legend so as to conserve at least the memory of the club that had always been part of Merton.

On the strength of the pride and determination of the supporters and serial victories recorded by the team, in just a few seasons the club rose from the lower reaches of the football pyramid and returned to the professional ranks in 2011/12, writing one of the most romantic pages in the history of the English game.

So it was that a few years later, in November 2017, I too had the honour of getting up close and personal with the community that is AFC Wimbledon. Standing on the Kingsmeadow terraces that cold autumn afternoon, I saw with my own eyes the passion of those supporters, people who just can't live without their football. Theirs is real football, based on love and sound values. Feelings that made the impossible possible, starting from the basement and reaching the upper floors thanks to people prepared to start from zero, investing their own money and doing their damnedest to take AFC Wimbledon back to Plough Lane, where the club belongs.

And they succeeded. A few hundred yards from the site of the old Plough Lane ground, on 3 November 2020, AFC Wimbledon's new stadium was officially opened, making it clear once and for all: the real Dons are not in Milton Keynes, they're south of the Thames. That's where the history of Wimbledon is, and it's theirs.

Final note: In 2003 Wimbledon FC were taken into receivership and compelled to sell all their best players, while AFC Wimbledon enrolled as an amateur club in the Premier Division of the Combined Counties League, football's ninth tier.

The following year Wimbledon FC were relegated to League One and changed their name to Milton Keynes Dons FC. In the same season, AFC Wimbledon won their league title and were promoted to the First Division of the Isthmian League, a feat they repeated in 2005, winning promotion to that league's Premier Division, the seventh tier.

In 2007 MK Dons gave back to AFC Wimbledon all the silverware won by the defunct Wimbledon FC, including the FA Cup famously conquered by the Crazy Gang in 1988.

Onwards and upwards. In 2016, the minnows of AFC Wimbledon gained promotion to League One, where Milton Keynes Dons were also playing. Two years later, AFC Wimbledon finished the season above Milton Keynes Dons; never before had a club founded by supporters reached such a high level. What's more, the end of the season saw Milton Keynes Dons relegated to League Two.

Those are the bare bones of the story. It's hard to do justice to the history of this great little club in a few lines. So for anyone interested in finding out more, I'd advise reading Stefano Faccendini's book *Noi siamo il Wimbledon* (We Are Wimbledon). His love for the game, passion and attention to detail have produced an enthralling history of the real Dons.

FAREWELL GRIFFIN PARK

There we stood, in the middle of the Brook Road Stand, silently savouring a moment we knew we'd never forget. Up to then I'd broken many a rule, sneaking into dozens and dozens of football grounds without a word of permission, but on that cold January morning we risked more than I'd ever done.

I'd only just met Michele and Elisa, two more lovers of English football, not far from Stamford Bridge. As we enjoyed a cup of hot tea and a biscuit or two, they looked earnestly at me with shining eyes and asked me to go with them to Griffin Park.

How could I say no? But when we got there the lady in reception said it wasn't possible to go in for a visit, so we tried to make the best of it with a walk around the surrounding area. It's a quiet corner of London, with typical terraced housing on all sides of the ground. The old-time charm of the setting sent Michele into dreamland – he'd been hankering after a visit to Griffin Park for years.

Then, walking along Brook Road, we came across a gate that had been left open. Hearts hammering, without a second thought we slipped inside the heavy gate and reached the ground's historic terraces. We were overwhelmed by the beauty of the place in the silence of the morning, but not so much that we didn't try to get on to the pitch. Until, that is, a burly-looking figure appeared from the middle of the New Road Stand.

Carrying some small metal girders on his shoulder, the man started to yell at us. Too excited to take any notice, we continued to take photos of the glorious interior of Griffin Park, but then the worker with the girders got really cross. Still shouting, he chased us out of the ground and into the street. As we walked off, the three of us smiled at each other, aware that that good man could never understand the fascination that had drawn us to Griffin Park.

Alas, a few months later that great little ground would close its gates for the last time, leaving a huge hole in the local community but a wonderful memory in our hearts. The memory of the one and only Griffin Park, the true home of Brentford Football Club ...

⚽ ⚽ ⚽

The first time I ever set foot there I was breath-taken. That October afternoon in 2015, when my English pilgrimages were just beginning, I turned up for a Championship match against Rotherham United with my brother Francesco, known to me as Ciccio, and we gazed upon perfection.

At that time I'd only been to about 30 grounds and seen fewer than ten matches, so the experience of being in those places had the sheen of fairyland. Looking back, those moments stand out as the most memorable of my long journey. Every little thing gave me an unrepeatable tingle of excitement.

Walking around London's many districts has always made me happy. Just being there was enough to start me daydreaming. I'd think how nice it would be to live in one of the little houses in those terraces, which had a charm all their own. A charm I've often tried to explain to anyone who fails to understand it, repeating, to myself as much as to them, that I felt at home there, strolling in the streets of that beautiful nation – one that has shown me that diversity is not a problem, but a resource for our development and our life.

So as the years have gone by, I've been able to discover and experience the world of English football in all its variety, watching more than a hundred matches around the country. Including another visit to Griffin Park, over two years after that first and unforgettable experience. That was an adventure I've recounted, misty-eyed, many times over, captivating like-minded listeners and igniting interest in that historic ground – whose possibly unique claim to fame is having a pub standing outside each of its four corners.

There, as you can imagine, beer flows plentiful. And on Boxing Day 2017, the day of a Championship match against Aston Villa, it was going down by the quart, lubricating me and the supporters packing the Princess Royal, one of the four pubs where matchday passion would be whipped up before the Griffin Park turnstiles started clicking. Old-style turnstiles, each with an old-style gent to let you into the little stadium nestling among the houses. Being there on that day took me back to far-off days. To a time when everything was different from today's world ...

It was in 1926 that Harry Curtis pitched up at Brentford to take over as manager. Photographs then were still black and white, and the little west London club plied its trade in the Third Division South. Times were hard, the shadow of the Great War still loomed large and the club's only supporters were local ones.

With the arrival of Harry Curtis, things began to change. Under his guiding hand the club consolidated and improved its standing, winning more games and making more money – money invested in a new stand, which brought more people to Griffin Park.

In the 1932/33 season their patience and support were rewarded when Brentford won the Third Division South. They didn't stop there. Two years later the club won the Second Division title, ushering in the most successful period in its history.

Brentford started the 1935/36 season in the English First Division for the first time ever. And the end of the season saw them in fifth position – above Arsenal, above Chelsea

– as London's best-placed club. This astounding success took Brentford's supporters, at least for a few seasons, to a new level. From trooping into dilapidated Third Division grounds they'd begun to follow their team to England's most prestigious stadiums, proud to cheer on their west London underdogs.

So there I stood on that freezing Boxing Day afternoon in the middle of hundreds of fans in the Ealing Road Stand, watching the match against Aston Villa. We sang non-stop for 90 minutes, on our feet from the first minute to the last. The whole place was jumping, and the explosion of roaring joy that greeted the winning goal remains one of the best memories of all my journeys.

In truth, it wasn't a particularly hard match – Brentford dominated proceedings from kick-off to the final whistle. It harked back to the reign of Harry Curtis, club manager for 23 years, architect of the club's finest hours.

A small club in a tight little ground, Brentford played at Griffin Park for more than a hundred years, from September 1904 to the summer of 2020. A venue with a charm all its own, enhanced by its homely setting, but now, alas, replaced by a new stadium carved out on a site a few blocks away.

More than a football ground, Griffin Park was a home, which I was lucky enough to visit three times: first with my brother in the Braemar Road Stand, then on the vibrant terraces of the Ealing Road Stand, and in 2020 by sneaking in unnoticed, something of a weakness of mine. It was my way of saying a last goodbye.

In memory of Harry Curtis and the place that was yesterday, is today and always will be the true home of Brentford Football Club. The little, the captivating, the irreplaceable Griffin Park.

CRAVEN COTTAGE: ENGLAND'S MOST BEAUTIFUL STADIUM

I was 16 years old when Fulham made history by beating Juventus 4-1 at Craven Cottage. At the time I was a fan of the *Bianconeri* from Turin, but when I saw the beauty of that ground on the banks of the Thames I was spellbound. Never had I been so struck by such charm on a television screen, not only because of the old-time splendour of the ground itself but in particular the houses surrounding it – one of which was actually in a corner of the stadium. Little did I know that about nine years later that part of London would become my favourite place in the world, the backdrop for my daily walks on the banks of the river. Relaxing strolls that started from West Kensington, where I lived for about two years, and always ended on Stevenage Road. Not any old road but one of those places defined by their history and atmosphere. Get your rucksacks ready and follow me. This time we're going to Craven Cottage, where the unique home of Fulham Football Club awaits …

❀❀❀

Have you ever given up on a dream? I have, just once. It was awful. Every time I think about it I still get torn up. To abandon my playing ambitions was the hardest decision I've ever had to make. It wasn't so much having to relinquish everything that made me happy as the fact that I was closing the door on my greatest dream, one that I'd cherished for ten years or more, without really making much headway.

Fair enough, I was no Alessandro Del Piero, but the village where I grew up didn't help much. It's a tough little town just outside Naples, with dozens of kids growing up in the streets, chasing a football, chasing hopes and dreams.

I left football – my best friend – in September 2013 when the chance of a well-paid job came up. By well paid, I mean the equivalent of £140 a week, working ten hours a day, six days a week. Not the greatest prospect, obviously, but my desire to make something of myself induced me to accept it. Not just to redeem myself after my recent failure in London but mainly to earn enough money to take me back to England. What kept me going was thinking about my return to the places I'd seen. As I dreamed of that fresh departure, though, those days at work seemed endless.

Each day would start and finish in the same way, with my dreamy gaze wandering over all the photos of Craven Cottage hanging on my bedroom wall, wanting nothing more than to immerse myself in those colours and never come out.

Then in March 2014 I got what I wanted, awarding myself a couple of days in London. I lived every moment of that visit to the full. And the excitement came not just from my return to the city I loved but, above all, from football – from the first Premier League match I ever saw in person.

Fulham against Newcastle was the realisation of a dream. Partly because of the unique charm of Craven Cottage, and partly because I was becoming a Fulham fan. So I did what fans do: when Ashkan Dejagah rifled in the winning goal, I exploded with joy, hugging all those around me and singing my heart out for the team that had stolen it.

On that sunny March afternoon I could have stayed in that ground forever. When I did leave, and found myself walking along Stevenage Road, I broke down in tears. Those tears were a distillation of all my love for football and for England.

Shortly afterwards I was in Bishops Park, right behind Craven Cottage's Putney End. As I stared at the calmly flowing waters of the Thames I made myself a promise: I would go back there and I would make my dreams come true.

Five years and many a sacrifice later, I'd done it. Not just because I'd spent a good fraction of my life in London but mainly because I'd been living in the birthplace of Fulham FC, a stone's throw from Craven Cottage.

The club was formed through the efforts of some of the worshippers at St Andrew's church, a building I was able to admire for two years from my bedroom window. As I did so, I'd think back to how I used to lose myself gazing at the photos of Craven Cottage in my old bedroom in Italy. In those days Craven Cottage was a far-off place, seemingly beyond reach. It was opened in 1896, with the enchanting cottage and what later became the Johnny Haynes Stand built in 1905 by renowned Scottish stadium architect Archibald Leitch.

Over a century later, the cottage and the stand are still there, shrouded in a sense of times gone by, a feeling I had the honour of sampling one mid-October Sunday morning thanks to the kindness and good offices of Penny and the stories told to me by Morgan Phillips, whom I met in that church where Fulham were founded.

A dyed-in-the-wool supporter, Morgan sipped his hot tea as he began to tell me of when his grandfather first came to London in 1907 to work as postman. It didn't take him long to fall in love with the area around Craven Cottage and, of course, the team to which it was home. Two years later he got married and rented a flat in Fulham Palace Road. That's where Morgan's mother was born the following year, within hailing distance of Craven Cottage.

As in many English families who worship at the altar of football, she too grew up with the local club in her heart, as did her future husband, whom she met in 1928 at the tender age of 18. So it was only natural that when Morgan came into the world, in 1940, he should follow his parents and grandfather into the faith.

He first stood on the terraces at Craven Cottage at eight years old in 1948, when his parents took him to a match. The atmosphere worked its magic on him too, and in the following years he did his best never to miss a home game. The tradition started by his grandfather was in safe hands.

A couple of days later I was at the Cottage for a Championship match against Luton Town, and my imagination went into rewind. I found myself reliving Morgan's stories. Lost in these thoughts as the ground gradually filled up, the Thames flowing quietly to the right of the Hammersmith End, I looked at the pitch and felt the tears pricking behind my eyes.

Deeply touched by Morgan's stories, as the teams took the pitch I tried to picture myself on that same terrace when the Fulham shirt was worn by champions like Johnny Haynes, George Best, Bobby Moore, Bobby Robson and George Cohen, all players who had or would become legends well beyond those homely horizons.

Speaking of legends who have trod the grass of Craven Cottage but who never wore a Fulham shirt, the history books and some memorable photographs record the great Eusébio and the magical Pelé, who both appeared in friendlies there. When I was first inside the hallowed walls of the Cottage I saw the proud display of a match ball signed by Pelé. It represented years of glorious history, as did every other treasure conserved in that place – a place that had been home, even if just for one night, to a host of players and managers. A special home, whose guests could awake to a romantic view of the River Thames and the most captivating ground in the whole of England.

When I was a young boy, those places were the stuff of daydreams. Then, as time went by, I was able to visit them, to experience them. First with my own eyes and then through what I learned from Morgan, who since 1948 had watched his beloved Fulham more than 1,600 times. His love for the club has led him deeper into its history. Numerous stories unearthed from his local bookshop have enabled him to discover everything that happened before he was born, and he has written books on Fulham's history. With Guy Alexander Wilkinson, vicar of St Andrew's, he had the idea of suggesting that Fulham Football Club install a plaque in the church in official commemoration of its founding by members of the congregation.

Years later, I admired that church every day. Any hour of the day, walking through the streets where the founders of Fulham FC would meet. Experiencing those streets, that stadium, that church and that quarter is one of the most significant stories of my journey. It's a long journey, which started in a little room in the village where I grew up and passed through West Kensington, where Fulham Football Club was founded. A club that has played for over a hundred years in the unique setting of Craven Cottage, where the Johnny Haynes Stand and the historic cottage have been named as listed buildings, preserved for posterity.

West Kensington is a place that everybody should experience at least once in their lives. Not just for Craven Cottage on matchdays, but when everything is quiet and peaceful. Perhaps walking from St Andrew's church down to Stevenage Road, where stands the one football ground in the world that leaves me speechless every time I see it.

A special ground, of unparalleled romantic charm. That's Craven Cottage – England's most beautiful stadium.

BLUE IS THE COLOUR

Jen cried twice that day. The first tears were of joy – she'd realised her dream of meeting Antonio Conte, one of the coaches she loved best. A few hours later she took part in the minute's applause in homage to the deceased Ray Wilkins, Chelsea stalwart and one of her favourites, and shed tears of sorrow. It was sorrow unexpected on that April afternoon before a Premier League derby against West Ham United, felt by everyone there at Stamford Bridge. A stadium with over a hundred years of stories to tell.

Jen had lived through more than 30 years of them, driven by her passion for Chelsea. No ordinary love, one that makes your heart beat fast even when things are going badly, one beyond all logic, overcoming all obstacles. It's a love I've had the honour of knowing, of sharing, and now, to the extent that I'm able, of relating. Her story is not only of a supporter but of a friend, one who opened the door of her home and took me into her world. She took me back in time and in the blink of an eye I was standing on the terraces of Stamford Bridge. More than a football ground, a home – her home.

⚽ ⚽ ⚽

The first time I met Jen I felt as if I'd always known her. Her eyes were alive with love and passion, and as we walked serenely along the wall of the historic Shed End, she quietly took my hand and led me on a tour of her personal scrapbook. It's an album full of tears and smiles, victories and defeats, long journeys and sacrifices, all made with guts and passion.

It was 7 May 1983 when this passion first visited her, sitting on her sofa at home. A feeling that crept up on her unexpectedly, and came out in the final minutes of a Second Division match between Bolton Wanderers and Chelsea.

Anything less than a victory would send the Blues down to the Third Division; terrified at the very thought, Jen sat waiting to hear the final result. Things were a bit different in those days, though. There were no instant updates on match scores, any changes were communicated from time to time on the radio, and the final results beaten out on the BBC's *Grandstand* teleprinter from about a quarter to five on a Saturday afternoon.

She couldn't tear her eyes from the screen, not because she didn't love Steve, her boyfriend sitting beside her on the couch, but because she could think of nothing but Chelsea in their hour of need. Steve didn't see it quite like that – he was moved to ask her if in her madness she cared more about that damn team than about him. Jen, a fan since the age of seven, when her brother had given her a blue rosette after watching a match at Stamford Bridge, replied that she was just anxious about the result and the horrendous consequences of the wrong one. But Steve wasn't having any of it. He wanted Jen all to himself, and unable to stomach the thought that a football match could distract her from his pretty face, he flew into a rage and demanded an answer.

At that precise moment, Jen was in no doubt. Wracked with worry about the result, she promptly replied, 'Chelsea. I care more about Chelsea!' She couldn't have been clearer. The boy picked himself up, walked through the door and out of her life. A life that since that day has seen Chelsea put above everything and everyone. Not just because of what happened with Steve, who had vowed to love her, but on the strength of the emotion that overcame her when she saw the result of the Bolton match, something she'd never felt before. And it wasn't even the simple fact of avoiding relegation, it was the discovery of a love that from then on just grew and grew.

As a young girl she'd had to follow her passion by halves. Not through any fault of her own, but because of her strict father, who was dead set against football. She'd have liked to play, but time and time again he said no.

Back then, when she was 12 years old, times were different. Without the internet and all the conveniences we take for granted today, the only way she could see anything of Chelsea and the goals they scored was in the highlights on *Match of the Day*. The problem, of course, was that the programme started at half past ten, which her dad thought was well past her bedtime. Sometimes she managed to persuade him to let her stay up, but more often than not she had to go sadly to bed and wait until the next day to find out how the team had played from the papers.

The years went by, and every time she looked at her dear old rosette she felt a blue spark, fuelling the desire in her to move to London and get closer to her beloved club.

Jen has always lived in Salisbury, about two hours from London. One February morning in 1978 she went to its post office, where she worked for over 20 years, to send a letter to Stamford Bridge, applying for two tickets to the Arsenal match scheduled for 27 March. It was to be her first visit to Stamford Bridge. After about a month, the longed-for tickets arrived, and then came the great day.

With her parents' permission she made the trip with a friend of hers, and was awestruck by the sight of Stamford Bridge. But once they'd gone through the turnstiles and taken up a position in the Shed, a thought came to her. She realised the importance of the glasses she needed and had always been too ashamed to buy. So her Stamford Bridge debut was spoiled by her inability to see most of the action. That made up her mind. She bought a pair of glasses as soon as she could, putting her devotion to Chelsea above any worries about what people might think of her looks.

As the seasons rolled by, Jen's dream gradually came within reach. No longer of an age when her parents dictated her bedtime, she was able to enjoy *Match of the Day* and look forward to going back to the Bridge.

Finally, after years of enforced patience, she managed to get hold of a season ticket for 1989/90. That ticket was a dream come true, and no matter how much she loved Mike, her then boyfriend and future soulmate, she laid down the law straight away: 'Chelsea are and always will be the love of my life. On Saturday, when Chelsea are playing at home, we won't be eating at your parents' place because I'll be at Stamford Bridge. And you needn't think you can change my mind, because this is the most important thing in my life. Okay, Mike?'

They'd only been together for a few weeks, but Mike knew where he stood. Previous amorous disappointments had hardened her heart, and anyone who decided to love her would have to remember to love her greatest passion too.

That passion entailed great sacrifices for Jen, not only in the many little things she had to do without during the football season but above all in the summer, when she took any job she could get, leaving the house at dawn and coming back just in time for dinner. All of which was to pay for her season ticket at Stamford Bridge.

And one day in November 2017, for a match against Norwich City, she had a hard time getting into the place. Not because of the crowd but because she turned up on crutches with a bandaged knee. Which just goes to show that when you want something badly enough you'll always find a way to get it.

In addition to home matches, in all these years she's been hitting the road to follow her team all over England and beyond, clocking up attendances in 15 European cities. Not to mention Chelsea's two Champions League finals, in Moscow in 2008 and four years later in Munich. For good or ill, those journeys gave her the most powerful emotions of her life. In

Moscow her tearful eyes saw Manchester United put paid to her Champions League dreams, but in Germany she climbed with Chelsea to the summit of European football, courtesy of the decisive penalty scored by the one and only Didier Drogba.

In their time at Stamford Bridge, Drogba and other champions have given Jen and thousands of fans unforgettable moments, making their names in history and taking the club to the very top – a club that Jen began to follow when they were struggling in the basement of the Second Division. A club she's immensely proud of, a club for which she'd lay down her life. A life spent on the terraces and in the stands at Stamford Bridge, where she has been a season ticket holder for over 30 years and where the pitch still pulls at her heartstrings every time she sets eyes on it.

I felt a little bit of the same in February 2013, when I first experienced that historic ground. It's a place that has blessed me with so much joy and memories galore. Not only when I was watching matches there with my good friend Jen but also when I actually had the opportunity of working there. I loved that job from day one, when I found myself, purely by chance, in the private box allocated to the family of young Chelsea player Callum Hudson-Odoi. It was 22 September 2019.

For the rest of the season, for every home match, I had the pleasure of working as a waiter for Callum's family, sharing all their joy and suffering, their victories and defeats. As I observed their eyes during every match, I perceived the whole range of emotions: from serenity to anger, from sadness to joy.

And there's one joyful day that will stay with me for the rest of my days: 5 January 2020. In the sixth minute of Chelsea's match against Nottingham Forest, Callum scored the goal that put them one up, sending Stamford Bridge wild. Jennifer, Callum's mum, hugged me in a flood of tears. Bradley, Mike and Bismark sprang from their seats, smothering each other in violent embraces.

After weeks of hysterical criticism and mounting pressure stoked up by some supporters and several newspapers, Chelsea's youngster had shown everyone what he was made of – his goal was just one contribution to an excellent performance. His explosion of pent-up emotion on the pitch and that of his family in the stands went straight to my heart. I was lucky to be there. It seemed like a dream. I was at Stamford Bridge, in the private box of one of English football's brightest prospects and, thanks to his family, who had taken me into their hearts, I was watching every match with them, and Chelsea were gradually making me one of their own.

My time with the club was an intense experience, not only within the confines of Stamford Bridge but also at their training ground at Cobham, where I acquired one of my most treasured memories, when I worked as a waiter at the club's Christmas dinner. That was on 18 December 2019.

I say training ground, but I'd never seen a sports centre anything like it. I saw more than 20 football pitches, each manicured to perfection. I thought I was in fairyland. No sooner had I arrived than I found myself having breakfast with Jorginho, Kovačić, Azpilicueta, Barkley, Pulisic and Kanté. I fantasised about turning up there one day as team manager – coaching is a long-time ambition of mine. Then my daydream was interrupted. Before my eyes appeared the greatest of them all: Frank Lampard, no longer a player but the Chelsea manager. All my tasks for the day took second place as I concentrated on observing Frank. Following his every move, I thought of all the times I'd admired him on television, seeing him put in one sensational performance after another.

Now that I think of it, after observing all those champions, that day confirmed one thing for me: dreams can come true, and some of mine did just that in the splendid historic setting of Stamford Bridge. The home of Chelsea Football Club – and Jen's home.

CHAPTER 8
BE KIND TO YOURSELF

Always celebrate your achievements!

Taff Rahman

MY JOURNEY of discovery around English stadiums has not only given me the opportunity to visit places I always dreamed of but, along the way, I've had the opportunity to meet dozens of new people, many by chance. One of these is Taff Rahman.

We first met thanks to Simone, another person whose acquaintance I owe to this ongoing journey of mine. Taff has coached at international level and founded Just Play FC, a grassroots club. He also happens to be one of the most inspirational people I've ever had the fortune to meet. Working alongside him as a coach with Just Play FC was one of the most wonderful and formative experiences of my life. He's a straight shooter who doesn't talk much and observes keenly. The sort of person I wish I could talk to every day, because he always enlightens me in some way or other.

When he talks, he comes across as relaxed, smiling and confident. I've always felt at ease in his company, in both good times and bad. Sometimes he has been unceremonious in imparting his views to me; other times, he has taken me by the hand before letting me go, encouraging me to ask myself the right questions.

That's what happened one cold Friday evening in early November. During a training session, he came over and asked me what was wrong. He'd seen the empty look in my eyes and the difficulty I was having managing the children. He asked me a series of questions that helped me delve deep inside myself and realise things I'd never have imagined. Some of his words touched me so profoundly that I was unable to hold back the tears.

That conversation, which I shall never forget, lasted around 20 minutes, as the kids ran around playing football in the incessant rain. Of all the questions he asked me, only one left me speechless: 'Ivan, what achievements have you celebrated in the last year?'

I felt a tug at my heartstrings as I replied: 'I haven't celebrated any achievements in the last year. Actually, I can't remember the last time I celebrated anything. All I do when I achieve something is think about the next target. I don't really savour anything.'

He responded with a smile. 'Always be kind to yourself. Working hard to achieve your dreams is a wonderful thing but don't be too hard on yourself, Ivan. Learn to celebrate your successes and every little achievement. There have always been three stages in life. The first is the hunt (working hard); the second, the most difficult, is killing your prey (achieving your target); and the third, Ivan, is satiating your hunger, just as the hunter enjoys the prey he has captured (celebrating the achievement).

'Be kind to yourself and remember to celebrate your successes and everything you achieve. That's the only way you'll be able to achieve everything you desire. Celebrate your achievements. Always.' With those words still ringing in my ears and the training session nearing completion, I found myself looking up to the sky in gratitude for another life teaching I'd received. I promised myself that, from that day on, things would improve and I'd change my attitude to life and to my dreams. I'd be kind to myself and would celebrate every achievement, big or small, on my life journey.

London, 2 December 2019

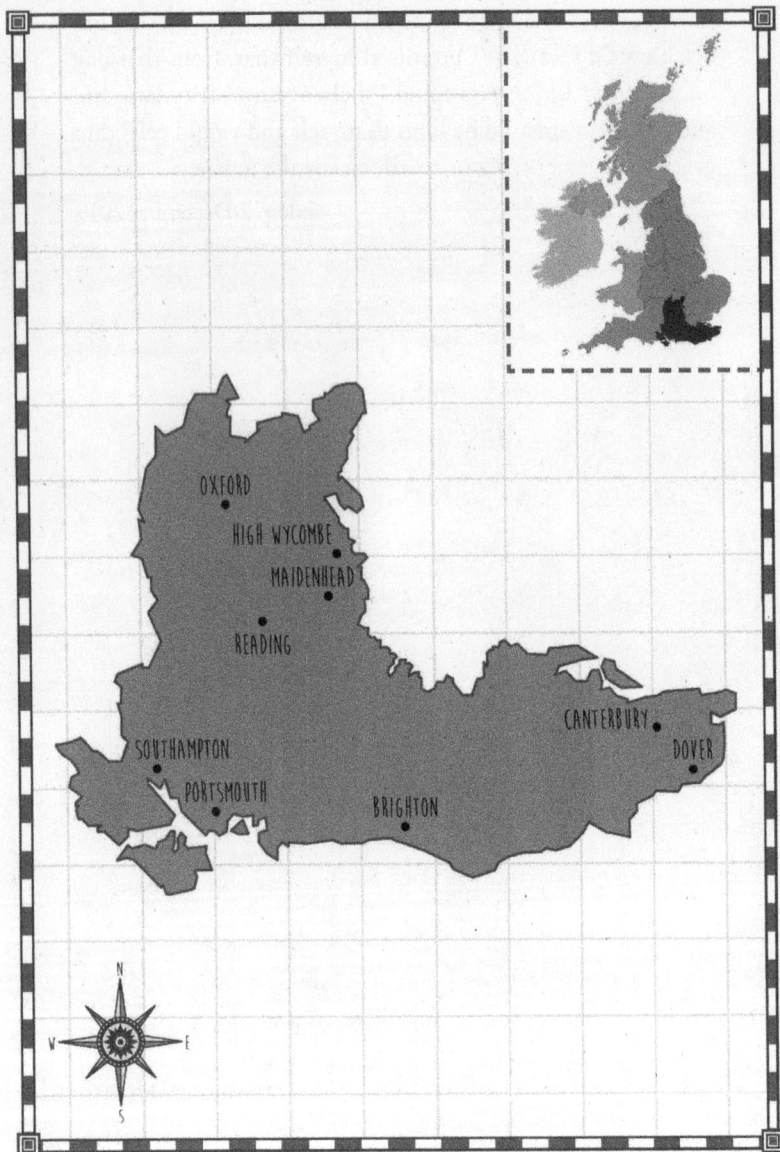

OXFORD

HIGH WYCOMBE

MAIDENHEAD

READING

SOUTHAMPTON

PORTSMOUTH

BRIGHTON

CANTERBURY

DOVER

N
W   E
S

SOUTH EAST

There we were, running around without a care in the world on the green grass above the majestic cliffs of Dover. Giuseppe was in a state of bliss as the sun beamed down upon us, accompanying us in that magical moment we were indulging in. Before then, we'd only been able to admire those white cliffs in photos. And while a photo can convey much of their mystique, seeing them with our own two eyes was a feeling impossible to put into words. As we trod our way carefully along the narrow footpaths overlooking the sea, strong winds swirled around us all morning. When we visited Dover Castle, standing tall above the city, it felt like we'd taken a step back in time.

I got the same feeling as I sauntered around the streets of Southampton with Lucio, taking in the history of the city where the inimitable Matt Le Tissier – Le God – became a legend.

We're off on another journey. Over the coming pages, I'll transport you to new places, relate magnificent meetings and detail centuries-old stadiums. We won't be visiting Matt Le Tissier's Southampton but there will be plenty of thrills nonetheless!

BRIGHTON, HOME OF THE SEAGULLS

Dozens and dozens of seagulls flew above my head, squawking incessantly, and a light breeze swirled around me making the air feel much cooler. On the horizon, the calm, flat sea merged with the darkening blue sky as day turned to night.

A magnificent full moon lit up the sky while I trudged back towards the railway station to catch my return train to the centre of London. But when I reached the station, I suddenly felt a void inside me.

It was a hot day in early August, and sun, sea, serenity and football were my daily bread. As the train pulled out of the station heading for London, I looked out the window and felt my heart overflowing with gratitude for the wonderful, unforgettable day I'd just had.

⚽ ⚽ ⚽

The clock hands pointed to 9.00am as I alighted from my carriage and left the station. A small flock of seagulls circled above me, welcoming me to Brighton. Invigorated by the sight of the deep blue sea on the horizon, I hastily made my way down to the beach in just over ten minutes. When the ocean opened up before my eyes I suddenly felt like a little kid – I couldn't resist the urge to take off my shoes and go for a paddle.

I did so, and then, after walking a fair way along the shore, I lay down to enjoy the sun. In that moment I heard a familiar sound behind me. Four young lads, all wearing Atlético Madrid shirts, were playing keep-up with a ball. I put aside any feeling of awkwardness and politely asked if I could join in. They agreed without a moment's hesitation. We messed about together for a good half-hour before jumping in for a dip. The water was very cold and the unrelenting cool breeze didn't help. But then I caught a waft of fish and chips. I quickly dried myself down and a few minutes later I was ordering that most typical of English dishes, my mouth watering.

I sat down with my prize next to Brighton Pier and savoured every morsel of it, until I realised that time was passing and my mission here was not just sun, sea, and fish and chips. I was here for the football, of course!

A few miles away stood my destination, Falmer Stadium, nestled in the rolling hills of the South Downs. That day a prestigious friendly was to be played between Brighton & Hove Albion and Atlético Madrid. It would be the cherry on top of a fantastic day.

Hundreds and hundreds of blue-and-white striped jerseys swarmed around the stadium, the relaxed, party atmosphere reminding me that football in England is much more than just a sport. Families, pensioners, men, women and children were all enjoying the moment – and the return of their team to the big time.

Brighton hadn't played in the English top flight for 34 years – long before the advent of the Premier League – and having a top European club visit them was a source of great pride for all the fans. You could read the joy on the faces of the people.

When I passed through the turnstiles I took my seat and sat there dumbfounded. It was like being in a cartoon. Everything around me seemed perfect. The blue seats, representing the sea, were the perfect match for the white seagulls – the symbol of the club and the city. The finishing touch was the green hills, which could be glimpsed between the corners of the stands.

Believe me when I tell you that everything about that day was utterly marvellous. It was like a dream. I expect the Seagulls fans felt something similar the first time they set foot inside their new home when it opened in 2011. Their previous home, the historic Goldstone Ground, was sold by the owners in 1997 to pay off crippling debts. A decision they took without consulting the fans in any way and, even more disgracefully, without having another stadium to play in.

Those were dark years. For two seasons the club played their 'home' games at Gillingham's Priestfield Stadium, over 70 miles away. Then they returned to Brighton and played at Withdean Stadium, just a couple of miles from the city centre, from 1999 to 2011.

At the peak of the crisis, in 1997, Brighton were knocking about in the old Third Division. When the board was eventually ousted, Dick Knight took control of the club – much to the supporters' delight. A local businessman and lifelong Brighton fan, Mr Knight became chairman and quickly restored stability, steering the club back up through the divisions.

When another potential owner eventually threw his hat into the ring 12 years later, in May 2009, Dick Knight only stepped aside after making sure the new chairman was able to provide the funding for the new stadium. As promised, Tony Bloom delivered and, in July 2011, Falmer Stadium, the Seagulls' new home, was opened.

When the home side and Atlético Madrid entered the field of play, the squeals of joy from a nearby child, to a backdrop of chants and rhythmic clapping, stole my heart. That sunny August afternoon was witness to a fast-paced game of attacking football. The visitors edged it 3-2, but that didn't dampen the spirits of the home supporters one iota.

As the players made their way back towards the dressing rooms at full time, the screams of support and long, drawn-out applause brought down the curtain on a magnificent day of football. Indeed, I was enjoying myself so much that I only left the stadium when the stewards kindly ushered me towards the exit.

When I left that beautiful green turf, where all my dreams and those of millions of other people lie, I found myself in the midst of a group of kids having a kickabout, all wearing the blue and white stripes of their beloved Brighton. With a happy heart, I savoured every minute of that match as it took me back to when I was a child playing in the streets with my friends just like them, dreaming of emulating my heroes and playing for the best teams in the world.

For them, however, it was different. They didn't imagine themselves playing for a big club. The dream in their hearts was to turn out for their beloved Brighton, a unique club by the sea, basking in the sun's rays with seagulls as friends. Their dream was to fly high like the seagulls in their city.

WELCOME TO YORK ROAD: HOME OF MAIDENHEAD UNITED FC

It was 16 February 1871 when the first fans of Maidenhead witnessed a ball being kicked around in York Road. Since that day, nothing has been able to stop them playing in the same charming little stadium. I've had the honour of standing on those concrete stands, patched up in various spots, on three separate occasions.

York Road reeks of history and tradition – nothing like those squalid brand-new stadiums without so much as a hint of history about them. The clubhouse provides shelter and warmth on those cold, rainy, non-league football days, and that's exactly where I found myself before, during and after their match against Barrow AFC in March 2018, sipping a pint with the Magpies fans while taking in other games on TV. It was the sort of atmosphere I'd only seen in films before.

As I observed the smiling, relaxed patrons with Maidenhead United scarves wrapped around their necks and a pint glass in hand, I fell in love with that beautiful, unfamiliar world. It's a special place steeped in history with football at the heart of it all.

⚽⚽⚽

I've passed through hundreds of turnstiles in my time. From those at the majestic Old Trafford to those at tiny, enchanting facilities in the tenth tier. At first glance they may all appear the same, but as I went through the York Road turnstiles, after buying a ticket from an old man sitting on a comfy chair next to a little heater, I realised that something was different. It was somewhat of a struggle to squeeze through those very narrow turnstiles with decades of history behind them.

In that precise moment, overcome with the excitement of being where I was, I tried to imagine how many football lovers had passed through there before me, since 1871. Then when York Road opened up before my eyes, it felt like I was stepping into a fairy-tale book, which we dreamed of doing as children.

The giant letters reading MAIDENHEAD UNITED on the walls at the Bell Street end with pretty rooftops dotted around behind it caught me unawares. The smell of history reigned supreme, together with the passion of the proud fans who filled the York Road terraces despite the cold and rain. The thrashing wind slammed against our faces and I could barely feel my frozen hands. The fans' chanting made the atmosphere slightly warmer but as soon as the ref blew for half-time nearly everyone in attendance – including the away fans – made a dash for the clubhouse to warm up and recharge with some beer.

The rest of the match was played out in near silence, and when Barrow took the lead – with the sky becoming darker by the minute and my feet now as numb as my hands – all I wanted was to be somewhere warm. Before leaving, I went to say goodbye to Neil Maskell, the club secretary whom I'd met shortly before the match.

'Ivan, come back for our match against Sutton United. You'll be our guest and we're going to tell your story in the match programme!'

When I returned exactly two weeks later I was greeted by even colder climes. Snow and rain had been falling all night, and the pitch, despite being well looked after, wasn't exactly in pristine condition. The game was at risk of being called off.

'Hi, Ivan. Welcome back to York Road. We're so happy to have you here!' Neil greeted me as you would a friend. After opening the doors of the clubhouse and offering me a drink, as promised he showed me the match programme with my story told within its pages. I cannot put into words the thrill I felt seeing myself in a match programme for the first time.

After half an hour in the warm, welcoming clubhouse, Neil came back and told me the match was going ahead and that he'd take me on a tour of some of the out-of-bounds areas of York Road. A few minutes later, giddy and in disbelief, I found myself in a little room where the club's history was safely guarded. As I immersed myself in the photos, the old pennants, paintings of York Road and black-and-white newspaper cuttings, Neil called me over to show me a trophy of great value to the club.

'This is the Berks & Bucks Senior Cup, set up in 1878/79. The FA Cup had only come into existence seven years earlier and there was no Football League at the time. What you're holding there, Ivan, is a piece of history!'

Neil was elated to take me on a journey through his world, and I couldn't stop smiling, so in love with it as I was. Placing my hands on such an ancient trophy was a special, emotional experience.

'This cup is played between the non-league teams of Berkshire and Buckinghamshire. We first won it in 1894/95 and since then we've won it over 20 times.' I was at a loss for what to say but my sparkling eyes spoke for me.

Neil sensed my emotion and, when we parted, he told me I'd always be welcome back – perhaps to present my book or to work in their academy as a coach. Still incredulous and over the moon for the marvellous reception, I thanked him again and again. As I edged towards the clubhouse, holding my hand on my heart in gratitude and telling him I'd never forget his kindness, the rain continued to tumble down incessantly. The pitch was looking less and less playable.

I was quite enjoying the atmosphere inside the warm and welcoming clubhouse by now, but when the referee blew the opening whistle, with the deluge showing no signs of abating,

I ran up to the top of the terraces in the Bell Street stand, singing at the top of my voice with the home fans, in the vain hope that I'd warm up more quickly.

The players, soaked to the bone and caked in mud, slid around on the heavy and by now rather sorry-looking turf, whipping the fans on those glacial terraces into a frenzy. These fans follow and support their team home and away, braving whatever the British weather has to throw at them – more often than not, cold, wind and rain – to spend 90 minutes of their time standing on the concrete terraces of a stadium that offers no creature comforts, a far cry from the bright lights of the stadiums on TV.

Sadly, on some occasions, such as that afternoon in late March, rain ran out as the winner. At half-time, with the pitch now completely unplayable and Sutton United leading 3-2, the referee was forced to abandon the match, evoking sadness in all of us. However, that sadness was soon replaced by the feelings of joy and excitement that magical place had bestowed upon me.

A magical stadium with a train running past it, with the rooftops of those typically British houses sprouting from behind the Bell Street stand, with Neil and the other fans making me feel at home at the ever-so-charismatic York Road. A stadium whose charm stretches back 150 years, through the generations, to 1871, making it the oldest football ground in the world continuously used by the same club.

That ground and that club won my heart, made me feel at home and gave me feelings and memories that will accompany me forever on my life journey.

MY STORY ON MAIDENHEAD UNITED'S MATCH PROGRAMME

IVAN: YORK ROAD DREAM

York Road has always been a popular venue for ground-hoppers. The history of our much loved old home combined with our town centre location and proximity to the railway station makes the ground an attractive proposition for those with an enthusiasm for ticking off visits to genuine places of footballing heritage.

Our recently elevated status as a National League club with larger crowds and increased publicity has only served to spread the word yet further. At the recent home game with Barrow a 'calcio inglese' enthusiast made his first visit to our ground for a match and intends on featuring Maidenhead United and York Road in his planned book on the subject.

Ivan Ambrosio is a 24 year old Neapolitan who has moved to London from Italy and has fallen in love with English football. Quite extraordinarily, York Road is one of 316 football grounds that Ivan has visited in the UK and Ireland alone. Ivan had heard all about the long and significant history of our home and he braved the bitterly cold weather to attend the Barrow match. And it was clear that York Road left a lasting impression on him. "It was fantastic and I really like the stadium. The thing I liked best was the name 'Maidenhead United' spelled out at the back of the terrace against the backdrop of the roof-tops". The Barrow match was hardly a classic encounter as the

Magpies slipped to a single-goal defeat but Ivan remained enthusiastic: "I was sorry for the defeat, but the guys tried to do their best. Congratulations to the fans, it was nice to be part of you for one day of my life!".

Ivan intends to include his York Road odyssey in his forthcoming tome which has the working title 'Story of a Dream'. Ivan explains: "Completing this project, for me, would be the realisation of a dream that I have been carrying forward for years with passion and love for England and for English football. Moreover, I hope with all my heart to transmit healthy and important values of life. In the book we will not only talk about football and stadiums, but above all about how to face the difficulties to reach a dream, never give up and always believe in what the heart tells us. We must believe in dreams, because sooner or later they will come true."

Stirring stuff! Ivan you will be most welcome back at York Road one day, perhaps to sell copies of your book. Ivan has indeed promised to return and perhaps Alan Devonshire needs to watch his back as he explains "I hope to come back soon. Maybe as a coach, my big dream!" Having watched so many matches in 4 years Ivan would at least make a very knowledgeable scout!

STAND UP IF YOU LOVE WYCOMBE

The sun was beating down on High Wycombe on that balmy May day. The houses along Lane End Road, which leads to the stadium, were bedecked with flags and banners in Wanderers colours. A line of trees with thick, green foliage joined up perfectly with the bright blue sky, giving you the impression of walking inside a painting. The atmosphere was the sort that fans dream of all season long. Men of all ages, women and hundreds of chirpy, smiling children sporting their Wycombe Wanderers shirts teemed around Adams Park, with music blaring, flags waving and chant after chant being sung. They were celebrating promotion that day and there was no better place for a fantastic, unforgettable day of football.

❀ ❀ ❀

Green, and more green. Trees as far as the eye can see. Adams Park stands in a valley surrounded on three sides by the gentle hills of West Wycombe Park. For years I'd wanted to see it, and when I finally set foot on the little hill, it felt like a dream come true. A small but very pleasant dream. From the top of the hill, in the distance I could see the first fans passing through the turnstiles and slowly starting to fill the stands of their home. There was a party atmosphere, and I was looking forward to savouring every second of it with them, feeling part of their beautiful little family. Before then, though, there was time for a quick history lesson. A story that began in 1887.

As chance would have it, after leaving the hill I found myself telling my own story to Mark Burrell, a club director. Amazed by what I told him and in high spirits due to the party mood, Mark didn't think twice about opening up the doors to the ground and welcoming me into his home. Less than ten minutes later, I was being shown around Adams Park.

Walking around the heart of the stadium, I immersed myself in the club's history one photo at a time, starting with black-and-white images before working my way through to the day Martin O'Neill arrived at Loakes Park – Wycombe Wanderers' home from 1895 to 1990. Burrell explained:

> Martin is a legend here. He joined in February 1990 and none of us will ever forget what he did. We were playing in the fifth tier at the time. We missed out on promotion to the Football League on goal difference in 1991/92 but went up the following season, winning the Conference by 15 points. We also won the FA Trophy again that year, repeating the success of two seasons earlier. Having taken us into the professional Football League for the first time in our history, the very next season Martin got us promoted again, to the Second Division [third tier at the time], by winning the play-offs. We were in dreamland! From non-league to the Second Division!

The more Mark spoke, the more his eyes lit up with glee. It didn't take much to realise that the stories he was telling me with such pride were coming from the bottom of his heart. Having fallen in love with everything around me and quite content to sit there listening to Mark, I almost didn't want to leave – but there was a party waiting.

As eager as could be, I hugged Mark and ran to the turnstiles, rushed through and took my place on the terraces. The chants, drums, balloons and a sea of flags made for an electrifying environment. With just over half an hour to go before kick-off, Adams Park was completely packed. It was a beautiful sunny day and the only thing that could make it any better was the start of the match itself.

The players were in good cheer as they warmed up, waving to the crowd singing one chant after another in honour of their heroes. Meanwhile, the players who were due to start on the bench played with their kids. Every time one of the youngsters put the ball in the back of the net, the crowd erupted with joy and cranked up their singing voices. Some of the others, including the powerhouse fan favourite Adebayo Akinfenwa, went around signing autographs and dishing out smiles to the hordes of kids waiting patiently for a photo.

At long last, the two teams took to the pitch and the referee blew his whistle to commence play. As the minutes passed, the decibels seemed to spiral and I became more and more caught up in the Wycombe Wanderers spell. It wasn't long before I found myself singing along with them, jumping in unison. I felt like one of the family. When Matt Bloomfield gave us the lead in the 19th minute, Adams Park exploded. I don't really recall what happened in that moment but I was submerged by a tidal wave of elation that further accentuated the electric atmosphere. Looking back on that day now, years later, I can still hear the fans' chants and unremitting clapping reverberating in my head.

The remaining 70 minutes felt more like a party than a football match, with dancing and singing, balloons and bare chests all forming a crescendo until the final whistle. A pitch invasion was in everyone's mind, besides being one of my lifelong dreams. When the final whistle blew, I clambered over the low fence separating the terraces from the pitch and felt an uncontrollable feeling of joy.

All my life I'd dreamed of experiencing English football grounds first-hand, but never in my wildest dreams could I have imagined celebrating Wycombe Wanderers' promotion to League One as one of their supporters. It was astonishing. You can only begin to imagine how exhilarated I felt as we swept across that pitch with abandon. I remember the squeals of delight as I ran across the turf with hundreds of other fans, giggling like a child as I lapped up a moment I'd cherish dearly forever more.

Wycombe was a different trip. Unforgettable and soul-stirring. Whenever I think back to that gorgeous early May day, with the sun gently warming my skin as I walked to the stadium past those picture-perfect trees in bloom, I feel butterflies in my stomach. The sort of feeling only football can induce. Less a sport, more a raison d'être.

As I touched the gates of the former, glorious Loakes Park, which now stand outside Adams Park in reverential memory, I realised that, although time passes and everything eventually disappears, the most important thing is for us to hold memories in our hearts. And that I will, treasuring the emotions of that day at Adams Park with the small but mighty Wycombe Wanderers.

OHHH VITO MANNONE, OHHH VITO MANNONE

For many years, when I was younger, my chief concern was cheering for my favourite team and footballers. I'd scream with joy and celebrate in the silliest ways. I'd kiss posters of my favourite player and sleep with his shirt under my pillow. I'd cry, feel sick and anxious when things didn't go well. I'd sing for my team as I watched them home and away. I was always there for them. I'd get into an argument with anyone to defend them. And I was willing to give up anything to watch them. Now, years later, that's all changed.

The passion I felt for my team slowly waned, as did my level of support. My journey into English football has given me the opportunity to experience everything I always dreamed of, and now those years of chants, thrills and celebrations are but a fond, distant memory. I genuinely miss being a fan, but it's not something you can choose – it's a feeling that comes from deep inside.

Another feeling I had no control over came across me one afternoon towards the end of March in 2018. It was the 92nd minute of the match between Reading and Queens Park Rangers. The home side were leading 1-0 and the visitors had the opportunity to equalise with a penalty. QPR's No.3 Jake Bidwell stepped up to face Reading's No.1 Vito Mannone …

⚽ ⚽ ⚽

I didn't meet Vito for the first time on that cold March afternoon, but five months previously, before Reading's match against Nottingham Forest on 31 October 2017. And I owe that meeting to the kindness of a lovely chap called Alberto, whom I met by chance in Milan in June 2017, at the fifth Italian Connection tournament.

'Hi, Ivan. I saw your interview on Sky Sport a while ago and your story touched me. I'd really like to help you. I work for Gianluca Di Marzio. If you ever need anything, you can count on me!'

That's how Alberto introduced himself to me. It's been a few years now since we first met but I'll never forget his kind, sincere eyes – very similar to Vito's. A genuine person with good values.

'Hi, Ivan, here's your ticket. It's really nice to meet you. I'll see you after the game in the Players' Lounge.' That's how Vito welcomed me to the stadium.

As the other players got out of their cars and walked undisturbed towards the many fans waiting for them, my gaze became completely lost in the beauty of that moment. I stood and watched as a friendly, smiling Vito – together with his team-mates – signed autographs and brought joy to the faces of dozens and dozens of children, gifting them a special, unforgettable moment. I was moved by that scene, seeing how down-to-earth this man I'd previously only admired on TV was. That big man with a big heart had made his dreams come true one save at a time, working hard and overcoming the many obstacles life has placed in his path.

On that October evening, my own path led me to Gate 1 of the Madejski Stadium's West Stand for Reading's Championship match against Nottingham Forest. It was the same gate I found myself hurrying through five months later, when I returned to Reading for the game against Queens Park Rangers. I have a vivid memory of the cold, incessant rain on that 30 March 2018.

Vito's wife Fiorella, whom I'd also met a few months earlier at the Nottingham Forest game, was waiting for me.

'Ciao, Fiorella. Sorry I'm late but the traffic was atrocious. All the roads are blocked because of the bad weather.' I greeted Fiorella, still panting for breath, and took my seat just in time to hear the notes of 'Sweet Caroline' welcoming the players on to the pitch.

There would be no respite from the wind, rain and cold that day. But regardless of the inclement weather and the pitch being somewhat worse for wear as a result, the Royals desperately needed to win, as they were sitting just a few points above the relegation zone.

A wonder goal by Sone Aluko just ten minutes after kick-off sent the Madejski into raptures and gave the Reading fans hope, but the remaining 80 minutes felt like an endless ordeal. QPR were attacking from all angles and every time the ball entered Vito's territory my heart started beating wildly, giving me feelings of anxiety and fear – which then vanished with a sigh of relief once the danger had passed. All of a sudden, I realised the excitement of being a fan had gripped me again. Every time the ball went out of play, I checked how many minutes were left.

Fiorella's eyes were glued to the pitch every second. She was Vito's number-one fan and you could see the tension in her face – the same tension that had taken over myself and all the other spectators. Pain and suffering were a constant that evening.

It felt as if the QPR onslaught would never end, and when David Edwards brought down QPR's No.22 in the area in the 92nd minute, Fiorella and I felt the world crashing down on top of us. The ref awarded the visitors a spot kick with only a minute left to play. I felt anger rising up inside me as I held my head in my hands, but when I saw Fiorella's sad, almost tearful eyes, I told her and myself that Vito would keep it out.

'Vito will save it. I know he will. He'll save it for his mum and dad watching from above. He'll save it for us and for all these people who believe in him. Come on, Vito!' I shouted at the top of my voice, stirring Fiorella in the process.

I really believed he'd save that penalty. It had to be that way. Just a few months earlier Vito's mum had passed away, another pillar of his life no longer by his side. That penalty was his chance to become an idol for the fans and I was utterly convinced he wouldn't let such a big opportunity pass him by.

QPR's No.3, Jake Bidwell, picked up the ball and calmly placed it down on the penalty spot. Boos of fear swirled around him, piercing the surreal silence. You could cut the atmosphere with a knife. There were mere seconds remaining of a game that Reading couldn't afford not to win. Their fate lay in the hands of their goalkeeper. Vito bowed his head and did the sign of the cross to feel the presence of his parents even closer. He stretched his arms out and stared into his opponent's eyes. Jake took a brief run-up, hit it with full force … and Vito saved it!

Yesssss! Yesssss! Yesssss! Fiorella and I glanced up towards the heavens with tears in our eyes as we celebrated wildly, saying over and over again that we knew he'd save it. This was his night and he deserved it more than anyone. A few moments later the final whistle sounded and the Madejski Stadium erupted with elation. All around me people were smiling and hugging each other, jubilation and love written all over their faces.

I'm sure Vito's parents looking down from above will have felt incredibly proud of the boy they'd raised, making all sorts of sacrifices. That boy with a big heart, who had worked his way up from the bottom, was named man of the match that day. I got the chance to spend some time with him after the game and he invited me to have dinner with him and the woman of his life. That's when he began telling me about the key moments from his long career.

He had some incredible stories to share, from joining Arsenal as a 17-year-old to making his Champions League debut for the Gunners. The years spent at Sunderland and a magical night against Manchester United at Old Trafford, when he saved two penalties to take Sunderland into the League Cup Final against Manchester City at Wembley. Idolised by the Sunderland fans, he was named both supporters' player of the year and the club's player of the year that season (2013/14). Finally, he told me about the famous stadium chant he was so proud of, which began life in the stands at the Stadium of Light and journeyed with him all the way to the Madejski, where it rang out loud and clear on that cold March afternoon after his penalty save: 'Ohhh Vito Mannone, ohhh Vito Mannone, ohhh Vito Mannone …'

Much more than a goalkeeper. A friend and my favourite No.1. Simply, Vito Mannone!

OURS

It was 27 November 2008 when I was first mesmerised by one of the most beautiful stadiums in England. I wasn't quite 16 at the time and I spent that Thursday evening playing happily on the PlayStation. I nearly always played FIFA. I'd pick an English team then choose one of the stadiums available. Often it was Old Trafford and I'd dream of the day when I'd get to see it in person.

Even back then I nurtured a deep fascination with English stadiums. And when I saw that the AC Milan side of Kaká, Seedorf, Pirlo, Inzaghi, Ronaldinho and other stars were playing away at Portsmouth – a club whose name I couldn't even pronounce properly then – I was dumbstruck.

At that point in my life I was only used to seeing Italian stadiums, so when I realised the Portsmouth fans could watch the game from as close as two metres behind the white lines around the pitch, without the usual barriers, I could hardly believe my eyes.

Beside myself with excitement, I told my mum and dad, as they listened lovingly, that one day in the not-too-distant future I was going to experience that stadium for myself. It's a special stadium with fans whose passion and veneration for their team's colours are off the scale.

Pack your bags: it's time to set off on a new adventure. I'm taking you to a place by the sea where the working class rules: the historic, glorious home of Portsmouth Football Club awaits. Welcome to Fratton Park!

❂❂❂

My journey to the south coast by bus and train began at 2am on a cold, rainy night in Manchester. It was long and tiring, and when I finally reached my destination I had to be woken from my slumber by the train guard telling me we'd arrived in Portsmouth.

On that late October morning in 2017, Portsmouth welcomed me with a beautiful blue sky and warm sunshine, putting a spring in my step. The happiness I felt wasn't just for the weather and the latest journey I was on but also – and especially – because I'd soon be getting the real Fratton Park experience, something that until then I'd only witnessed and admired on TV.

I'd actually visited the stadium once before, back in July 2016. I managed to sneak in through an open gate and was able to walk undisturbed alongside the green turf that had inhabited my dreams for years.

Since its inauguration in 1899, it has been the battleground for some epic encounters, the stage for some incredible, exhilarating matches. And not just in the league and the FA Cup, for Pompey have enjoyed some memorable European nights too, including that game against the great Milan side in November 2008.

The previous season, Harry Redknapp had guided Portsmouth to victory in the FA Cup, earning the club their first-ever European campaign, in the UEFA Cup. They beat Vitória Guimarães in the first round but were unable to make it past the group stage.

With the likes of Peter Crouch, Sol Campbell, Jermain Defoe and Nwankwo Kanu, among others, Pompey fans had good reason to be genuinely excited about the possibility of seeing their beloved club reach even greater heights. Sadly, though, Pompey would soon find themselves entering the darkest years of the club's history: within four years of playing in Europe, they'd plummeted down the divisions and been relegated to League Two.

It's a chilling tale indeed. When Pompey superfan and lifelong season ticket holder, John Portsmouth Football Club

Westwood began describing those years to me, his words penetrated so deep that I felt myself welling up.

A succession of poor owners between 2006 and 2013 meant the club found itself saddled with tens of millions of pounds of debts, having paid stratospheric fees for players and handed out multi-million-pound contracts, further aggravating the situation. Several changes of ownership and a seemingly never-ending series of problems saw the club go into administration, twice, and reach the verge of bankruptcy.

At the end of this sorry story, the threat of bankruptcy was eventually staved off by the love of the Portsmouth fans. Tired of an absurd situation, they rustled up around £5 million through thousands of donations and tireless efforts over an 18-month period and finally succeeded on 19 April 2013. What they managed to do was buy a majority stake in the club. It thus ended up in the hands of the Pompey Supporters' Trust and its 2,300 members, the names of whom shine proudly outside the stadium. Without their unconditional love, Portsmouth Football Club would have vanished for good.

That love was on full display at Pompey's League Two opener against Oxford United on 3 August 2013, when over 18,000 fans – including 10,000 season ticket holders – squeezed into the stands at Fratton Park. Despite setting a new attendance record for League Two, the crowd didn't see their team triumph that day as they were roundly beaten 4-1 by the visitors. Nonetheless, the match will remain memorable for the incredible welcome offered by the supporters before kick-off, including a giant tifo that read 'OURS'. The club was finally in the hands of the fans and, win or lose, all that mattered to them was being able to watch Portsmouth play, cheering and supporting them to the end.

As John PFC Westwood told me, you have to support your team in the difficult times, not just when everything is rosy. 'And when you lose, you have to sing even louder. Everyone can sing when you're winning.'

John's love for the club is simply astonishing. The man hasn't missed a single Portsmouth match since 1979 – a feat I struggled to believe initially. In the ultimate show of allegiance, besides sporting over 50 Portsmouth tattoos, in August 1989, two months after getting married, he decided to change his name by deed poll, adding the name of his beloved club between his name and surname and thus becoming one with Portsmouth Football Club.

John's eyes brimmed with unbridled passion – the same passion I sensed rippling through the thousands and thousands of spectators surrounding Fratton Park when I visited it on that Saturday afternoon in autumn. It's a stadium steeped in history, full of shabby charm in every corner, from the delightful pavilion up through Specks Lane behind the away stand – a run-down, largely neglected street, lined with graffitied walls and garages, weeds and back gardens with washing hung out to dry. It's not hard to imagine the unsavoury incidents that unfolded there years ago.

Back in the day when hooliganism was rife, that ominous little lane witnessed violent scenes between rival groups. Fortunately, when I walked down it, everything was very peaceful, despite the presence of both home fans and those of Bradford City, who had travelled many hours down from the north. It turned out to be a worthwhile trip for them as Bradford left the south coast with all three points. Albeit without ever silencing the Fratton Park faithful in the stands.

It's a magical place where passion and charm reign supreme. Where you can stretch your arm out and touch the turf. Where signs warn you to 'beware of players falling into this area'.

For 90 minutes those fans did nothing but sing and chant fervidly – not just for the boys in blue on the pitch, but for the shirt and the club they love. The team's colours run through their veins, giving them a feeling of complete happiness only when they're in the stands at Fratton Park. A place they call home and that, in the darkest days of their history, they defended with honour, fighting with gritted teeth against everyone and everything to save their beloved club.

These are exceptional, unique fans who firmly believe in the 'support your local team' philosophy. Theirs is a team that will never be abandoned, regardless of the division they play in. Because for them there's nothing better than Portsmouth Football Club!

CHAPTER 9
FIND YOUR OWN WAY

*A ship is always safe at shore, but that is
not what it is built for.*

Albert Einstein

THERE I was, blubbing in front of everybody. I lay my head
on the desk in shame, wrapped my arms round it and shut my
eyes. The tears just wouldn't stop. As my classmates and the
teacher laughed at my pathetic attempts to read in English,
all I wanted was to disappear.

Then the lesson resumed as if nothing had happened,
and I raised my tearful gaze and stared into nothing. Sitting
next to me in the silent classroom, my girlfriend whispered
words of encouragement; I turned to her and quietly sobbed:
'I'm never coming back to school, and before long I'll be going
to England. You see if I don't.' Asking no one's permission, I
stood up and walked out.

That day was in October 2012. I was 18, attending my
fourth year of a hoteliers' training course. It was a bad time
for me: my life looked bleaker with every day that passed.
Nothing made me happy – alas, not even football.

The village where I lived did nothing but constrain and
frustrate my dreams. The prevailing mentality there made
me feel like a misfit, so all I wanted was to get out for good.

Problems at home didn't help, and my chances of making it as a footballer had dwindled to zero. I felt lost and increasingly out of place. But getting away was far from easy. My family has never had much money and at that time my dad was out of work for a while, making things even harder. So I decided to find a job, at least to earn enough money for a one-way ticket to London.

As I've already recounted, that ticket took me away from everything and everyone, bringing me face to face with failure, but giving me the best, the greatest and most formative experience of my life. That move to England made me find out who I really am, and I learned to appreciate – even love – everything that confronted me on my path. I can't honestly say I liked washing dishes or flipping thousands of burgers in a Manchester McDonald's, but I can say that it was because of those jobs and others like them that I've learned so many of life's lessons.

I've learned to appreciate people, from managers to kitchen skivvies. There's no distinction. In fact, truth to be told, I've seen more honesty in the eyes of washers-up than in those of a host of bullying managers. I've learned to look people in the eye, and to listen when someone's got something to say. I've learned to hold my tongue, because I've understood that there's a time to speak and a time to shut up.

I've learned how to get my hands dirty, doing all kinds of jobs without a fuss. From cleaning the toilets in a restaurant to working as a private waiter for the family of a Chelsea player, at Stamford Bridge, watching the match.

I've learned – and I'm still learning – to speak my mind, and I've learned to judge people not for what they say but on the strength of what they do. I've learned how to get on with everybody, and then decide who I can do without. It's crucial to be able to recognise good people and shady types alike.

I've learned that there's nothing better than to see others smile, particularly if they're happy because of something you've done.

I've learned to say please, thank you and sorry. I've learned to be kinder all the time, but never forgetting what I absorbed as I grew up in the streets of my village at the gates of Naples. Kind all right, but no mug.

I've learned to talk about my fears and insecurities. I've learned to ask for help, and how to give it. I've learned to recognise my weaknesses. I've learned to face and get through the stormiest of days, knowing that after every storm comes a rainbow, after every rainbow comes the sun. I've learned to have faith. It has saved and changed my life. That, I owe to my wonderful mum.

I've learned to act always and only with love in my heart. And to recognise my mistakes and analyse them, so as not to repeat them. I don't always succeed, but I'm trying.

I've learned to appreciate the village where I was born and grew up, and, importantly, to love Italy, in the hope that it will soon be able to give me what it has thus far denied me.

I've learned to love my family, all the more so from afar. I've learned – and I'm still learning – to live in the here and now. I've learned to live life my way, by my rules. I've learned to reach out to others. Sometimes, though, even now, too often forgetting myself …

I've learned how to live with the bare necessities. And I've learned English, mindful of when the teacher and most of the class were laughing at me. I've learned all this and more besides, as I hope to learn many other things, tomorrow and every other day of my life. I've learned that nothing in life comes free, that you've got to build your own path to your dreams – fighting, more often than not, against everything and everyone.

Lastly, I've learned to have courage, to face my fears and to find my own way. It's a long and winding road, starting from a Neapolitan village and passing through England, with an uncertain future, but one sure thing, wherever I may be: a happy heart – today, tomorrow and forever. Nothing more, nothing less.

And you, have you found your own way?

London, 6 February 2020

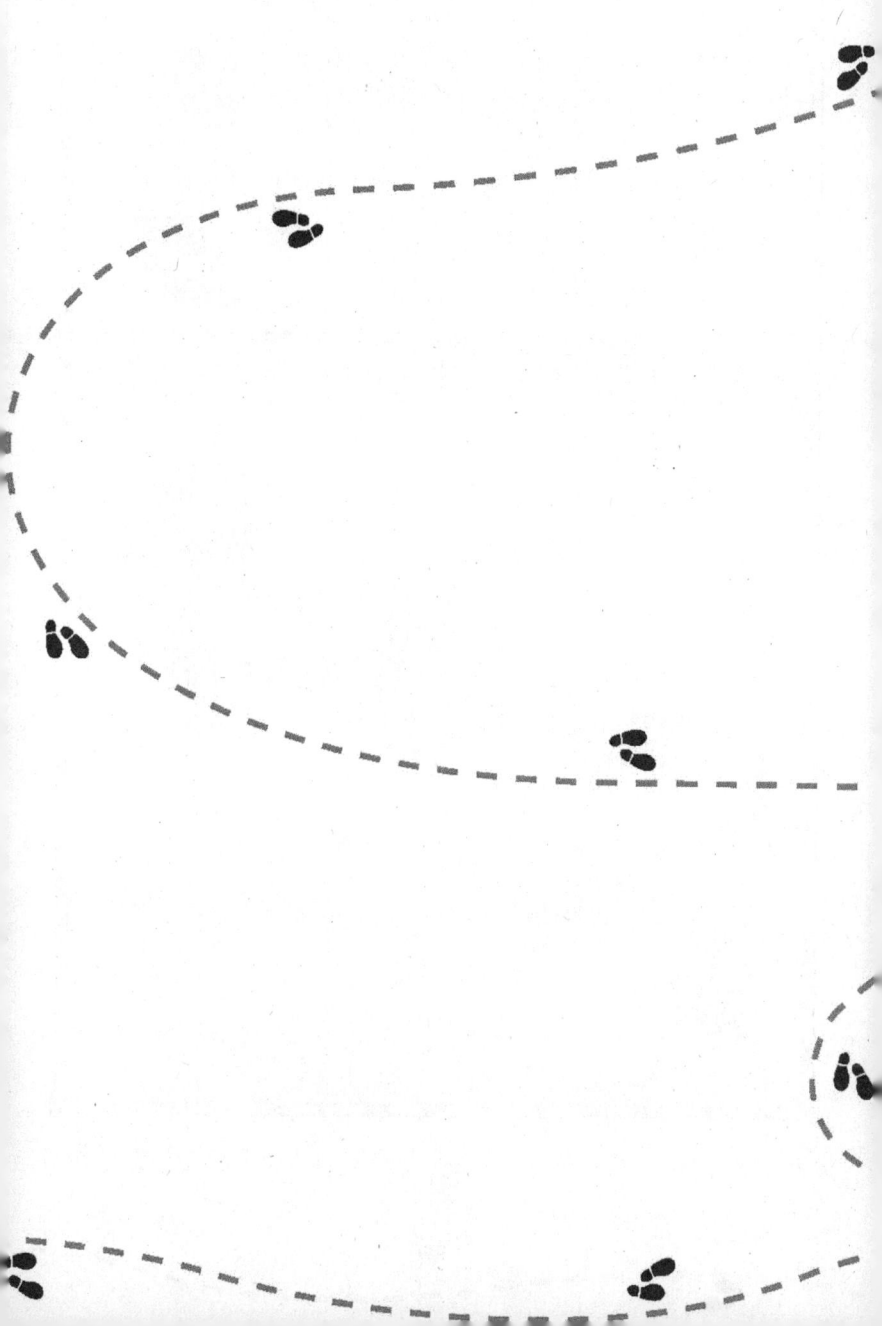

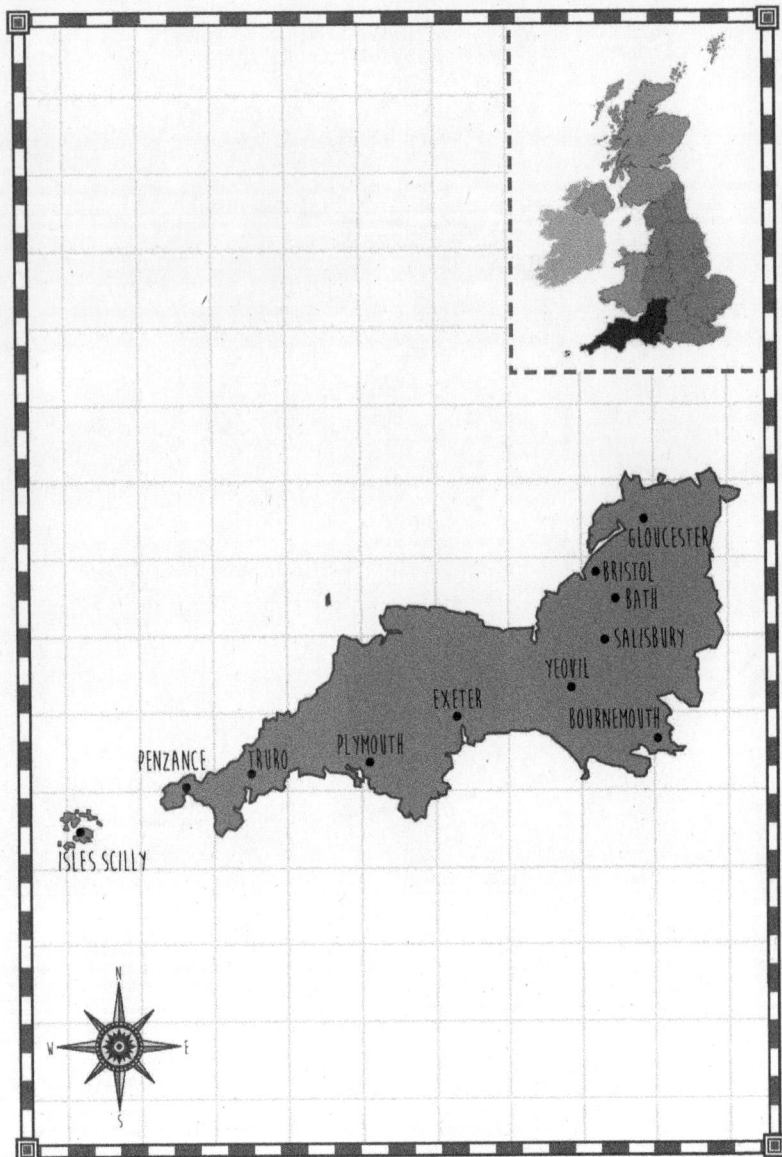

SOUTH WEST

The ancient mystique of Stonehenge, the magnificent arch of Durdle Door on the Jurassic Coast and the bucolic charm of Castle Combe. The splendid cities of Bath, Exeter and Bristol and the seaside attractions of Bournemouth. The picture-postcard beauty of Penzance and nearby St Michael's Mount. The Scilly Isles and the whole of Cornwall.

The South West is a marvellous area, one of those that you simply must visit at least once in your life. Its magic is particularly strong in the summer, its hundreds of beaches ideal for relaxing in the sun. But it's not just magical scenery and historical sites – it's home to a diverse range of football clubs. The tiny Forest Green Rovers, famous for being the world's first vegan football club, is in the quiet heart of the Cotswolds. Time there seems to have stood still: visitors drive past centuries-old cottages as the road signs warn of the possible presence of elderly pedestrians along the way. The South West is all this and much more.

The following pages recount my discovery of football clubs great and small, and also my journey to the Scilly Isles. Those islands are home to the world's smallest football league championship – the Isles of Scilly Football League.

All ready? We're off again.

TOGETHER, ANYTHING IS POSSIBLE

I got up at dawn that morning. I picked up my rucksack, made my way to the beach and sat down quietly near the waterline. The gentle lapping of the breakers and the continual cries of the seagulls relaxed my mind. The sun was about to anoint a new day. I'd have loved to stay there like that for hours, but a new adventure awaited me. The previous evening's match between Bournemouth and Middlesbrough was now a pleasant memory and the train to Glasgow would be leaving in a few hours – it certainly wasn't going to wait for me.

I left Bournemouth that morning with a heavy heart, as I always did. That cosy south coast resort had conquered me again, won my heart and raised my spirits, first with the sun and then with the rain. And with its heroic stories, battles won with gritted teeth, football at the centre of everything. The stories of great little AFC Bournemouth.

⚽⚽⚽

Sometime before, late one afternoon towards the end of July, the sky over Bournemouth began to turn red, orange, pink and yellow, regaling the eyes and heart with one of the most romantic visions life has to offer. The sun was about to set, the moment enhanced by the delicacy of the wavelets descending on the wet sand and discreetly withdrawing whence they came. Dozens of seagulls swirled and bantered overhead. As the sun took its leave and bade welcome to the night, I turned my gaze heavenwards and made a promise: 'Dear Bournemouth, in just a few hours you have stolen my heart. We shall meet again.'

And so we did. I returned to the Dorsetshire coast 15 months later, not only to visit the ground, as I had the first time, but to watch a League Cup match against Middlesbrough. On that late October Tuesday in 2017 I was met not by holiday sunshine but by rain, cold and a fierce wind – England reverting to type.

For more than an hour I walked on the beach that had so moved me the first time. Then I tore myself away and set out for Dean Court, the neat, unpretentious home of AFC Bournemouth since 1910, when the club went under the name of Boscombe Football Club. It took me half an hour to walk from the beach to Bournemouth's ground. I was still a few hundred yards away when I saw the floodlights above the houses surrounding it.

An old couple slowly walked hand in hand towards the entrance to the Main Stand, while a group of children, decked out in the club colours, kicked a football around. My eye was caught by a motto displayed on Dean Court's main façade: 'Together, anything is possible.' For the club and the people of Bournemouth it's an article of faith, a principle that has enabled them to achieve ever-greater ambitions, starting low and reaching high.

Theirs is a story that almost beggars belief, especially in the 2008/09 season. Beset by financial problems and on the verge of bankruptcy, the club began the campaign having been docked 17 points. Playing under that handicap in League Two, with the fans' morale at an all-time low, relegation out of the Football League seemed to be only a question of time.

Against all the odds and all predictions, Bournemouth managed to stay up. Thanks first to the arrival of the ridiculously young manager, Eddie Howe, and then to the return of their much-loved striker Steve Fletcher.

A product of the club's youth system, Eddie Howe racked up 270 matches in a Bournemouth shirt before having his playing career ended by a series of knee injuries. Having gained his coaching badges, at the tender age of 31 he was offered and accepted the job of manager on 31 December 2008. With the support of his players, club chairman Jeff

Mostyn and, in particular, all the devoted fans, he pulled Bournemouth back from the brink of disaster. But he did more than that. He laid the foundations for their future, built on a solid work ethic and the togetherness of a family spirit. A spirit that in the following season lifted them to promotion to League One.

Far from sated by that remarkable turnaround, in the space of five years Eddie Howe succeeded in taking the club to a level it had never reached before – the 2014/15 season saw Bournemouth make their debut in the Premier League.

Walking around the tiny Dean Court ground, I could almost relive that remarkable story – huge photos bearing witness to those moments of pure joy, with the fans, as ever, at the centre of everything. Fans I could only admire on that cold October evening as they gathered for the Middlesbrough match; I'd never seen so many old people and family groups filling up the stands of a football ground.

I went through the turnstiles just over half an hour before kick-off, and when I saw Eddie Howe take the time to say hello to a group of children I understood the meaning of 'Together, anything is possible'. Love, passion, unity, courage, humility, determination, hope and a sense of belonging. Bournemouth is all this and more.

I looked at the eyes of the older supporters as the match got under way, and I tried to conjure the difficult years they'd lived through when their beloved club was on the brink of collapse and relegation into the semi-professional ranks. A fate that – it bears repetition – was miraculously averted, to be followed up a few short years later by dreamland: competing on level terms with Manchester United and Liverpool, Chelsea and Manchester City – the cream of English football.

Age made no difference; all the fans erupted with joy at each of the three goals their team put past their opponents. As the teams trooped off the pitch after the final whistle, I stayed there for a while, marvelling at the brave little world I'd just discovered. It's a simple world, where passion and devotion to the club matter above all else, irrespective of league status and current circumstances.

Bournemouth is the place of golden sands, where the sky meets the sea on the southern horizon and seagulls circle undisturbed all year long. It's a magical place where anything is possible. It's like a family, going to the beach on a sunny mid-August morning, having fish and chips for lunch and then going to Dean Court, currently known as the Vitality Stadium, to support their team.

Humble beginnings, now standing proud; always believing, never giving up – because in Bournemouth they know: dreams can come true and 'Together, anything is possible'.

THE ROMANS

Enchanting in their elegance, the roofs of the city of Bath, thrown into picturesque relief by the green fields alongside the River Avon, vanished rapidly before my eyes, dazzled as they were by the rays of the setting sun. Ensconced in the Somerset countryside, this historic jewel retreated into the distance behind the clear windows of the train that was carrying me to London. For a second time Bath had succeeded in soothing my spirits, at the same time enlivening them with powerful emotions, leaving me with lasting memories and another story to tell …

⚽ ⚽ ⚽

Standing since 1909, Bath City's Twerton Park ground had seen better days. In its tumbledown charm, an air of the past inhabited its every corner. Fixed high on the wall between the players' tunnel and the pitch, the club crest was cracked and mildewed.

It was a cold grey afternoon in March 2017, and all around me was peace and quiet. The only eyes following my wanderings around the ground's old terraces belonged to the sheep grazing serenely on the hill of Innox Park, which rises behind the roofs close to the main stand.

Terraces all around, wooden benches and a somewhat threadbare pitch. The magic of the non-league football world had bewitched me once again; I spotted a ball lying in the corner of one of the goal nets and without a second thought I ran on to the pitch and started playing as if I was in my back garden. Invigorated by the smell of wet grass, I started to shoot at goal. Every time the ball bulged the net I imagined the crowd chanting my name. As we did when we were kids, diving on to our parents' beds, picturing ourselves in the world's most famous grounds. Playing and shouting our own names in the conviction that we'd grow up to be real footballers.

After spending more than half an hour walking down that memory lane, I realised it was time to go. I picked up the ball and kicked it as high as I could, promising it that sooner or later I'd be back. And back I went, just over a year later. Waiting for me this time was not an empty ground all to myself, but a National League South match against Hungerford Town.

That wasn't the only difference. This time I was welcomed to the city by a blue sky and bright sunshine. So I spent the morning exploring the intriguing streets and alleys of the city renowned for its Roman Baths.

Bath City's nickname, The Romans, was emblazoned on the club shirt worn by a supporter who, holding his young daughter by the hand, slowly made his way towards the entrance of the clubhouse, which was all decked out for Family Day. I decided to follow them. As I sipped a pint of Carling and browsed the match programme, dozens of children were having a whale of a time kicking sponge footballs and jumping around on the playground equipment laid out for them. The atmosphere was fabulous.

A short while later, as I bought a match ticket at the turnstiles from an old fellow sat comfortably on his stool, I found myself once again rewinding the tape of time. The narrow old turnstiles were redolent of times gone by. When I'd passed through and was approaching the pitch, old memories resurfaced and I had the sensation of being back home. The grass was crowded with children, playing their little matches and chasing each other round the pitch of Twerton Park.

Rather than attending a fixture in the sixth tier of English football, it was like being in a film. Hundreds of happy children and their families filled the ground, some of them accompanied by their faithful four-legged friends. This was football as I'd always dreamed of it. Made up of sound life teachings passed down to children, giving them a bedrock of values to grow up with and that will stand them in good stead in their everyday lives as much as in sport. The beauty of small things was all there, in the smiles of their loved ones and the mothers' warm embraces of the children as they happily left the playing pitch.

By that time the atmosphere was perfect, the sun beat down on our heads and we couldn't wait for the match to start. Songs and chants, banners unfurled on the terraces, the roofs of the houses around the ground and the backdrop of the surrounding hills – an unforgettable feeling.

Before then I'd had more than my share of experiences around the country, but that day went beyond them. The five goals Bath City put past their opponents rounded off a perfect day for the fans. But for me it had other delights: savouring the history in which the city's streets are steeped, bearing witness to the values of the beautiful game, the children's laughter and their families' contentment. And non-league football played in the quaintly faded charm of Twerton Park. A wonderful setting, impossible to forget and fantastic to relate ...

WELCOME TO ASHTON GATE: THE HOME OF THE ROBINS

On Corn Street, one of Bristol's oldest and most-renowned streets, crowds of people swarmed into and out of the traditional focal point that is St Nicholas Market. Scents of all kinds filled the air, which was cool and sunny on that late September morning in 2017. The city's streets still wore their summer attire, the parks full of flowers and the trees not yet displaying the autumn livery that heralds falling leaves.

With my sometime fellow traveller Andrea, I spent the morning on walkabout in the city's most popular spots. We felt part of those people and places we were seeing for the first time, and went home fulfilled by the experience.

Bristol was a great trip, replete with tastes and smells, rich in history and colour, but above all full of the passion and love devoted by the fans to the game of football and the red of their own special Robins. Welcome to Ashton Gate, home of Bristol City Football Club …

⚽ ⚽ ⚽

The first time I saw Ashton Gate the familiar urge took hold – as soon as I saw an open door I was through it, without a thought for the consequences. I didn't see anyone around me and all I could hear was the sound of my steps and my breathing, so I carried on.

Although the whole ground had recently been refurbished, I could feel I was walking in the midst of history – a history going back as far as 1887. After more than ten minutes of wandering around the stands I began to head for the dugouts with the idea of walking on to the pitch and feeling at the centre of the world.

'Oi! Who are you?' I was stopped in my tracks by the voice behind me, which turned out to belong to a far-from-friendly six-footer. 'How did you get in? And more to the point, what are you doing here?'

I tried to explain that being there was like making a little dream come true, and that after all my pilgrimages I'd write a book about them. That didn't cut much ice. 'You realise I could report you for coming in here without permission. You could even have a bomb or something in that rucksack for all I know.'

'Oh, mamma,' I muttered to myself. My story just didn't wash with that big bald bloke. But although I knew I was in the wrong, I pressed on. I lived in Manchester, so I couldn't come to Bristol every day. And, in any case, the most dangerous thing I could do was get hold of a ball and try a few shots at goal.

'Interesting,' he said. 'So you're visiting all the grounds in England. Have you been to Bristol Rovers by any chance?'

The conversation was beginning to take a delicate turn – the last thing I wanted was to get involved in local football rivalries. Looking into his eyes I could see that he was a good-hearted fellow, so I garnished my reply with a big smile: 'Yes, I was there a couple of hours ago, but this one's much better!'

That drew a laugh – he'd obviously realised I was no terrorist and meant no harm, so he told me his name and invited me to tell my story.

Sitting on the bench about ten minutes later, after I'd related a few of my adventures, he looked at me. 'I like your story,' he decided. 'Come on, I'll show you round Ashton Gate.'

I didn't know whether to be overcome with relief or excitement. Just a few minutes earlier Big Mike seemed to be on the point of chucking me out – bodily if necessary – but now, as we wandered around the silent terraces of Ashton Gate, he began to talk about himself:

You know what, I understand exactly how you must feel. Now you're having a hard time, not only because your dream's still a long way off but because doubts and fears crowd in on you every day.

It takes guts to believe in a dream, but remember that having one is what life's all about. Insecurity, fear of failure, doubts, choices you have to make, sacrifices, tears shed alone, in your case being a long way from home – these aren't easy things to face and overcome. But it's when you do overcome all those things that you'll understand just how much you want to realise your dream. I've been supporting this club for more than 40 years. I'd have loved to play for them, and in a way I've managed to do that. This club is the essence of my life and working here is a real privilege. I'd never have believed I could work for Bristol City – which, by the way, I've got tattooed on my skin – but, step by step, I got there. I've made one of my dreams come true, and I'm sure you'll do the same.

I was bowled over; he spoke to me as though we'd known each other all our lives. When it was time to go, he said, 'Ivan, it's been a real pleasure to meet you and I'm sure your book will make you a rich man.'

I put my hand on my heart:

The pleasure's all mine, Mike, but I'm not bothered about getting rich. Although it's important to have a bit of money in your pocket, what I want is to communicate something healthy and positive to whoever reads the book. In these years. I've realised that life's too short to get lost in fears and insecurity, which is why I think the best thing you can do is to seek out your own happiness. By happiness I mean being well in yourself and with those around you. In my case, I've had to come all the way to England to find happiness. Long story short, I want to make it clear that you have to believe in your dreams and not leave them to mould in a drawer.

Today the very thought of abandoning my dreams makes me shudder. If I'd given up because of fear of failure, where would I be now? Probably somewhere else, living a dissatisfied and unhappy life. The life that millions of people have chosen simply to avoid taking risks. We've only got one life and nobody's going to give us a second chance. The future's in our hands.

Mike had nothing to add to that, but after looking me in the eye and wishing me luck he urged me to return to Ashton Gate to see a match, to experience first-hand the love and the passion of the people of Bristol.

That feeling of belonging was all around six months later, when I went back to the city for a Championship match against Bolton Wanderers and stood on the Ashton Gate terraces again – only this time they were full.

The pre-match atmosphere was one joy after another. Hundreds of children wearing the club kit crowded around the ground, some holding on to their fathers' hands, others in an improvised kickabout in front of the statue of local legend John Atyeo, no doubt dreaming of emulating him.

Live music, craft beers and the club shop with adjoining bar and restaurant left me gaping in wonder. And when I passed through the turnstiles and saw the luminous green of the pitch open up again before me, I understood that Bristol is a city that lives and breathes football.

Fans of all ages filled the Ashton Gate stands, club shirts on their backs and red-and-white scarves around their necks, supporting their players with continual hand-clapped rhythms and songs and chants to tell them of their undying love for the team. A devotion on this occasion reciprocated with a clear-cut 2-0 victory, which excited the fans even more.

These are supporters who thus far have not been able to celebrate great triumphs. But as I celebrated that win with them I understood that the essence of their passion was and always will be encapsulated in the happiness those colours give them every day. On that September evening those colours and those fans touched my heart, taking me back six months to the moment when I walked alone through the gate to the silent stadium. And thinking again of big-hearted Mike, I was reminded of something: dreams can come true and we are the artists of our lives.

COLIN: THE GENTLE GIANT

For about three years of my life I spent more time travelling around England than within the walls of any house, jumping from one train to another and visiting dozens of towns and cities. Train carriages and stations were my daily bread, day and night. Interminable journeys, hundreds of trains I must have ridden, visiting every corner of the country. From north to south, east to west, never missing a train or waiting on the wrong platform. Except once. In Exeter, county town of Devon, I got something wrong. But on that March day life lent me yet another helping hand, giving me one of the most remarkable experiences of my never-ending journey ...

❂❂❂

An open gate on St James Road had given me the chance to explore every nook and cranny of St James Park, home of Exeter City since 1904. I spent half an hour exploring undisturbed in the ground's Old Grandstand. Most of it was built in solid wood, so, run-down though it was, it had its own particular charm.

Walking alongside the pitch I could see the roofs of the houses in the city; I think after all these years that it was one of the most evocative views a football ground has ever offered me.

The railway station, standing behind the Old Grandstand and bearing the same name as the football ground, was enveloped in silence that afternoon. After exploring the ground, I ran into the station, calculating the minutes remaining until the arrival of the train that would take me on to Torquay. It would be stopping at platform 1; for some reason I went to the opposite platform and stood there in incredulous silence when I realised my mistake. I can remember every detail of the moment when I watched helpless as the doors closed and the train left. My heart sank.

The next train would be passing in an hour, and since there was nothing else in the vicinity but the football ground and hundreds of houses, I decided that there was nothing for it but to go into the city centre. I've always hated wasting time, but what else could I do? I was kicking myself because I'd missed the train, and since after Torquay I was supposed to go to Plymouth, where I'd spend the night, to avoid hanging around in the station I decided to go into the centre and find something to eat. As it always does, though, my heart won out.

As I hurried off, wondering how I could have been so stupid, I was struck by the memory of when Jürgen Klopp's Liverpool team came down to England's deep south for an FA Cup third-round tie against the Devonshire lads. And it all came back to me, especially Klopp's famous post-match interview in the little press room at St James Park. Why on earth hadn't I thought of that before? Without further ado, I did an about-turn. Hungry or not, all I wanted was to touch what I'd seen on television a year earlier.

Running back, grinning like a boy on his way to the sweetshop, in a few minutes I was standing outside the ground, this time on Stadium Way, in front of the club shop. I was looking around in the hope of finding a kindly soul who might help me, when I saw a six-footer hefting two big bags of rubbish. 'Hello, mate,' he smiled. 'Need any help?'

'Hello, there. I'd really like to see the changing rooms in the stadium, if possible,' I smiled in return.

'Sure. Come on then!' That's how Colin Baker welcomed me – with open arms. For more than an hour and a half he showed me round the ground, telling me story after story, giving me a conducted tour of true football – football away from the bright lights, where simplicity is its daily bread:

With my family, I've been supporting this club for more years than I care to remember. That's because of my dad, who passed his love of Exeter City on to me. I'm so proud to be actually part of the club, and that's because of what happened in the terrible season of 2002/03. We were on the brink of collapse, and when the chairman and vice-chairman were arrested for fraudulent trading, the club was taken over by its supporters. It was a bad time – after spending most of its life in the Football League, in that year the club suffered its first relegation to the Conference League. It was living the nightmare, and the only way out of it, the only way to keep the club going was to join all our forces.

Loads of fans, including me, donated money to the Exeter City Supporters' Trust, and that summer a group of us took care of the ground. I remember painting the goalposts, sprucing up everything I could find that wasn't in decent condition. Even now, when I'm cleaning the changing rooms or any other part of the stadium I feel pride in what we, the supporters, have achieved.

Colin had so much to tell, and everything he told me came straight from his big heart – it was clear straight away. With a twinkle in his eye he opened the door to the changing rooms and started giggling as he gave me permission to enter, should I be curious to do so.

'Away team. Welcome to St James Park' ran the legend on the door. I walked through it and into fantasy land. Just a year before, that threshold had been crossed by the Liverpool team, and in 2005 by Alex Ferguson's mighty Manchester United. It was a neat and simple place, all the essential things within arm's reach. Two toilets, a tiny washbasin and eight or so showers, with timed cut-offs (of course) so as not to waste water.

'This is real football, Ivan. Sad to say, television companies are only interested in the big clubs, but here we're a family, we all know each other and we're proud of what we have. These changing rooms and this stand have been here since 1926. A lifetime.'

After we'd left the changing rooms and other places accessible only to the few, Colin opened another door. I went through it and found myself surrounded by dozens and dozens of club shirts, historic photos and footballs with who knows what stories behind them. But nothing seemed as important as the walls in a corner of the room. It was there that he began another story:

> After that 2002/03 season, when we were on the brink of closure, we picked ourselves up thanks to the money that the supporters collected for the club. But, to tell you the truth, what really got us out of trouble was a match – against Manchester United in the third round of the FA Cup in January 2005. We came away from Old Trafford, would you believe, with a 0-0 draw, and the replay was here at St James Park. We lost it 2-0, thanks to goals by Cristiano Ronaldo and Wayne Rooney, but our share of the ticket revenues and television rights enabled us to pay off all our debts. Despite the defeat, that was one of the best days in our history. So in this room we've dedicated this corner to commemorate that great event.

By this time I felt as though I'd known Colin for ages. Although I've travelled the length and breadth of the country in my exploration of English football, I don't think I've ever met anyone as kind, helpful and funny. He was always ready to laugh, and he was at it again when he took me into the place I'd come for: the interview room.

A blue basin, a green duster and dozens and dozens of teacups. Everything was there, exactly as it had been when the great Jürgen Klopp was interviewed. I could hardly believe it. At that moment I should have been on a train to Torquay, but there I was enjoying one of the greatest experiences of all my travels.

'It's good to see you so happy!' Colin exclaimed. I smiled and put my hand on my heart, to thank him for everything he was showing me. We were about to go back out to the pitch, when he pointed at a small mirror bearing the club crest: 'You see that little mirror below the TV? It was a present I gave my dad and he donated it to the club. My dad's no longer with us, he died a while ago, but I say hello and talk to him every day.' His expression turned serious. His big smile had given way to a sadness behind what he was about to tell me. A sadness that began to trouble me as we walked slowly towards another part of the ground.

A couple of minutes later we were standing in front of a high red-brick wall bearing a series of plaques in memory of well-known supporters, employees and Exeter City players who had died over the years. Among them were Colin's dad and Adam Stansfield, a footballer who died at the age of just 31.

'Every day when I get to the ground I stop here for a bit, take my hat off and talk to my dear old dad. Mum always tells me to say hello, and after I've told him the latest about how my family's doing we start chatting about football. Sometimes it feels like he's always by my side.'

As his words came out, Colin began to well up, as I did when I tried to put myself in his shoes. He changed gear: 'On the other side of the ground you'll find my name, my wife's and my daughters' names. For just over £30 per person, the club offers fans the chance to have their names inscribed on the walls of the stadium. It's a good way of supporting the club financially and the great thing is that our names will stay up there forever.'

Shortly before I left, Colin – as kind as he was big – gave me a match programme and a booklet commemorating the club's Brazilian tour of 1914. Thanks to him and then from the pages of the book, I made the astonishing discovery that the Brazilian national team's first-ever match was against – you guessed it – Exeter City, on 21 July 1914. I was flabbergasted. 'You're lucky to be here today, Ivan. In a few months the Old Grandstand won't be here any more; it's going to be demolished to make way for a new stand. You've been able to see and touch the history of our club.'

His words brought me close to tears; then, as I thought of the train I'd missed and what I'd gained, I looked thankfully skywards and broke into a smile. I hugged Colin and thanked him over and over, not knowing if or when I'd see him again.

'Come back whenever you want, Ivan, and remember us. Here, we're a real family. Don't ever forget that.' That's how he said goodbye. When I got to the station and started waiting for the train to Torquay, this time on the right platform, it struck me that nothing in life happens by chance. As we tread the path to our dreams with love and passion, if there are places we can't reach, life takes us to them, opening doors that we could never have opened by ourselves.

Which is what Colin Baker did. Working with other volunteers on the running and maintenance of St James Park, for me he opened the doors of the stadium and then of his heart. A great heart, full of love and rich in stories to tell. The best of which, for me, takes me back to the unforgettable day that I met him.

A LESSON IN GENEROSITY

The happiness of that moment was almost overwhelming. For a few minutes, as I was waiting for the train that would take me to the pretty seaside town of Penzance, I was moved by such a demonstration of generosity. A spirit of nobility that I've tried to emulate over the years, giving to whomever is in need. The very thing that had happened a few moments before the train pulled into the station at Truro. Happily clutching the presents I'd just received, I was smiling through the tears when an old lady in the seat beside me, wearing a long black dress and a yellow scarf entwined in her hair, benignly enquired, 'What's happened to you, young man? How come you're so happy?'

That kind lady, with eyes the colour of the sea and a voice as soft as snow, reminded me of my grandmother, Anna. So it was moments I'd spent with her that came into my mind as I replied, 'I'm living what I've always dreamed of, and I owe it all to football and to England.'

She smiled as she heard my words, turned her blue eyes skywards and for a few seconds said nothing. Then she looked at me again and said, 'It's a delight to see such a young lad follow his dreams. I hope you can make them all come true, but remember always to lend a helping hand to others and appreciate life every single day. In time you'll learn that happiness lies in little things, and there's nothing finer than making other people smile. Good luck, my boy, I wish you the best of luck.'

I'd have liked to stop time for a moment, to listen to those sweet words of advice again. That dear old lady's eyes seemed to want to say something more, but since the train I was waiting for was about to arrive, all I felt able to do was thank her and gently squeeze her shoulder, saying that I'd never forget her and always cherish her lesson in life …

✦ ✦ ✦

On a cool mid-March afternoon, the streets of Manchester were lit by rare sunbeams, as was my tired face. Another long day of hard work was over. As I made my weary way home, starting to imagine what my next journey would bring, my thoughts were interrupted by an unexpected phone call. It was 17 March 2017.

I'd made a mistake. In the post I put up on Facebook a few hours earlier, instead of mentioning the page of Truro City Football Club, I'd inadvertently referred to the one belonging to Truro Community Football. That's what Dele was calling about.

I apologised profusely for my oversight, promising to put it right pronto. 'Don't worry about it, Ivan, I like your story. If you want, I can take you to Treyew Road, where Truro City play. I know a few people there.' There wasn't much I could say to that. I thanked him for his kindness and continued on my way home, thinking that the journey I'd been looking forward to so much had already begun – with an unexpected turn.

The days of work still separating me from the trains that would take me to deepest south-west England sped by. When I walked through the ticket barrier at Truro station, Dele was there waiting for me. It was 28 March, 11 days after his phone call.

He greeted me as two old friends would; then, to break any remaining ice, he told me that his dear friend Edwina was already expecting us at the ground. As we walked there we passed the time by telling each other about our lives. When we reached the entrance to Treyew Road, Edwina hugged me like a lifelong friend and welcomed me into the clubhouse with a cup of piping hot tea and some delicious caramel biscuits.

For over half an hour I felt Edwina's and Dele's eyes on me in their curiosity to know more about the long journey I'd undertaken. I told them of my love for English football, and how and why I'd decided to leave home at such a young age to pursue my dream.

'England has literally changed my life. Living here is making me a better man, and if I should ever achieve my greatest ambitions, perhaps becoming the coach I'd so love to be, I'll owe it all to this wonderful country.'

The two of them seemed impressed by what I had to say. When I told them that after that long journey I intended to pursue a coaching career, Edwina exclaimed, 'What? Why do you want to be a coach, Ivan? You're so young! If you want, you can come and play for us. We need a good attacker!'

Her words had me cracking a huge smile and for a moment my heart started racing with excitement as I thought of all the times I'd dreamed of playing for an English team, of how great it would be to play there with those people who made me feel so at home. I told them how much I missed running after a ball, that ten years of playing football are not easily forgotten.

They could see my sadness as I tried to explain how I felt about failing to become a footballer, but I don't think they really understood me. Nobody could have understood. Deep down I've always known that I didn't try as hard as I could have done, partly through my own fault and partly because my home village never really gave me the chance.

But here was Edwina offering me a real chance. It was with a heavy heart that I pretended not to hear – I'd decided to pursue other dreams. Dreams that wouldn't comprise the pitch at Treyew Road but other wonderful places, with football, as ever, at the centre of my world.

Edwina gazed at me incredulously. I could see that she'd read my expression, that of a sad little boy who's seen his footballing dreams fade and die, but determined and optimistic about the adventures still to be experienced. So, before we left the ground, which by this time was almost familiar to me, she opened the club shop and smiled: 'Choose anything you like, Ivan. Pick something and take it with you, so you'll always have us in your heart.'

I hardly knew what to say, embarrassed by so much kindness and generosity. 'You decide what to give me,' I choked, my voice filling the little shop. 'Whatever it is, after a day like this, you'll always be in my heart.'

'Here. This shirt to remind you of your playing days, and a hat to wear against the cold on your next trips. And you can hang this pennant in your room to remember us by every day; oh, and this computer game to bring you luck in your coaching career.'

Humbled by her generosity, I thanked her and Dele over and over again for the warmth of their welcome, hugged them both and, before setting off for the station, I asked Edwina if I could walk on to the pitch to feel the grass one last time. Grass that could have been mine.

I scampered to the centre circle, stroked the grass and for a moment imagined how it would have felt to score in one of those goals, run to the fans and hug them close. Then I retraced my steps. I had a dream to pursue. The train that would take me to my next adventure was due soon. After sharing a last embrace with Edwina and Dele, I set off for the station with joy in my heart.

Another journey was about to begin – the Scilly Isles were waiting for me. I got on the train knowing that I had more than presents in my rucksack. I'd learned that in life you should always be ready to stretch out your hand to others. In the name of love, with a smile on your face and in your heart.

WELCOME TO GARRISON FIELD: THE HOME OF THE SMALLEST FOOTBALL LEAGUE IN THE WORLD

The dripping leaden sky just didn't want to know. The rain continued incessantly and there wasn't much left to do in the pretty little town of Penzance. The sea was too rough for some of the local fishermen, who reluctantly decided to stay at home rather than risk their small boats. Bobbing at its moorings, one of them was fire-red, just like the colour and heat emanating from the hearth in The Longboat Inn, a stone's throw from the sea. The raindrops ran down the window panes and, as I savoured a delicious meal of the freshest fish and chips, I could think of nothing but what I'd experienced a few hours earlier on the deserted roads of St Mary's, the largest of the Isles of Scilly.

Large is a relative term, given that it has a population of under 2,000 and occupies an area of 2.5 square miles. But there, despite its distance from the British mainland, football is not only followed on television but played, Sunday after Sunday and year after year, from mid-October to the end of March, on the mud and grass of Garrison Field.

All aboard, *Scillonian III* is about to set sail. Our destination is a place you won't easily forget and, at least for a while, will heartily envy. It's the home of the smallest football league in the world ...

❂ ❂ ❂

As sullen as it could be, on that March morning the sky was nothing if not ominous. The rain kept on coming and the state of the sea inspired no confidence whatever. *Scillonian III*, the ferry that would take me from Penzance to St Mary's, was ready to depart, and despite my excitement at the forthcoming trip, my heart began to give the odd lurch. The three-hour journey on a swirling rain-lashed sea was heavy going, but when we reached the island and finally dropped anchor my mood changed altogether. Delighted to be on land, without a thought for the freezing wind and drenching rain, I made a beeline for Garrison Field.

Garrison Hill, the lane from the centre of Hugh Town up to Garrison Field, was utterly deserted. I was forced to hopscotch my way around the innumerable potholes in the road, filled to the brim by the constant rain. Between hops and skips I caught glimpses of the spectacular sea view as I approached the Field and finally felt its soft mud beneath my feet. I looked around repeatedly in the hope of finding some kind soul who could give me the lore on this football shrine, and then realised that in this weather nobody in their right mind would stick their nose out of the house. So I started to search for myself.

'Garrison Field – Home of the smallest football league in the world.' That's what was written on a pretty little wooden hut, with the names and crests of its two teams on either side: Woolpack Wanderers and Garrison Gunners.

I already knew their singular history, but although the internet carries all the information you could wish for, the temptation to see their tiny football world was too much to resist. So strong that it led me to undertake one of my longest journeys. I was living in Manchester at the time, and the hours I spent on buses, trains and the ferry didn't bear counting, but I didn't care. To tell you the truth, at that time I didn't care much for anything except achieving what I'd set out to do.

I had hardly any money and the pay at McDonald's was miserable. After paying the rent on my tiny room in Moss Side and scraping up the funds needed for the trips I was planning, all I could afford was dry bread rolls and a banana or two for breakfast. Yet that was a time when I appreciated everything, including every difficulty, learning to focus on solutions, not problems.

Which is how it was on that March day in the Scilly Isles, as I savoured every moment in spite of the rain and the sacrifices I'd made to get there. And 'there' felt like the middle of nowhere, with nothing but the freezing wind sweeping in from the sea and that wooden hut standing in front of me.

A curious peep through the keyhole in the door of the hut revealed little of interest until my eye was caught by a small noticeboard on the left-hand wall. The results and final league tables of the last ten years had been written on some sheets of paper and pinned up. A while later, when I was drying out and warming up in The Scillonian Club, the pub where the players from the two teams meet up after every match, the fascinating history behind those bare statistics began to emerge.

It was about 1920 when football began to take hold among the people living in the Scilly Isles. In the early years there were five teams who played each other, one from each of the main islands. Then in 1962 it all changed and there were just two teams, both from St Mary's. At that time they were simply called Rangers and Rovers, but in the mid-1980s they took on the names of the two teams that nowadays play every Sunday at Garrison Field: Woolpack Wanderers and Garrison Gunners.

That was the background provided by John, the pub landlord, whose words were followed by Anthony Gibbons, one of the lads lucky enough to play every Sunday on the pitch at Garrison Field. My eyes bulged as he told me how the teams were organised:

To prevent the same team winning every season we choose two captains. After writing down the names of all the other players we toss a coin to see which captain gets first pick and they work their way through the list. That way we get two teams at the same level, which means that all the matches are a good hard fight.

To me that was the stuff of fairy tales, on which I continued to muse as I left The Scillonian Club and returned to the wet and windswept roads of the island. I still had a bit of time before the ferry back to the mainland left, so I decided to go back up to Garrison Field.

I began to convince myself that I'd known the place for years. I felt my feet sink deep into the muddy grass of the pitch as I walked on it. A glance at my watch reminded me it was time to go (if I missed the ferry, I'd have to wait days for the next one) but I sat for a couple of minutes on the bench near the wooden hut and imagined what it would be like to play every Sunday in that splendidly wild setting.

The rain seemed to be observing a ceasefire, but the cold wind continued to buffet my face. I tried to picture myself as one of the players, marking out the touchlines or planting a corner flag before the match began. Then, obviously, I was scoring a goal, but immediately afterwards returned to the real world and had to run down to catch the ferry or risk being stranded.

On that island, where the lads of Woolpack Wanderers and Garrison Gunners face each other every Sunday from October to March in league matches and cup matches, they know and show the whole world that you don't have to play in the Premier League to feel important. What matters is playing football. And if you can play it at Garrison Field, in the world's smallest football league, it's even better.

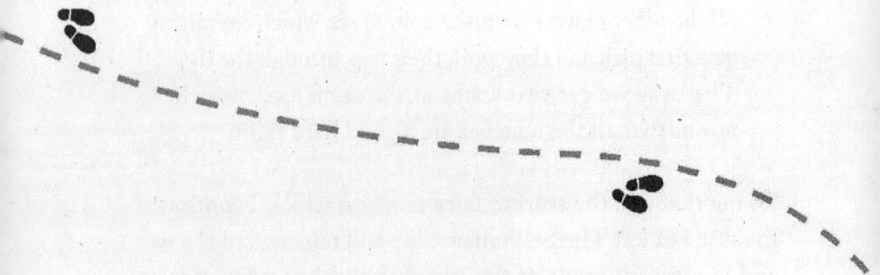

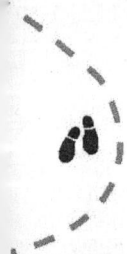

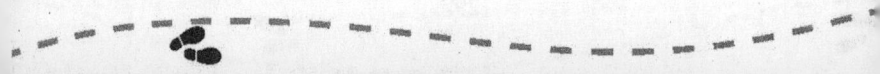

CHAPTER 10

TO YOU, YOUR DREAMS AND YOUR HAPPINESS

I'M LEAVING the introduction to the last chapter to you. You have complete freedom. Pick up a pen, a pencil or some crayons. Write whatever you like. Write about your dreams and ambitions. Write about your forthcoming journeys, if it makes you feel good. Write about everything you'd like to achieve in your life, setting no limits. Age is no barrier, obviously. You've got everything needed to achieve any aim, no matter how great or small. I believe in you, I really do! Even though I don't know you.

To finish, here's a thought from Mark Twain, one that's stayed with me for all the years I've been pursuing my dreams:

> Twenty years from now you'll be more disappointed by the things you didn't do than by the ones you did. So throw off the bowlines. Sail away from the safe harbour. Catch the trade winds in your sails. Explore. Dream. Discover.

Now it's up to you.

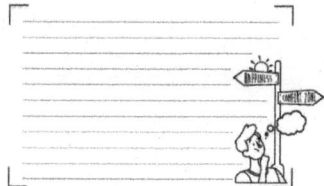

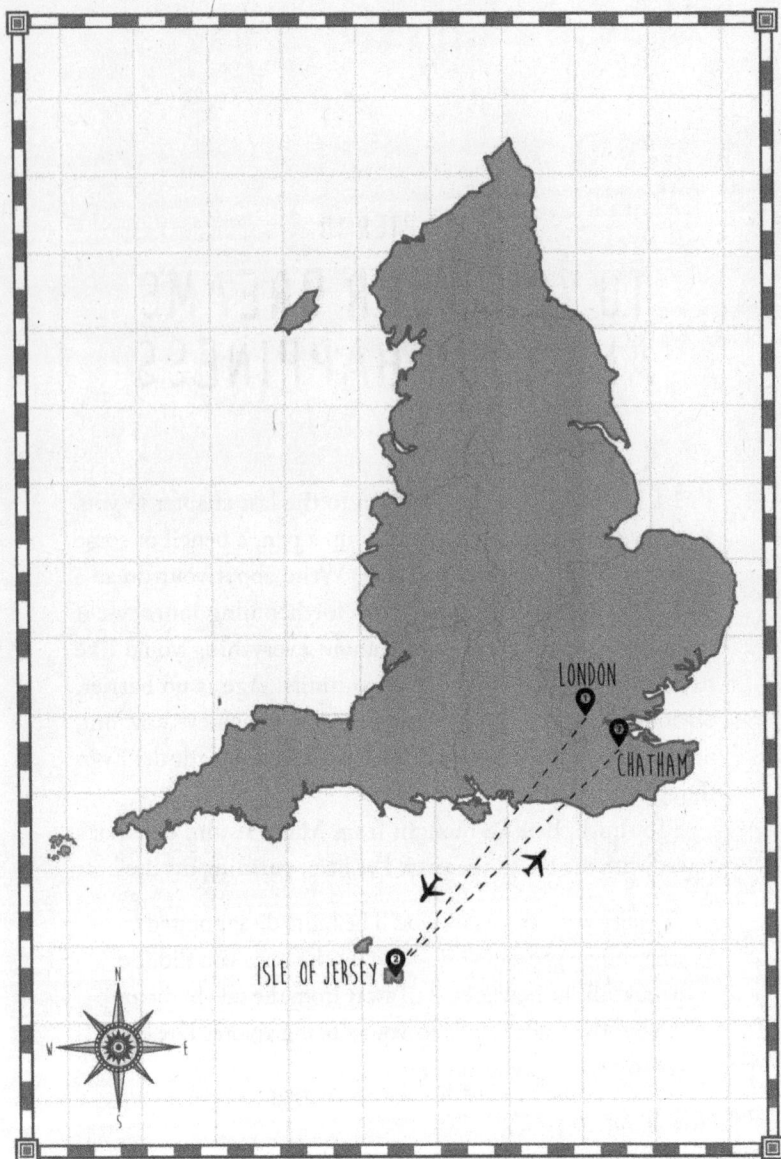

BETWEEN A DREAM AND REALITY

London, 21 October 2017

If I'd tried one more time that evening to get those tickets for Sheffield and Edinburgh, today there would probably be no story to tell. Obviously, I don't mean the many unforgettable journeys that have taken me all over England, I'm talking about something that, when I'm recounting it, often seems unreal even to me.

I'm talking about a story that's hard to tell, full of emotions and inexplicable situations. A story that follows no rules, involves some wonderful people and has regaled me with one of the biggest joys of my life. A life spent in love with England, its people and the football they adore, and it's thanks to the beautiful game that I'm here to tell you one of the best stories that English football has ever given to me.

Make yourselves comfortable – in these last pages I'm going to tell you all about Upton Park FC. A club with more than a century of history, a club I've experienced and even represented, in fulfilment of the dream that in February 2013 took me to England for the first time …

IT ALL STARTED HERE!

London, 5 November 2017

Billy, Jonathan and all the others gave me goodbye hugs as if they'd known me all their lives. They thanked me many times over, wished me luck and reminded me to keep my wits about me as soon as I set foot outside the East Ham Working Men's Social Club, since that part of London has some people you might not want to meet. I smiled and told them not to worry.

A few minutes later I was walking down Green Street, just where the famed Boleyn Ground used to stand, and I began to weep. Not just because in a few hours I'd be going home and would miss England, but because of the emotional roller-coaster that day had been, impossible to forget but almost as difficult to relate.

⚽⚽⚽

A blue sky and wan sunshine welcomed me to London's East End, immersed in the quiet of an early November Sunday morning. The yellowed leaves falling from the trees, which were bracing themselves for the rigours of winter, came lightly to rest on the roadside, giving a picturesque feel to the walk. The birds chirruped happily as they flitted about, filling me with a sense of peace. After a short time I was standing outside one of the gateways to West Ham Park reading about the event on a poster, and I felt that I was touching the sky.

'Did you know that the first-ever goal in the history of the FA Cup was scored in West Ham Park in 1871 by Clapham Rovers player Jarvis Kenrick?' Those were the words written on the poster carefully hung beside the park gates.

A couple of hours later, when I happened to find myself telling the story of my travels to Jonathan Hunter, chairman of Upton Park FC, I couldn't believe my luck. With a warm smile he asked me to give him my phone number. He'd been thoroughly charmed by my story, he said, and in a few months' time, when Upton Park FC were flying to the island of Jersey to celebrate a match played over a century ago, he'd do what he could to take me with them.

For a moment I found it hard to believe what Jon was telling me, and when he began to recount the glorious history of the club he'd re-founded, it was like travelling back in time:

> Upton Park FC, Ivan, was founded as long ago as 1866, and is one of the 15 teams that took part in the first-ever FA Cup competition, held in 1871/72. Nowadays, every year more than 730 clubs play in the world's oldest football tournament.
>
> Knowing that this park, where we're standing now, was on 11 November 1871 the venue of one of its first-ever matches fills all of us with pride. I'm sorry to say we've never won the cup, but on 20 September 1900, in Paris, we represented Great Britain in the second modern-day edition of the Olympic Games, which was the first one to feature football.
>
> That day we beat France 4-0, and since medals were not awarded then we had to wait for a few years before the International Olympic Committee decided to assign them, but we got them.
>
> After that unbelievable victory, though, the Upton Park lads only played a limited number of matches, including some against the two Channel Island teams, and in 1911 the club went bankrupt and disappeared altogether.

Not for the first time I was dumbstruck. I'd been listening to a series of revelations I'd never have believed possible. My only certainty was that I'd been regaled with a unique story.

The sort of story I might have dreamed up when I was a schoolboy as, instead of following the lesson, I'd look through my English textbook in search of photos that would reveal something about that country.

When Jonathan realised the state I was in, his face broke into a smile – he was almost as moved as I was. His eyes were sincere. As his words came out, the love and the passion behind them were crystal clear. Giving me two match programmes, he began to tell me how and when he had the idea of re-forming Upton Park FC. As he did so, the world seemed to stop:

> The idea of re-founding this historic club came to me when West Ham United were about to move away from the Upton Park area. Before long everyone was going to forget about the place, which for Hammers fans isn't just a district, it's an identity. So I thought of starting the old club up again. The hope is that in time it can go back to being an important part of the lives of people with ties to the area.
>
> Our first match was played at the Boleyn Ground on 30 May 2016 against Royal Engineers, another historic club in English football. Not many people know that the last match ever played at the Boleyn Ground was that match, our match, not West Ham's game against Manchester United on 10 May. For our history, that's something to be really proud of.

Once again I was lost for words. Jon had led me to the discovery of a series of historical gems I could never have found out about sitting on my settee at home.

But there was more to come. He went on to tell me that the match to be played that day, between Upton Park and Clapham Rovers, would be commemorating the first-ever goal in the FA Cup, scored by Jarvis Kenrick on 11 November

1871. Where? Right there, in the middle of the park we were standing in.

Back in time. With my eyes closed, in complete silence, I pictured myself among the 1,500 spectators watching that historic match on 11 November 1871 in the heart of West Ham Park. I imagined worming my way to the edge of the pitch, ready to enjoy the sight of the young Jarvis Kenrick scoring that historic first FA Cup goal in the 11th minute of the match, unaware that his goal would go down in the history of the world's most famous competition.

My train of thought was interrupted by the sudden arrival of Billy Jenkins. 'Hey, Ivan, I've just been hearing all about you. Great stuff! Thanks for coming, I'll see you after the match.'

Player-manager of Upton Park, Billy rapidly introduced himself. After Tom Godfrey and David Bauckham had heard my story, without understanding how or why, I suddenly found myself captured in the moment in a photograph with the two teams – I'd have a memento of one of the most exciting surprises of my life.

I was on cloud nine. A little more than an hour later I was being regaled with more football stories, unaware that when the referee blew his whistle for the kick-off the best of that day was still to come.

> In the eleventh minute the match will be stopped and everyone will join in the applause to celebrate the first-ever FA Cup goal, which Jarvis Kenrick scored in the eleventh minute on the afternoon of 11 November 1871.

That's what was written in the match programme. Although everything happening to me that afternoon seemed too romantic to be true, between the dying seconds of the tenth minute and the first seconds of the next, Upton Park, before the incredulous eyes of all those present, scored in the exact same instant in which the match was supposed to be stopping – the 11th minute. Which meant that 146 years later, with the boot on the other foot, history had been rewritten. Shaun Griggs, the goalscorer, couldn't believe his eyes, and neither could the 62 spectators and a dog who were there.

Everybody fell about laughing at what they'd just witnessed. The lads on the pitch, stunned though they were, didn't take their eyes off the ball for a second, and after hard tackles, balls booted high into the trees and a generous helping of goals, they reached the end of an exhausting match. Not a 3-0 victory for Clapham Rovers, as it was a century and a half ago, but 5-1 to Upton Park.

Six goals, of which the first was on the stroke of the 11th minute, another unbelievable story to tell, a photo with the two teams to treasure and so many new friends. My day in the East End was coming to an end, and, as I made to say goodbye to everyone, Billy came up to me and said, 'I'm really pleased to have had you here with us today and I hope you had a good time. In a little while we'll all be off down the pub, and I'd like you to join us. We'll have a drink and something to eat. On the house!' Happy as a sandboy, how could I say no?

The colours of the day were gradually fading to make way for the darkness of night. Waiting for the players to finish showering, I walked in silence towards the centre of the pitch, trying to process the day's events. It didn't seem possible. Two goals, a huge green field and just the rustling of leaves around me. That apart, all was quiet. Shortly afterwards, when I was in the pub surrounded by all the others, happiness flooded over me. I'd hardly ever had the privilege of experiencing such carefree moments.

After having something to eat, I found myself chatting to Billy Jenkins's dad, Rob, and yet again I couldn't believe my ears:

I was the West Ham physiotherapist for more than 20 years. I started in 1966, when I took over from my dad, and stayed there until 1990. I was there with a lot of great players, but the one who stole my heart was Bobby Moore. An absolute legend, on the pitch and off it. Having had the chance to look after his bones makes me so proud.

With a weary voice and a slight stutter, Rob told me about his life. Billy looked on proudly and together we drank to his father's health.

Not long after that, having finished my umpteenth pint, I reluctantly announced that it was time for me to go. In a few hours I had to be in the airport to get on a flight back to Italy. With smiling eyes, Billy told me it was a pleasure to have met me, put his beer on the table and gave me a big hug, as though we'd known each other for years.

He called the others over to say goodbye and, after a minute or two, reappeared holding an Upton Park club tie and said, 'Here's a little thought from all of us. Not just because we're glad to have had you here, but, more than anything else, to say welcome to our family. From now on you're a member of Upton Park Football Club!'

Then and there the words wouldn't come. I'm sure my eyes spoke for me, sparkling from everything that the day had unreeled for me, from the delightful gift, but above all from the spontaneous affection those people had shown me. People I'd known for just a few hours had opened their hearts to me, taken my hand and led me into a world replete with history.

I had to hold back the tears, repeatedly putting my right hand on my heart and relishing the prospect held out by a promise: to meet again soon, and to go with them to Jersey.

ONE STEP FROM THE DREAM
Jersey, 28 March 2018

Since that November day a lot had changed in my life. After that extraordinary encounter with Upton Park FC, in December I returned to England for about ten days. At that time I was based in Italy, and after living for a while in the Lake District and then in Manchester, in January 2018 I was faced with an important decision: should I move to London or go back to Manchester?

I had my doubts about returning to the capital, partly because of the bad experience I'd had in February 2013, but mostly because of the cost of living there. Despite that, in the end I decided to follow my heart – London it was.

Facing those fears and with nothing in the way of certain prospects, on 22 January 2018 I began my new life in England.

At the time I had no way of knowing how things would turn out, but now, more than two years later, I can say London has been the best experience of my life. That's where I discovered the story of the Upton Park club, and that fact alone would be enough …

⚽⚽⚽

'Jon said you're more than welcome if you want to come to Jersey with us, but you'll have to pay for the outward flight and the hotel because we've already booked everything. The only problem is that the flight and the hotel will probably be full because of limited capacity. One thing, though – if you do come, you won't have to pay for the return flight because we've got an extra place, and you can have that.'

That's the message I got from Tom Godfrey on the evening of 16 March. Unfortunately, all I could say in reply was this: 'Thanks, Tom. I'm really grateful. I don't know if I'll be able to get the time off work, but I'll get back to you.'

And the next day things didn't look too good. The manager of the shop where I was working, a woman almost perpetually angry at life, told me with a smirk that there was no way I could have three days off. Stifling the rage and disappointment I felt at that flat refusal, there and then I kept my mouth shut. That was a job I needed badly, so I tried to repeat to myself that the trip just wasn't meant to be. Until, on the evening of 26 March, my phone rang.

'Chairman Upton Park FC' said the display on my iPhone, which kept on ringing. For a few seconds I stared at the screen, wondering why I was being contacted by someone I hadn't seen or heard from since November. I answered the call. 'Hello, Ivan. It's Jonathan Hunter, chairman of Upton Park Football Club. I hope I'm not bothering you. How are you?'

In the few seconds that passed as Jon was saying those words, my thoughts went back to how, not five months before, he'd invited me into his world and given me one of the best days of my life. No, he wasn't bothering me at all. And I was delighted to hear from him.

'I'm glad to hear you're all right. I'm calling to tell you that tomorrow we're leaving for Jersey, and since one of the lads on the list has got a problem and has given up his place, I thought of you. Obviously, it's all on me, flight and hotel. What do you think? Do you want to come with us? If you confirm it, I'll get the passenger name changed straight away and send you the tickets.'

That put me right in a spot. Going to Jersey with them would cause a hell of a row at work. Nonetheless, I told Jon I'd get back to him in an hour. In that time I tried repeatedly to call the manager. I tried to contact all my workmates and even wrote a message to one of the higher-ups, but I didn't get a single answer.

For a few seconds I tried to convince myself that I should just tell Jon that if I went with them, I'd be landing myself right in it at work, and he'd probably understand. Then my real feelings welled up and chased all that nonsense away. So, not giving a damn about the job, the manager or any of the possible consequences, I called Jon and said, 'Listen, I don't think I'll be able to take any time off work, but I just don't care. You don't get chances like this every day, so I'm coming with you. I'll be one of you!'

I could hear the enthusiasm in Jon's voice. After I'd said goodbye and ended the call, the happiness I felt told me I'd done the right thing.

The next morning I got up at dawn so I could get into work two hours early. As soon as I'd told the manager all about it, she told me I wasn't going anywhere. I made it clear that she wouldn't be able to stop me. I was telling her the truth, not making it all up. As a grown-up, she should be able to understand and meet me halfway.

At first she wasn't having any of it, but then I managed to get her to soften up a bit. After at least ten minutes of back and forth, she came round to the idea of meeting me halfway. I'd have been willing to get the sack rather than not go on tour with Upton Park.

What with one thing and another, the morning's work flashed by. Shortly after lunch I was in Victoria station with Billy and Tom, ready to go to Gatwick Airport, happy and without a care in the world.

When we got to the airport I caught sight of Jon. With a great big hug I thanked him profusely for everything he was doing for me. With his customary smile he offered me a drink and told me to enjoy everything around me.

Just like a little boy, I did exactly that, and when the plane landed at Jersey Airport, a bus, which we had all to ourselves, took us to the hotel, where a hot dinner and more beer was waiting for us. After the meal Jon pulled out another story from his peerless repertoire. He took us back to 1897, when the club organised its first tour – to the Channel Islands:

It was on 23 September 1897 that Mr J.H. Jones, goalkeeper and secretary of Upton Park, had a letter published in the *Guernsey Star*. The letter supplied the newspaper's readers with all the details of the matches that the London club would be playing there and in Jersey. The aim was to popularise the game of football in the Channel Islands.

Once they'd got to Guernsey, to arouse as much interest as possible the boys in the club decided to display the Grays Charity Cup trophy, of which they were the proud holders, in a shop window. There was a problem, though. A local solicitor said in public, wrongly, that the trophy would be offered as the prize for Upton Park's match against Northerners Athletic Club, the local team.

The news spread fast. Not only did the idea of playing for an important trophy attract a huge crowd to the ground, the Upton Park players were faced with the prospect of equally large quantities of egg on their faces if they lost.

Fortunately the Londoners won 12-0 and the cup remained in their possession. From then on, since the first tour had been a resounding success, it was repeated every year.

To mark the tenth anniversary of that historic first tour, the club came up with the idea of donating a cup, the Upton Park Trophy, to the Guernsey Football Association. To this day, not only is the cup played for by the champions of Guernsey and Jersey, it's the one the islands most want to win. Unfortunately, though, the last tour took place 108 years ago because, as I said, in 1911 Upton Park went bankrupt.

I wasn't the only one – everybody listened to Jon's story in rapt silence. The thought of being there to represent a club that had played such a fascinating part in football's early history was itself a reason for pride. And joy. So much so that it was gone midnight by the time we went to bed. As goodnights were being exchanged before we went off to our rooms, Jon put a hand on my shoulder and said, 'From the moment I met you I was struck by your passion for football. I'm so glad to have you here with us. I hope you've brought your boots, because tomorrow morning you're going to be training with us. If you do all right, in the evening you can have an Upton Park shirt of your own ...'

Not knowing what else to say, I thanked him over and over again and went to bed in dreamland. Two days before, even the thought of having the chance to pull on the shirt of an English team and train with them had seemed impossible. Now I was just hours away from making the dream come true.

The next morning I jumped out of bed at dawn, prepared the boots I'd fortunately decided to bring with me, and went to the beach. The salt air and the lapping of the waves on the shore gave me a sense of peace. But when it was time to go back for breakfast before training, I could feel the excitement mounting. What with the banter, joking and reading about ourselves in the local papers, it wasn't until I went back to my room that I realised I had no kit for the training session apart from my boots.

I was saved by Matt Kenny, who lent me his Royal Engineers training strip. A historic club, the Engineers, with a host of fascinating stories behind it – as had Charlie Sheringham, son of striker Teddy, with whom I had the honour of sharing the training pitch. The son of an English football legend was there to represent Upton Park and I –

having started out from nothing – was there with him and the rest of that special team.

I scored four goals in the three-a-side training match, and when Charlie came up to compliment me, I thought of all the years I'd spent chasing a football. And wondered why I couldn't have been born there, in that great country with so many opportunities. Then those thoughts vanished.

'Congratulations, Ivan! That was a great session. As promised, tonight you'll have your own Upton Park shirt.'

Jon and Billy couldn't have given me a greater gift. Over lunch, as we enjoyed the fine food and the first beers of the day, I was overwhelmed by the interest and esteem that all the boys showed towards me. They could hardly believe the admiration and passion I had for their homeland.

Just as I had to suspend my own disbelief a little later as the bus took us, after a game at the local bowling alley, from the hotel to the Springfield Stadium. On the way we stopped at a supermarket to stock up on fruit, energy drinks and bag after bag of chewy sweets. Knocking back the sweets, from the bus windows we could see the floodlights as we approached the ground, and I think it's as easy to imagine the feelings I had as it is hard for me to put them down in words.

We filed out of the bus, picked up our bags and, like real footballers, perhaps as the gentlemen representing Upton Park had more than a century before, went into the changing room. Not long afterwards we were standing in a group in the centre of the pitch, a pitch that had been there since 1885.

The pride at being part of that tour was plain to see on all our faces. Just after our arrival at the ground, when Billy handed me that historic club shirt, time seemed to stand still. My head was full of all the stories Jon had told us the night before.

Although I was delighted and felt more than lucky just to be there and have such an experience, when Billy read out the names of the first team and put me on the bench, I felt the burn of disappointment. Then I realised that the other striker was no less than Charlie Sheringham, so there was nothing more to be said – in any case, I was short of fitness.

Music playing during the warm-up, team photos, spectators crowding on to the terraces, the prestigious Upton Park Trophy being held up by the two captains and, just before kick-off, a moment I'll never forget: the stadium announcer reading out the teams, making my name reverberate (with an impeccable English pronunciation) around the walls of the Springfield Stadium. In all that, more than once it seemed I was in one of those dreams you never want to end, then the referee blew for the kick-off and my feet returned to earth.

It was a hard-fought match, particularly in midfield. The home team took the lead a few minutes into the game, but the Upton Park lads never let their heads go down. We fought and fought until the last second but the run of the ball was against us – we couldn't find the net.

When the referee blew the final whistle Billy turned to me and said, 'Ivan, I'm sorry I didn't send you on, but the match was in the balance and it was a fight to the very end. What made me happy was to make you feel one of us and our great club. That's what counts, my friend.'

Billy's heartwarming words made me realise how important it was, and is, for a coach to offer their unstinting support to the players. In the face of defeat, that gesture showed he cared about me – which was confirmed a little while later when, as was his wont, he started ordering pints all round. Although I don't usually drink more than a half, his generosity included me.

The first half of the evening's proceedings were spent in the clubhouse. After sinking the first rounds and eating everything offered by our hosts, Billy, Jon and all the others decided it was time to get serious. So we went to one of the island's many pubs.

What made a lasting impression on me that evening was this: to keep track of how much they'd be drinking, they took a pint glass and filled it with all the money they were going to spend on beer. Only when the glass was empty would we – perhaps – be going back to the hotel. I reckon it contained at least £400, and when closing time loomed just after midnight there was still some cash left in it. Which left us two options: find another venue to accomplish our mission or make our way back to the hotel and go to bed. Dispelling any lingering doubt, Jon took less than five minutes to find another place.

The beer flowed for another two hours. By the end, some of them had put away more than 25 pints. I ran up the white flag at seven. But that was a record for me – until then I'd never managed more than two. It was gone two o'clock by the time we left the bar and – somewhat the worse for wear – made for our hotel, with a cold wind in our faces and happiness warming our hearts.

Another great adventure was at an end. From the next morning, another story was preparing to make its way into my album of memories ...

BEST DAY OF MY LIFE

Brompton Barracks, 19 May 2018

'Ivan, what are doing on 19 May? We're playing the Royal Engineers and kick-off's at 11 in the morning. It's a veterans' match but there are four places for the under-40s, so straight away I thought of you. Up for grabs is the Generation Cup. Do you fancy playing?'

It was 9am on 10 May 2018 when Jon sent me that message. After the fabulous time I'd had with them in Jersey, of course it was an offer I couldn't refuse. Playing for an English team had always been one of my greatest dreams. Being able to do it against a historic club like the Royal Engineers would be the crowning moment of what was for me an epic. A story of special encounters and never-ending journeys on which I'll embark again every time I think of how and where it all began …

⚽⚽⚽

Bright sunshine coloured my face, a clear blue sky lit my way towards the train that would take me on this new adventure. Step after step, my eyes shining with happiness, my thoughts took me back to the last months of 2012. Caught up in memories, I was sitting in the train almost before I knew it.

And the memories flashed by, some of them faster than the train itself. That had been a hard time for me. My life's ambitions seemed a long way off, almost impossible to achieve. The dream of being a footballer was fading into the distance, partly because the opportunities where I lived were so few, and perhaps because I'd never really given all of myself. Giving yourself to a dream requires enormous energy, and if that energy isn't renewed, it's gradually spent. That's how I felt, each day a little more spent. Sometimes dead inside.

The only light I could see at that time was England, and the only thing I wanted was to leave and never go back. 'England is the only place where I can change my life. I feel I belong in that country.' That's what I often repeated to my mum and dad, so without further ado I bought a one-way ticket and left.

As I've said before, I left school, football, a good job, the friends I'd always had, my family and my girlfriend. Not only because I was besotted with that distant unseen land but because I needed to find myself and, most importantly, needed to be happy. But at that time I didn't know what being happy meant. These days, being happy is synonymous with being mad. I think that happiness is something to be conquered, worked for, achieved through your own efforts, because no one's going to hand it to you as you sit comfortably on your settee. I've always thought that happiness abides in all of us, but it's our job to bring it out.

Roberto Benigni said:

We must always think of happiness, and even though it sometimes forgets us we must never forget it, until the last day of our lives. Because it's in us. We were endowed with it when we were little, and since it's such a wonderful gift we've hidden it away like a dog that buries a bone. And many of us have hidden it so well that we can't remember where we put it.

Those words are for the benefit of people who lose their way in fear and insecurity, closing their hearts and suppressing happiness.

So as the train pulled into the station at Chatham, where the Royal Engineers are headquartered, I wondered what would have happened if I'd never had the desire and the guts to pursue my dreams and my happiness.

Happiness – which is what I felt when I met up again with Matt Kenny, who welcomed me with a smile to 'his home', drawing me into yet another story that only English football can come up with.

'Ivan, first of all welcome to our home. Besides being proud to belong to the British Army and having the opportunity to represent and defend our country, we're just as proud of the history of our football club. Our FA Cup victory in 1875 is the greatest thing we've ever achieved. As you can see, the cup and the year we won it are sewn on to the official badge on our shirts.'

For the umpteenth time, what I was hearing took my breath away and I could only respond with a great big grin. Although Jon had told me something about the history of Royal Engineers, hearing it from Matt Kenny, who represented not only the club but the engineering corps of the British Army, was a spine-tingling experience.

When Billy, Jon and the others from Upton Park arrived at the pitch shortly afterwards I had the impression of meeting up again with lifelong friends, even though it was only the third time I'd seen them. We had a job all squeezing into the changing room. When Billy read out the starting XI and I heard my name in it, I felt I was reliving the tension we all used to feel years ago on a Sunday morning when the coach gave us our positions and his final instructions for the match.

For my whole footballing life I'd almost always played as a striker, but that morning Billy told me I was playing on the wing. Although I wasn't match fit, and playing in an unfamiliar position, all I wanted was to get on the pitch and start chasing the ball that embodied, and will always embody, all my dreams – all our dreams.

Before pulling on the historic club shirt, I held it tight in my hands and kissed it, then I closed my eyes for a few seconds and remembered where I'd come from. As I thought of everything I was trying to achieve for my life and for the people I love, I opened my eyes, put the Upton Park shirt on and ran on to the pitch with the others, a ball under my arm, all fired up and as happy as can be.

I went through the warm-up routine in the same mood, but when the referee blew for the kick-off I was almost in a state of disbelief at how I'd managed to make my debut for a club with the glorious history of Upton Park.

The beginning of the game was really tough for me, but after ten minutes or so I got my second wind and adapted to the pace. I didn't see much of the ball that morning, but I gave my best, running and sweating for the colours I had the honour of wearing and representing. I played for just over half an hour, and when Billy and Jon gave me a high five and told me to take a rest, I gave them a hug and thanked them for everything they were letting me experience.

The rest of the match was a battle. The score was 2-2 with just a few minutes left when we were awarded a penalty, and the whole bench, Jon and me included, jumped for joy, hoping for all we were worth that we could get the ball in the net and take home the Generation Cup.

Up stepped Billy, our redoubtable player-manager. Cool as a cucumber, he trotted up and sent the ball one way and the goalkeeper the other, leaving us with a short and happy wait for the final whistle, since our keeper was untroubled for the rest of the match.

Adversaries on the pitch, the two teams were united by respect and friendship, by love and passion for football. We had a photo taken all together and adjourned to the pub to celebrate that memorable occasion and the spirit of football history that the two clubs encapsulated.

Pint upon pint, live music, beautiful sunshine and unforgettable people gave me one of the best days of my life, not just because they'd given me the chance of playing for an

English team but more because they confirmed for me that I'd done the right thing when I dropped everything to pursue my dream of happiness. After all, as Peter Pan said, 'Only those who dream can fly.'

And nothing in life tastes as good as realising your dreams.

Craven Cottage, the stadium that made me fall in love with English football

Griffin Park: a little gem that no longer exists

With the Hudson-Odoi family

Me and my friend Jen

Me and John Portsmouth Football Club Westwood

Me and Colin with part of the old Grandstand in the background

One of the best pics of my long journey: the 'interview room' at the old Grandstand, which now no longer exists

With Upton Park FC in West Ham Park, the first time I met them

Team photo at the end of the match against Jersey FA

All of us with the cup after winning against Royal Engineers AFC

All of us with the trophy at the end of the game against Rappresentativa Vesuviana in Ottaviano, in Italy

Happy faces after winning the Anglo-Italian Cup against US Agropoli – one of the best experiences ever!

Me at Craven Cottage: A dream come true: playing (and scoring) at Craven Cottage!

With my brother Francesco at the historic City Ground

Stamford Bridge: a stadium I've called home for many years and for many reasons

With Eleonora, the love of my life, at Craven Cottage

WHAT'S LEFT ...

It seems like only yesterday that it all began. It feels incredible that we've reached the end of this unforgettable journey. With each stadium, with each match, I've realised many of my dreams, experiencing everything I'd have loved to see as a footballer.

Living in England and travelling from one city to another completely changed my life. It has helped me discover myself and taken me to places I could never have imagined from the comfort of my sofa. Travelling has taught me to interact with the world, to become a better person and, above all, to believe that anything is possible in life. Travelling has taught me to build bridges, not walls; that the essence of life is in what we do, not what we say.

Setting off from San Gennarello di Ottaviano, the small town where I grew up, and getting to experience some of the finest stadiums in the world one after another is not just the realisation of a dream, it has given me unending satisfaction – contentment that I've wanted to share from day one. I love the word 'share'. The mere thought that someone is sharing something of theirs makes me happy.

That's why I decided to spend over a year of my life putting this book together. One word at a time, one page at a time, through smiles and tears, joy and sadness. I did it because I felt the need to share with you the greatest experiences I've had, in the hope that it touches you in some way and makes you feel a part of everything I've had the good fortune to experience myself. In all honesty, there's a whole lot more I'd have liked to share with you but haven't been able to for now. I'd have liked to tell you about my trips to Scotland, Wales, Northern Ireland and the Republic of Ireland. I'd have liked to take you to Glasgow and describe the unbridled passion of Celtic Park and the open arms I was shown at Ibrox, the legendary home of Rangers Football Club. I'd have liked to tell you about Cathkin Park, and my trips to Dumbarton, Dundee, Aberdeen, Inverness and Fort William. Not forgetting Edinburgh, one of Scotland's most beautiful cities.

I'd have liked to tell you about my travels in Wales and in Ireland, where football is 'soccer'. Lots of people prefer rugby in those parts of the world but there's plenty of football – the game we all love – to be enjoyed there too. Wrexham vs Chester is the best derby I've ever witnessed. The rivalry is immense. I'd have loved to tell you about that match but haven't been able to, for lack of time and energy. I'd have liked to tell you about my trip to Bala, a tiny Welsh town in Snowdonia National Park. Not far from there, slightly to the north, is a special village that I was lucky enough to see with my own eyes:

Llanfairpwllgwyngyllgogerychwyrndrobwllllanty-siliogogogoch.

The name alone takes up more than a whole line. See if you can pronounce it! Further south, on the coast of the Irish Sea, is Aberystwyth, a town I have a wonderful memory of. There the stadium groundsman let me kick a ball about for a good two hours – and even let me take a shower when I'd finished playing. s

Across the sea from Aberystwyth lies Dublin, a marvellous city. I'll never forget the reception I was given at Shamrock Rovers' stadium, nor Cork, Galway, Sligo, Dundalk and Drogheda. I'd have needed to write at least two books to share all that with you.

And that's not forgetting my spectacular trips to Northern Ireland. The legend of George Best lives on in Belfast through the murals on the city's walls. Visiting the house where he grew up, the neighbourhood where he first kicked a ball and his grave in Roselawn Cemetery is up there with the best adventures I've had on my long journey.

I could go on for hours and hours, but for now I'll stop here. The time has come to say goodbye, with more than a hint of sadness – to leave all this behind and dive headlong into a new adventure. With huge sacrifices and immense dedication, my dream of becoming a football coach is slowly taking shape. As wonderful as it has been to travel around discovering British football, it's time to get serious. I don't want to experience those stadiums that I always admired from afar and have now seen in person, as a fan, just from the stands any more. I want to experience them from the touchline. A new journey awaits and I'm willing to put everything into it. My heart and soul, as always.

Ivan Ambrosio

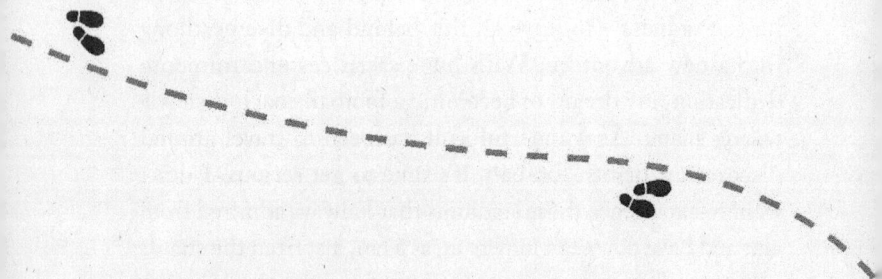

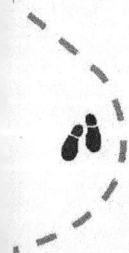

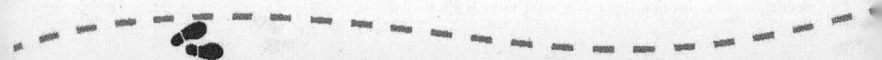

AFTERWORD BY FILIPPO GALLI

ENGLISH GROUNDS, THOSE TEMPLES OF FOOTBALL

I DON'T know exactly when I fell in love with English football. I only remember that as a child I was familiar with the names of Peter Lorimer, Joe Jordan, Mick Channon and Steve Coppell, and that the first English football match I went to see was Queens Park Rangers vs Coventry City in 1979, when my uncle and aunt, Giorgio and Carla, and friends Renzo and Piera took me with them to London.

A few days ago, as I was writing the afterword for this book and rummaging through my memories, I learned that in those days Coventry City had a player by the name of Mark Hateley – the same Mark Hateley I'd share a dressing room with at AC Milan a few years later.

I was fortunate enough to experience English stadiums during my playing career, in the old First Division (now the Championship), and more recently as a fan, at Liverpool, Everton, Manchester United, Manchester City, Preston North End, Leeds United, Norwich City, Brighton & Hove Albion and nearly all the London clubs.

It's not easy to describe the atmosphere you feel at an English ground. It's akin to entering a temple, each time so similar and yet so different. It beguiles you, enraptures you, and bestows a feeling that resurfaces every time you think about it. While it's true everywhere, it's even more the case in England that every match is a new dawn, whether you're a player or a fan. Everyone participates. It doesn't matter what happened last time, every game is a fresh start with the same passion and new hope. And that hope is exalted in every stadium, every temple, across the land.

Reading this book, which Ivan has filled with both his passion and that of the people he has encountered along his journey, has reinvigorated my own dream, one I've had for many years: to visit all the stadiums of England. I guess you probably felt something similar yourself!

Filippo Galli

TO BRADLEY
AND GIUSEPPE,
MY LIFE COACHES

BEFORE FINISHING this book, I want to tell you about two special people: Bradley Lowery and Giuseppe Bifulco. Crossing paths with them on my journey through life was one of the greatest things that could ever have happened to me, for so many different reasons.

Bradley, with his sweet, sweet smile, taught me a great deal. During my time in Manchester, all too often I'd wake up in the morning and not appreciate anything. Then one day, after hearing his story, I realised I had absolutely no right to complain. That's when I learned to appreciate the little (great) things in life.

His smile always gave me so much strength and that's why I decided to support the Bradley Lowery Foundation.

For similar reasons I also support the Associazione Marameo run by Giuseppe Bifulco. It's thanks to him that I learned to face life with courage and optimism. Without knowing it, just through his incredible example, he taught me to face difficulties without being afraid, with the belief that you can overcome any challenge.

The aim of the Associazione Marameo is to encourage people to fight illness, to foster social solidarity for people with leukaemia and other blood diseases, to promote and support research, to raise awareness about the fight against blood disorders. Over the coming pages, I'll tell you a little more about Bradley and Giuseppe, but first I want to say that I'm counting on you, hoping that you can make a small donation that would help lots of people (young and old) who find themselves fighting for their lives.

I'd like to thank you and remind you that we can't make a difference alone – but together we can! Which is exactly what's written outside Bournemouth's stadium: 'Together, anything is possible.' Remember?

With immense gratitude, I thank you from the bottom of my heart.

Ivan

TO BRADLEY AND GIUSEPPE, MY LIFE COACHES

THERE'S ONLY ONE
BRADLEY LOWERY

Hartlepool, 21 December 2016

Bradley was there, just a few metres away from me. For the first time, and quite unexpectedly, I saw his sweet smile with my own eyes. It was an intensely emotional moment that I'll never forget.

Just half an hour earlier, having walked over six kilometres, I was knocking on the door of his house to hand him in person the Christmas cards he'd asked the world for in his soft little voice. Sadly, I found no one home. So I headed to the beach, which wasn't far from there.

It was by pure chance that I found him at Blackhall Rocks Beach, where sky and sea meet on the horizon. Bradley was there with his dear dad, a small dog and other friends. As much as I wanted to go over to say hello and hug him, I didn't want to interrupt that beautiful father-and-son moment, so I just observed the scene without disturbing them.

Shortly before I met him, his story went around the world in a matter of weeks. That's why he received 250,000 Christmas cards that year, sending him love from across the globe. His story touched the hearts of millions of people, who all felt an immense loss when young Bradley flew up to heaven.

On 7 July 2017, the neuroblastoma, a rare form of cancer that mainly affects children, wrenched Bradley away from his mum, Gemma, and dad, Carl, who had fought alongside their little boy year after year without ever losing hope.

Bradley celebrated his sixth birthday on 17 May, not long before he left this world. His passing left a void in me, but one thing I'll never forget is the way he embraced life and his illness. With bravery and determination, he managed to keep smiling through it all, hugging his best friend Jermain Defoe. He left me with one of my most important life lessons: that you should find another reason to smile every day, never stop fighting, and appreciate every little thing.

Thank you, Bradley. Wherever I go, I'll always carry you in my heart.

If you'd like to support the Bradley Lowery Foundation, go to: bradleyloweryfoundation.com (and follow the instructions on how to donate.)

THE STRONGEST PERSON I KNOW

I still remember the first time I met Giuseppe. It was 12 October 2015. I owe that meeting to his cousin Antonella and my mum, who had told him about me a few months previously. At the time, Giuseppe was fighting the Big C. He'd been fighting that terrible disease for 30 years and, in spite of everything, had never given up. He kept fighting like a lion while remaining amazingly upbeat.

What I remember about our first meeting was how candidly he spoke to me. He never beat around the bush. That's one of the many reasons why I'm now writing about him and the Associazione Marameo, which, as I mentioned earlier, was set up to encourage people to fight the disease.

Before meeting him, I could never have imagined someone so strong and with such a positive outlook. Years on from our first meeting, I cherish every opportunity I've had to spend with him but nothing compares to the chat we had on 29 November 2016, at one of the restaurants at Stamford Bridge.

The Wyscout Forum had finished a few hours earlier and my journey had been told live on Sky Sport 24. What I wanted more than anything else was to stay in that world that had been, and was, my dream. Not go back to working in McDonald's in Manchester.

I told Giuseppe without mincing my words that I was fed up with all the adversities I was facing at that time of my life. Giuseppe listened and calmly replied: 'Your story has just been told on Sky Sport 24, you're young and, more importantly, you're not ready to work in football yet. Finish your travels, write your book and then you can focus on getting into football. Now is the time to sow and make sacrifices, so get your head down and keep at it.'

Giuseppe's words galvanised me enormously. That day, he unwittingly became one of the biggest points of reference in my life. In the following months, his words reverberated with me day after day. Since 29 November 2016 I haven't been afraid of anything. Thanks to him, I learned to tackle problems head-on, to remain positive in every situation and to be strong when life gives me tough knocks.

Years passed and every time I met Giuseppe or spoke to him on the phone it was always a real pleasure. Then, on the evening of 5 December 2018, I received a message out of the blue that left me speechless for a moment: 'They've called me in for the transplant.'

I told him my thoughts were with him and that we'd all be waiting for him. A transplant was all that Giuseppe wanted, despite all the risks associated with such delicate surgery. After a long operation, when Giuseppe opened his eyes again he felt reborn. That was 6 December 2018, in Rome.

Giuseppe's life is going well. He's continuing his work as a sporting director, spending time with the people he loves and running the Associazione Marameo, helping lots of other people who are going through what he has overcome. I hope each and every one of you gets to meet someone like Giuseppe on your life journey. He's without doubt the strongest person I know.

If you'd like to support the Associazione Marameo, go to: associazionemarameo.it (and follow the instructions on how to donate.)

ACKNOWLEDGEMENTS

I'VE ALWAYS believed that you can achieve nothing on your journey through life without the help of others. We weren't given life to spend it alone, but to share our time, our passions, to offer each other help, exchange ideas and become better people.

When I was a boy, my mum and dad taught me to share even the last few crumbs of bread, so that everyone could satiate their hunger. Thanks to that small gesture, I realised, as I grew up, that we're not worth much on our own and that, however nice and essential it is for us to take some time out for ourselves, the most important thing of all is never to feel alone.

That's why I want to thank you all, one by one, for making sure I never felt alone. With your gestures, your words, your messages, your hugs and your love, you've given me so much strength, helping me to overcome the toughest challenges and make this dream come true. This is our book. If I've managed it, it's partly – in fact, mostly – thanks to you. Grazie!

⚽ ⚽ ⚽

To **Giuseppe** and **Lucio**, who are much more than friends. There are no words to describe what I feel in my heart. All I can say is thank you, for everything.

To **Alfonso**, **Emiddio**, **Paco**, **Fiorello**, **Michi** and **Raffaele**, my lifelong friends. To all the staff at Bar Franzese and all my friends in San Gennarello. To the friends I grew up with at school, of whom I have fond memories.

To **Pasquale** and **Giuseppe**, for being like big brothers to me. To **Don Tommaso**, for always being ready to listen. A sincere thank you to the entire San Leonardo community, for always supporting me and providing me with great strength.

To **Nadia**, **Enzo** and **Stefania**, for welcoming me into your home like a son. It's the first time I've been shown so much love from another family. I'll give everything I have to make Eleonora as happy as can be.

To **Alessio**, for all the chats we've had and for getting me a ticket for the Wolverhampton vs Torino game. Without your help, I'd never have managed.

To **Gianni** and **Caterina**, for welcoming me into your home on numerous occasions and for always treating me like a son. I'll never forget the love you've shown me.

To **Gianpiero**, who's much more than a friend. More than once, you've spoken to me like a father and an older brother. Knowing you has been wonderful.

To **Giò**, **Gianluca**, **Giovanni**, **Pierfrancesco**, **Emmanuel**, 'bomber' **Gianluca**, **Martina**, **Dorotea**, **Filippo**, **Stefano** and all the other guys from Ischia. You supported me from day one. A special thank you to the Mazzella family, for welcoming me into your home and making me feel part of your lovely family.

To **Andrea**, founder of Il Calcio Inglese community. It was thanks to you that I discovered the importance of experiencing matches rather than just empty stadiums. Thank you so much for taking me into your home, together with mum, Ines, and dad, Paolo.

To **Taff**, **Matt**, **Walter**, **Toby** and all the others from the Just Play FC family. Your help has been immense. You'll always be in my heart, wherever I go.

ACKNOWLEDGEMENTS

To **Jon**, **Billy**, **Tom**, **Matt** and all the others from the wonderful family that's Upton Park FC. Thank you for welcoming me into your world and giving me the chance to make my dream of playing for an English team come true.

To **David**, **Felix**, **Frank**, **Biagio**, **Alberto**, **Enrico** and **Massimiliano**, for being so kind and helpful.

To **Jennifer** and all the **Hudson-Odoi** family, for always treating me like one of the family and being incredibly supportive. Words can't thank you enough.

To **Fabio**, **Antonio T.**, **Gabriele Q.**, **Gabriele M.** and **Silvio**, for the chats, for the advice and for your help. You've always been there for me, since the first day we met.

To **Enrico**, **Luca**, **Matteo**, **Massimo**, **Davide** and **Gerardo**, a heartfelt thank you for all the chats we've had about the clubs you love.

To **Gigi**, from *Romanzo Calcistico*. To **Andrea**, from *Non È Più Domenica*. To **Simone**, from *Il Calcio della Gente*. To **Tiziano** and **Daniele**, from *Passione Stadi*. Thanks to you and many others for telling my story on your websites and social media.

To **Filippo Galli** and **Claudio Ranieri**, for your help and kindness. It's an honour to see your names associated with my book.

To **Gianluca Iuorio**, for believing in me and giving me the chance to publish this book.

To **Jane Camillin** at Pitch Publishing and all the team, for your time and diligence, and for giving me this opportunity.

To **Matteo Albanese**, for giving me hours and hours of your time, at all hours of the day and night. Thank you for your patience and for improving the text of this book.

Thank you to everyone who supported me with the translation of this book. Your donations made the publication of the English edition possible.

A special thanks to Kevin for carefully taking care of every detail throughout the translation process.

To the rest of my family, cousins, uncles and aunts. To those who have been there for me, not because they had to but because they wanted to.

To those fighting for their dreams. To those offering help to others. To those who do their best to make the world a better place.

I'd have liked to thank so many more people but I'm sure that in person, with a hug or a handshake, with a message or with words, I've always shown and will always show my gratitude to everyone who has reached out to help and support me.

I hope with all my heart that you liked this book and that it touched your own heart in some way.

With immense gratitude and from the bottom of my heart, I thank you once again and wish you all the best.

With affection,

Ivan

MY JOURNEY, ENCAPSULATED
IN OVER 300 STADIUMS

Wolverhampton — 21
Wba — 42
Aston Villa — 43
Walsall — 44
Birmingham City — 46
Dumbarton (Scozia) — 61
Morton (Scozia)
St Mirren (Scozia) — 16
Celtic (Scozia) — 53
Rangers (Scozia) — 41
Partick Thistle (Scozia) — 64
Hamilton Acade West (Scozia) — 65
Motherwell (Scozia) — 23
Livingston (Scozia)
Arsenal Highb — 55
Arsenal Emirates
Tottenham
Dundee United (Scozia)
Dundee FC (Scozia)
Aberdeen (Scozia)
Arbroath (Scozia) — 30
Chesterfield — 35
Leicester City
Derby County — 19
Sheffield Fc — 51
Newcastle
Middlesbrough — 22
Hartlepool — 52
Sunderland — 47
Gateshead — 20
Glasgow — 58
Fulham — 49
Qpr
West Ham — 6 APRILE
Manchester United — 75
Manchester City
Liverpool — 37
Everton
Tranmere — 50
Halifax
Bradford
Salford — 4
Wembley
Lincoln — 9
Nottingham Forest — 59
Notts Co
Bradford — 24
Bolton — 40
Harrogate
Leeds — 2
York
Bury & R&D — 7
Morecambe — 6
Hibernian Edinburgh (Scozia)
Heart of Midlothian (Scozia)
Sheffield United — 38
Sheffield Wednesday — 36
Stockport — 15
Macclesfield — 10
United of Manchester — 60
Garfo — 1

Ivan Ambrosio

181 = FOREST GREEN
182 = SHORTWOOD UTD FC
183 = BRIMSCOMBE & THRUPP FC   6/2/17
184 = CHELTENHAM
185 = BISHOP'S CLEEVE FC

186 = STENHOUSMUIR   SCOZIA
187 = STIRLING
188 = ALLOA   8/2/17
189 = LOCHEND ATA EDINBURG CITY
190 = COWDENBEATH

191 = CLYDEBANK
192 = ALBION ROVERS
193 = AIRDRIE FC   13/2/17
194 = CLYDE   SCOZIA
195 = GRETNA
196 = ANNAN

197 = FYLDE   14/02/17
198 = LYE TOWN
199 = STOURBRIDGE   15/02/17
200 = HALESOWEN

201 = COVENTRY
202 = BEDWORTH UTD
203 = NUNEATON GRIFF FC
204 = NUNEATON TOWN FC
205 = TAMWORTH FC   16/02/17
206 = SUTTON COLDFIELD TOWN FC
207 = BOLDMERE ST.MICHAELS FC
208 = SOLIHULL MOORS FC.
209 = NEWCASTLE BENFIELD
210 = NORTH SHIELDS
211 = WHITLEY BAY FC   20/02/17
212 = WEST ALLOTMENT CELTICK
213 = MATLOCK TOWN
214 = BELPER TOWN   21/02/17
215 = PETERBOROUGH UTD   22/02/17
216 = LINCOLN CITY FC
217 = LINCOLN UTD
218 = GAINSBOROUGH FC
219 = WORKSOP TOWN FC
220 = STOCKSBRIDGE PARKSTEEL   23/02/17
221 = KIDDERMINSTER   26/02/17

Ivan Ambrosio

⑥② Barnsley — 12
⑥③ Burnley
⑥④ Accrington — 13
⑥⑤ Blackpool
⑥⑥ Blackburn
⑥⑦ Rotherham 87
⑥⑧ Huddersfield — 66
⑦⑨ Bury 38
⑦⑩ Bolton — 5
⑦① Oldham — 11
⑦② Rochdale — 17
⑦③ Preston
⑦④ Lancaster
⑦⑤ Kendal — 8
⑦⑥ Wigan
⑦⑦ Fleetwood
⑦⑦ Stoke City — 3
⑦⑧ Crewe — 14
⑦⑨ Hull City —
⑧⑩ Grimsby Town
⑧② Scunthorpe
⑧③ Millwall
⑧④ Crystal palace
⑧④ Charlton
⑧⑤ Watford
⑧⑥ Portsmouth
⑧⑦ Southampton — 57
⑧⑧ Bournemouth — 48
⑧⑨ Shrewsbury — 33
⑨① Telford — 34
⑨② Chester — 32
⑨③ Wrexham — 31
⑨④ Hampden Park (Scozia) — 21
⑨⑤ Ayr United (Scozia) — 30
⑨⑥ Kilmarnock (Scozia) — 19
⑨⑦ Queen of the south (Scozia) — 18
⑨⑧ West Ham (stadio olimpico) — 28
⑨⑨ Port Vale — 27
⑩⑩ Buxton — 26
⑩① ZEYTON ORIENT
⬜ 102 - ALTRICHAM
⬜ 103 - CURZON ASHTON FC
⬜ 104 - ASHTON UNITED FC
⬜ 105 - DROYLSDEN FC
⬜ 106 - STADIUM ACADEMY (NOW) MAN CITY
⬜ 107 - STALYBRIDGE CELTIC
⬜ 108 - MOSSLEY ATC
⬜ 109 - GLOSSOP NORTH END
⬜ 110 - HYDE UNITED FC

⑪① = PRESTATYN (GALLES)
112 = RHYL FC (")
113 = LLANFAIRPWLL FC (")
114 = BANGOR CITY (")
115 = LLANDUDNO (")   5|12|16

116 = ABERYSTWYTH (")
117 = NEW TOWN FC (")
118 = THE NEW SAINTS (")   8|12|16

119 = FALKIRK
120 = DUNFERMLINE
121 = RAITH
122 = ST. JOHNSTONE   12|12|16

123 = CLACHNACUDDIN FC
124 = INVERNESS
125 = ROSS COUNTY   13|12|16

126 = GUISLEY ATC
127 = DONCASTER ROVERS   23|12|16
128 = HALLAM FC
129 = BURTON ALBION
HAT   27|12|16

130 = LUTON TOWN
131 = ST. ALBANS CITY
132 = BOREHAM WOOD
133 = BARNET
134 = WEALD STONE
135 = HARROW BOROUGH

136 = BRIGHTON
137 = THREE BRIDGES
138 = CRAWLEY   28|12|16
139 = WIMBLEDON
140 = SUTTON
141 = CARSHALTON ATHLETIC FC
142 = TOOTING
143 = MAINE ROAD FC
144 = WEST DIDSBURY   1|1|17
145 = NEW MILLS   2|1|17
146 = ABBEY HEY

MY JOURNEY, ENCAPSULATED IN OVER 300 STADIUMS

222 = SLOUGH TOWN
223 = MAIDENHEAD
224 = READING
225 = SWINDON
226 = DIDCOT TOWN
227 = WINSOR

6 - 03 - 17

228 = DOVER
229 = FAVERSHAM
230 = GILLINGHAM
231 = CHATHAM
232 = MAIDSTONE

7 - 03 - 17

233 = NORWICH CITY
234 = IPSWICH
235 = COLCHESTER
236 = WITHAM TOWN
237 = BRAINTREE

8 - 03 - 17

238 = BIGGLESWADE TOWN
239 = BIGGLESWADE UTD
240 = STEVENAGE
241 = HISTON
242 = ST. IVES - CAMBRIDGE CITY
243 = CAMBRIDGE UTD

9 - 03 - 17

244 = KIDSGROVE
245 = CONGLETON

10 - 03 - 17

246 = WESTFIELD
247 = HEREFORD
248 = CARMARTHEN
249 = LLANELLI
250 = CARDIFF MET. UNIV
251 = TAFFS WELL

13 - 03 - 17

252 = BRISTOL MANOR FARM
253 = BRISTOL ROVERS
254 = BRISTOL CITY
255 = BATH CITY

14 - 03 - 17

256 = WYCOMBE
257 = OXFORD UTD
258 = OXFORD CITY

15 - 03 - 17

259 = EASLEIGH
260 = WINCHESTER
261 = WOKING
262 = WESTFIELD
263 = WALTON & HERSHAM
264 = METROPOLITAN POLICE
265 = ALDERSHOT
266 = RAYNES PARK VALE
267 = CORINTHIAN & CASUAL

16 - 07 - 17

268 = BOHEMIAN FC
269 = BRAY WAFERS
270 = SHELBOURNE FC
271 = UCD DUBLIN

20 - 03 - 17
IRLANDA

272 = ABINTFLEY
273 = GLENTORAN
274 = CRUSADERS
275 = CLIFTONVILLE
276 = WINSOR PARK
277 = CARRICK RANGERS

21 - 03 - 17
N. IRLANDA

278 = DROGHEDA
279 = DUNDALK
280 = PORTADOWN
281 = GLENAVON

22 - 03 - 17
IRL - N. IRL

282 = SHAMROCK R.
283 = ST PATRICKS AT.
284 = CROKE PARK
285 = AVIVA STADIUM
286 = HOME FARM FC

23 - 03 - 17
DUBLINO

287 = YEOVIL
288 = EXETER
289 = TORQUAY

27 - 03 - 17

290 = PLYMOUTH
291 = TRURO CITY

28 - 03 - 17

282 = GARRISON FIELD

28 - 03 - 17

283 = SOUTHEND
284 = BILLERICAY TOWN
285 = WINGATE & FINCHLEY
286 = HARINGEY BOROUGH
287 = ENFIELD TOWN
288 = COCKFOSTERS FC

31 - 03 - 17

298 = CATHKIN PARK
300 = FORT WILLIAM

3 - 04 - 17

301 = BROMLEY FC
302 = HAMPTON & RICHMOND BOROUGH

6 - 04 - 17

303 = SALISBURY FC

7 - 04 - 17

304 = KNOCKBRIDA FC

8 - 04 - 17

305 = DERRY CITY
306 = COLERAINE FC
307 = BALLYMENA UTD FC

10 - 04 - 17

308 = COBH RAMBLERS
309 = CORK CITY FC
310 = LIMERICK FC

12 - 04 - 17

147 = TRAFFORD ⌐ 3/1/17

147 = BURSCOUGH FC ⌐
148 = SOUTHPORT FC ⌐ 5/4/17

150 = M K DONS ⌐
151 = NORTHAMPTON ⌐
152 = RUGBY TOWN ⌐ 6/4/17
153 = LEAMINGTON ⌐

154 = MARINE AFC - AFC (LIVERPOOL ⌐
155 = BOOTLE FC ⌐ 7/4/17

156 = NEWPORT AFC ⌐
157 = SWANSEA ⌐
158 = PORT TALBOT FC (GALLES) ⌐
159 = AFAN LIDO FC (GALLES) ⌐ 11/1/17
160 = MILLENNIUM STADIUM ⌐
161 = CARDIFF ARMS PARK ⌐
162 = CARDIFF CITY FC ⌐

163 = BALA TOWN FC ⌐
164 = DRUIDS ⌐ 14/1/17

165 = BASFORD UTD ⌐
166 = ALFRETON TOWN ⌐ 28/1/17

167 = ATHERTON COLLIERIES AFC ⌐ 31/1/17

168 = COLNE FC ⌐
169 = NELSON TOWN ⌐
170 = PADIHAM FC ⌐ 1/2/17
171 = BAMBER BRIDGE ⌐
172 = CHORLEY FC ⌐

173 = CONNAH'S QUAY ⌐
174 = AIRBUS UK BROUGHT FC ⌐
175 = SALTNEY TOWN FC ⌐
176 = RUNCORN TOWN ⌐ 2/2/17
177 = RUNCORN LINNETS FC ⌐
178 = WARRINGTON TOWN FC ⌐

179 = BARROW RADCLIFFE ⌐ 3/2/17
    BROUGH
190 = BARROW ⌐ 4/2/17 x a 1

311 = GALWAY UTD FC ⌐
312 = ATHLONE ⌐ 13/04/17
313 = SLIGO ROVERS ⌐

314 = CLAPTON FC ⌐
315 = WEST HAM PARK ⌐ 5/11/17

316 = GREAT YARMOUTH ⌐ 22/12/17

317 = DULWICH HAMLET ⌐ 3/02/18
318 = JERSEY FA ⌐ 28/03/18

319 = ROYAL ENGINEERS ⌐ 19/05/18

320 = TOTTENHAM NEW STADIUM ⌐ 14/01/20

→

216 MATCHES LIVED ON MY SKIN, FROM 2014 TO 2025, CHASING MY DREAMS

15-03-2014: Fulham vs Newcastle United (Premier League)

12-05-2015: Manchester United U21 vs Manchester City U21
(Premier League U21)

14-09-2015: West Ham United vs Newcastle United
(Premier League)

15-09-2015: Manchester City vs Juventus (Champions League)

23-09-2015: Manchester United vs Ipswich
Town (League Cup)

30-09-2015: Manchester United vs Wolfsburg
(Champions League)

17-10-2015: Brentford vs Rotherham United (Championship)

17-11-2015: England vs France (Friendly game)

28-11-2015: Fulham vs Preston North End (Championship)

03-08-2016: Manchester United vs Everton (Wayne
Rooney Testimonial)

05-11-2016: Manchester City vs Middlesbrough
(Premier League)

09-11-2016: Manchester City vs Brøndby IF (Women's
Champions League)

19-11-2016: Manchester City U18 vs Everton U18
(Premier League U18)

28-11-2016: Huddersfield Town vs Wigan Athletic
(Championship)

03-12-2016: Ashton United vs Spennymoor
Town (Non-League)

10-12-2016: Ashton United vs Stourbridge (Non-League)

07-01-2017: Everton vs Leicester City (FA Cup)

10-01-2017: Manchester United vs Hull City (League Cup)

18-02-2017: Nottingham Forest vs Sheffield Wednesday
(Championship)

20-02-2017: Newcastle United vs Aston Villa (Championship)

21-02-2017: Sheffield Wednesday vs Brentford (Championship)

24-02-2017: Wolverhampton Wanderers vs Birmingham City (Championship)

25-02-2017: Leeds United vs Sheffield Wednesday (Championship)

25-03-2017: Liverpool Legends vs Real Madrid Legends (Charity game)

26-03-2017: England vs Lithuania (World Cup Qualifiers)

08-04-2017: Manchester City vs Hull City (Premier League)

14-04-2017: Shamrock Rovers vs Sligo Rovers (League of Ireland Premier Division)

04-08-2017: Sunderland vs Derby County (Championship)

05-08-2017: Celtic vs Heart of Midlothian (Scottish Premiership)

06-08-2017: Brighton vs Atletico Madrid (Friendly)

08-08-2017: Millwall vs Stevenage (League Cup)

26-09-2017: Bristol City vs Bolton Wanderers (Championship)

27-09-2017: Birmingham City vs Sheffield Wednesday (Championship)

29-09-2017: QPR vs Fulham (Championship)

30-09-2017: Aston Villa vs Bolton Wanderers (Championship)

21-10-2017: Stoke City vs Bournemouth (Premier League)

24-10-2017: Bournemouth vs Middlesbrough (League Cup)

25-10-2017: Rangers vs Kilmarnock (Scottish Premiership)

28-10-2017: Portsmouth vs Bradford City (League One)

29-10-2017: Leicester City vs Everton (Premier League)

30-10-2017: Burnley vs Newcastle United (Premier League)

31-10-2017: Reading vs Nottingham Forest (Championship)

01-11-2017: Preston North End vs Aston Villa (Championship)

03-11-2017: Notts County vs Bristol Rovers (FA Cup)

04-11-2017: AFC Wimbledon vs Lincoln City (FA Cup)

06-11-2017: Upton Park FC vs Clapham Rovers FC (Celebration of the first ever goal of the FA Cup)

22-12-2017: Norwich City vs Brentford (Championship)

23-12-2017: Luton Town vs Grimsby Town (League Two)

26-12-2017: Leyton Orient vs Dagenham & Redbridge
(National League)

26-12-2017: Brentford vs Aston Villa (Championship)

27-12-2017: Metropolitan Police vs Leatherhead (Non-League)

28-12-2017: Crystal Palace vs Arsenal (Premier League)

29-12-2017: Millwall vs QPR (Championship)

30-12-2017: Watford vs Swansea City (Premier League)

31-12-2017: WBA vs Arsenal (Premier League)

01-01-2018: Bromley vs Ebbsfleet United (National League)

03-02-2018: Dulwich Hamlet vs Metropolitan
Police (Non-League)

10-02-2018: Dagenham & Redbridge vs Aldershot Town
(National League)

16-02-2018: Chelsea vs Hull City (FA Cup)

17-02-2018: Burton Albion vs Nottingham Forest
(Championship)

22-02-2018: Arsenal vs Östersunds FK (Europa League)

24-02-2018: St. Albans City vs Chippenham
Town (Non-League)

03-03-2018: Southampton vs Stoke City (Premier League)

07-03-2018: Tottenham Hotspur vs Juventus
(Champions League)

10-03-2018: Stockport County vs Brackley
Town (Non-League)

11-03-2018: Wrexham vs Chester (National League)

17-03-2018: Maidenhead United vs Barrow (National League)

21-03-2018: Crawley Town vs Wycombe
Wanderers (League Two)

24-03-2018: Aldershot Town vs Boreham Wood
(National League)

28-03-2018: Jersey FA vs Upton Park FC (Friendly game)
*as a player

30-03-2018: Maidenhead United vs Sutton United
(National League)

30-03-2018: Reading vs QPR (Championship)

01-04-2018: Chelsea vs Tottenham Hotspur (Premier League)

02-04-2018: Sutton United vs Bromley (National League)

06-04-2018: Cardiff City vs Wolverhampton Wanderers (Championship)

07-04-2018: Swindon Town vs Carlisle (League Two)

08-04-2018: Chelsea vs West Ham United (Premier League)

14-04-2018: Bath City vs Hungerford Town (Non-League)

21-04-2018: St. Albans City vs Hampton & Richmond Borough (Non-League)

28-04-2018: Reading vs Ipswich Town (Championship)

05-05-2018: Wycombe Wanderers vs Stevenage (League Two)

06-05-2018: Derby County vs Barnsley (Championship)

09-05-2018: Chelsea vs Huddersfield Town (Premier League)

18-05-2018: Chelsea Legends vs Inter Forever (Friendly game in memory of Ray Wilkins)

19-05-2018: Royal Engineers AFC vs Upton Park FC (Generation Cup) *as a player

31-07-2018: Clapton FC vs Upton Park FC (Friendly game)

04-08-2018: Sheffield United vs Swansea City (Championship)

05-08-2018: Leeds United vs Stoke City (Championship)

11-08-2018: Bradford City vs Barnsley (League One)

18-08-2018: Barnsley vs AFC Wimbledon (League One)

25-08-2018: Corinthian-Casuals FC vs Croydon FC (FA Cup)

08-09-2018: Salford City vs Maidstone United (National League)

22-09-2018: Nottingham Forest vs Rotherham United (Championship)

02-10-2018: Accrington Stanley vs Doncaster Rovers (League One)

03-10-2018: Blackburn Rovers vs Sheffield United (Championship)

13-10-2018: FC United of Manchester vs Darlington (Non-League)

20-10-2018: Lincoln City vs Cambridge United (League Two)

29-11-2018: Chelsea vs PAOK (Europa League)

30-03-2019: Ipswich Town vs Hull City (Championship)

27-04-2019: York City vs AFC Telford United (Non-League)

18-05-2019: Manchester City vs Watford (FA Cup Final)

13-07-2019: Sheffield FC vs Hallam FC (The Alan Cooper Memorial Trophy)

29-08-2019: Wolverhampton Wanderers vs Torino (Play-off Europa League)

22-09-2019: Chelsea vs Liverpool (Premier League) *to work

05-10-2019: Hallam FC vs Nostell Miners Welfare FC (Non-League)

06-10-2019: Newcastle United vs Manchester United (Premier League)

19-10-2019: St. Albans City vs Bath City (Non-League)

22-10-2019: Millwall vs Cardiff City (Championship)

23-10-2019: Fulham vs Luton Town (Championship)

26-10-2019: Manchester City vs Aston Villa (Premier League)

30-10-2019: Chelsea vs Manchester United (League Cup) *to work

03-11-2019: Crystal Palace vs Leicester City (Premier League)

05-11-2019: Chelsea vs Ajax (Champions League) *to work

09-11-2019: Chelsea vs Crystal Palace (Premier League) *to work

23-11-2019: Charlton Athletic vs Cardiff City (Championship)

30-11-2019: Chelsea vs West Ham United (Premier League) *to work

04-12-2019: Chelsea vs Aston Villa (Premier League) *to work

10-12-2019: Chelsea vs Lilla (Champions League) *to work

14-12-2019: Chelsea vs Bournemouth (Premier League) *to work

05-01-2020: Chelsea vs Nottingham Forest (FA Cup) *to work

11-01-2020: Chelsea vs Burnley (Premier League) *to work

14-01-2020: Tottenham Hotspur vs Middlesbrough (FA Cup)

21-01-2020: Chelsea vs Arsenal (Premier League) *to work

17-02-2020: Chelsea vs Manchester United (Premier League) *to work

19-02-2020: Tottenham Hotspur vs RB Lipsia (Champions League) *to work

22-02-2020: Chelsea vs Tottenham Hotspur (Premier League) *to work

25-02-2020: Chelsea vs Bayern Monaco (Champions League) *to work

29-02-2020: Luton Town vs Stoke City (Championship)

01-03-2020: Tottenham Hotspur vs Wolverhampton Wanderers (Premier League) *to work

03-03-2020: Chelsea vs Liverpool (FA Cup) *to work

04-03-2020: Tottenham Hotspur vs Norwich City (FA Cup) *to work

08-03-2020: Chelsea vs Everton (Premier League) *to work

14-09-2021: Chelsea vs Zenit (Champions League) *to work

19-09-2021: West Ham United vs Manchester United (Premier League)

22-09-2021: Chelsea vs Aston Villa (EFL Cup) *to work

24-09-2021: Chelsea U23s vs Liverpool U23s (Premier League 2)

25-09-2021: Chelsea vs Manchester City (Premier League) *to work

02-10-2021: Chelsea vs Southampton (Premier League) *to work

20-10-2021: Chelsea vs Malmö (Champions League) *to work

23-10-2021: Chelsea vs Norwich City (Premier League) *to work

26-10-2021: Chelsea vs Southampton (EFL Cup) *to work

02-11-2021: Corinthian-Casuals vs Margate (Non-League)

06-11-2021: Chelsea vs Burnley (Premier League) *to work

07-11-2021: Upton Park FC vs Wanderers (Generation Cup) *as a player

07-11-2021: Upton Park FC vs Reigate Priory FC (Generation Cup) *as a player

16-11-2021: Westfield FC vs Badshot Lea FC (Non League) *as a scout

20-11-2021: Sutton Common Rovers vs Basingstoke Town FC (Non League) *as a scout

23-11-2021: Chelsea vs Juventus (Champions League) *to work

28-11-2021: Chelsea vs Manchester United (Premier League) *to work

04-12-2021: Hanwell Town vs Bedfont Sports (Non League) *as a scout

11-12-2021: Chelsea vs Leeds United (Premier League) *to work

16-12-2021: Chelsea vs Everton (Premier League) *to work

18-12-2021: Tooting & Mitcham United vs Westfield (Non League) *as a scout

20-12-2021: Fulham vs Sheffield United (Championship)

29-12-2021: Chelsea vs Brighton (Premier League) *to work

02-01-2022: Chelsea vs Liverpool (Premier League) *to work

05-01-2022: Chelsea vs Tottenham (EFL Cup) *to work

08-01-2022: Chelsea vs Chesterfield (FA Cup) *to work

23-01-2022: Chelsea vs Tottenham (Premier League) *to work

29-01-2022: Chertsey Town vs Chipstead (Non League) *as a scout

05-02-2022: Chelsea vs Plymouth Argyle (FA Cup) *to work

06-02-2022: Chelsea Womens vs Manchester City Womens (FA WSL 1) *to work

12-02-2022: Tooting & Mitcham United vs Uxbridge (Non League) *as a scout

22-02-2022: Chelsea vs Lille (Champions League) *to work

13-03-2022: Chelsea vs Newcastle United (Premier League) *to work

02-04-2022: Chelsea vs Brentford (Premier League) *to work

06-04-2022: Chelsea vs Real Madrid (Champions League) *to work

19-04-2022: Fulham vs Preston North End (Championship) *to work

20-04-2022: Chelsea vs Arsenal (Premier League) *to work

23-04-2022: Corinthian-Casuals vs Cheshunt (Non League)

24-04-2022: Chelsea vs West Ham United (Premier League) *to work

07-05-2022: Chelsea vs Wolves (Premier League) *to work

19-05-2022: Chelsea vs Leicester City (Premier League) *to work

22-05-2022: Chelsea vs Watford (Premier League) *to work

20-06-2022: Rappresentativa Vesuviana vs Upton Park FC
(Friendly game in Italy) *as a player

21-06-2022: US Agropoli vs Upton Park FC (Anglo-Italian
Cup in Italy) *as a player

31-07-2022: Fulham vs Villareal (Friendly) *to work
as a mascotte

14-08-2022: Chelsea vs Tottenham (Premier League) *to work

27-08-2022: Chelsea vs Leicester City (Premier League) *to
work

30-08-2022: Fulham vs Brighton (Premier League) *to work
as a mascotte

03-09-2022: Chelsea vs West Ham United (Premier League)
*to work

14-09-2022: Chelsea vs RB Salzburg (Champions League) *to
work

05-10-2022: Chelsea vs AC Milan (Champions League) *to
work

08-10-2022: Chelsea vs Wolves (Premier League) *to work

22-10-2022: Chelsea vs Manchester United (Premier League)
*to work

02-11-2022: Chelsea vs Dinamo Zagreb (Champions League)
*to work

06-11-2022: Chelsea vs Arsenal (Premier League) *to work

05-01-2023: Chelsea vs Manchester City (Premier League) *to
work

15-01-2023: Chelsea vs Crystal Palace (Premier League) *to
work

03-02-2023: Chelsea vs Fulham (Premier League) *to work

12-02-2023: Upton Park FC vs Clapham Rovers (Generation
Cup) *as a player

12-02-2023: Upton Park FC vs Oxford University (Generation
Cup) *as a player

12-02-2023: Upton Park FC vs Civil Service (Generation Cup)
*as a player

18-02-2023: Chelsea vs Southampton (Premier League) *to
work

04-03-2023: Chelsea vs Leeds United (Premier League) *to work

07-03-2023: Chelsea vs Borussia Dortmund (Champions League) *to work

18-03-2023: Chelsea vs Everton (Premier League) *to work

01-04-2023: Chelsea vs Aston Villa (Premier League) *to work

04-04-2023: Chelsea vs Liverpool (Premier League) *to work

07-04-2023: Watford vs Huddersfield (Championship)

15-04-2023: Chelsea vs Brighton (Premier League) *to work

18-04-2023: Chelsea vs Real Madrid (Champions League) *to work

26-04-2023: Chelsea vs Brentford (Premier League) *to work

13-05-2023: Chelsea vs Nottingham Forest (Premier League) *to work

28-05-2023: Chelsea vs Newcastle United (Premier League) *to work

01-10-2023: Nottingham Forest vs Brentford (Premier League)

06-12-2023: Fulham vs Nottingham Forest (Premier League)

16-12-2023: St Albans City vs Chelmsford City (Non League)

23-12-2023: Tottenham vs Everton (Premier League)

30-01-2024: Fulham vs Everton (Premier League)

24-04-2024: Crystal Palace vs Newcastle United (Premier League)

19-05-2024: Crystal Palace vs Aston Villa (Premier League)

24-08-2024: Hampton & Richmond Borough FC vs Salisbury (Non League)

04-01-2025: Hampton & Richmond Borough FC vs Spennymoor Town (Non League)

14-01-2025: Brentford vs Manchester City (Premier League)

25-02-2025: Chelsea vs Southampton (Premier League)

RECOMMENDED BOOKS

I have chosen to include, at this point in the book, a brief list of readings. These are books that offer a deeper exploration of topics and stories that I could only briefly address in this work.

In English:

- *The Countrymen - The History of Hallam Football Club*; JOHN A. STEELE (2010).
- *Men from the North - The Grand History of North Shields Football Club*; TRUDI THOMPSON (2019).
- *Red Rebels - The Glazers and the FC Revolution*; JOHN-PAUL O'NEILL (2017).
- *Annals of The Corinthian Football Club*; B.O. CORBETT (1906).
- *100 Years of the FA Cup - The Official Centenary History*; TONY PAWSON (1972).
- *From St Andrew's to Craven Cottage - How a Church's Cricket and Football Club Became Fulham Football Club*; Morgan Phillips (2007).

In Italian:

- *Noi siamo il Wimbledon*; Stefano Faccendini (2006).

PHOTOGRAPHIC COPYRIGHT

Il mio viaggio in Inghilterra

Il mio viaggio in Inghilterra

www.ilmioviaggioininghilterraa.it

englishfootballhome1462